New Dimensions

PROGRAMME DIRECTOR: JIM SWEETMAN

CollinsEducational
An imprint of HarperCollins*Publishers*

ISBN 0 00 323017 1

© 1991 CollinsEducational

First published 1991 by CollinsEducational, *an imprint of* HarperCollins*Publishers* 77-85 Fulham Palace Road, London W6 8JB.

Cover and book designed by Christie Archer Design, London.

Cover illustration by Simon Fell.

Typeset by Dorchester Typesetting Group Ltd. Dorset.

Printed and bound in Hong Kong.

Series Editor: Marion Rose
Project Manager: Philippa Sawyer
Production: Mandy Inness
Picture Research: Penni Bickle

Collins English Programme: *New Dimensions*

published by CollinsEducational

ERRATUM

The poem by Pat Arrowsmith appearing on p. 9 of the pupil's book and on Side 1 of Cassette 1 in the Teacher's Resources should read:

THE DAY I ONCE DREAMED

This is the day I first thought of
in my closed eyes,
deep in my eyes,
the day I first thought of;
with the sun strands weaving,
sun drops sparkling
in the high streams,
on the high seas –
the day I once dreamed.

This is the day I first saw
down in my mind,
deep in my brain,
the day I first saw;
with the wild gulls calling,
barley sheen swishing
in the high wind,
on the high hill –
the day I once dreamed.

This is the day I first heard
far in my head,
away out of sight,
the day I first heard;
with the streets all glittering,
coloured throng shimmering
in the bright lights,
under the lamps –
the day I once dreamed.

That was the day I then saw,
the day I then heard,
when I opened my eyes,
when I unblocked my ears;
the day I then knew
when I focused my mind,
the day I then knew;
with the huge cloud thundering,
thick sky asphyxiating
right overhead,
night overhead,
all over the land –
that was the day I then knew:
the terrible night,
the night of the Bomb,
the night of the doom.
That was the night I then knew –
the night of the end of the world.

We apologise for the incorrect printing and recording of this poem.

Contents

In this unit you are going to explore your dreams and the ways they relate to real life and your future.

Why do we dream?

Everybody dreams. Some people remember their dreams in vivid detail while others remember almost nothing but scientists are now convinced that everyone dreams and that dreaming performs a vital function as part of our normal sleep.

you will be....

Sharing ideas

Relating personal experience

Writing a poem

Responding to a range of texts

Presenting non-literary material

There are five stages in a normal night's sleep which often starts with what are called **myclonic jerks** where the sleeper may have a sudden sensation of falling. This is the start of Stage One sleep where muscles relax and the heart rate slows down. This is followed by three further stages where the sleeper's blood pressure and pulse slow further. Stage Four sleep is the one which it is hardest to wake up from and many sleepers will not respond to even a bright light shone directly into their eyes then. However, it is Stage Five sleep where we dream most and Rapid Eye Movement (REM) phases indicate that a sleeper is dreaming. In REM sleep, the eyes do not have to be open but can be seen to be moving under the eyelids. If you are woken up during REM sleep you will probably remember a dream. At this time, the body's systems all speed up, the sleeper uses more oxygen and his or her muscles tense. REM sleep periods last, usually, for between ten and twenty minutes with quieter periods of relaxation in between and there can be four or five of them in a normal night's sleep. In total you are likely to spend about six years of your life dreaming in REM sleep

Scientists have known for some time that REM sleep is very important. Some drugs stop REM sleep and when a patient stops taking them the intensity of their dreams can be very powerful for several nights afterwards. Sleep deprivation is a form of mental torture sometimes used in interrogations and a prisoner who is not allowed to dream will start to have vivid waking hallucinations. However, while scientists appreciate the importance of sleep, and know a lot about what happens to the brain and body during sleep, they cannot really answer questions about exactly why we dream, why we sometimes remember dreams and why we dream about the things we do

Brenda Mallon is a dream researcher who has conducted hundreds of interviews with children and young people about their dreams. Below are some of the things they said about why they dream.

ROXANNE (16): *I am sure dreaming is a way of getting rid of all the loose ends of thoughts in our minds. I usually find that I can connect my dreams with something which has recently happened or with something I have seen or heard.*

We dream so that we don't get fed up while we're asleep. **BRIAN (13)**

CAMILLE (7): *I think we go into the land of dreams because our brain switches off . . . it has a rest . . . it relaxes.*

Dreaming is just like thinking in the day except no one disturbs us and we can see things more clearly because we have nothing else to think about. **MARI (11)**

LUCY (12): *Dreams tell us what we are really like on the inside. Our subconscious is letting us know what we think.*

I think we dream because it adds another world to our own and we need another place to escape to. Things can happen in dreams which might never happen in life but you have the experience from your dreams. **GWENDOLYN (15)**

HELEN (13): *I think that while we're asleep we're still thinking and the thoughts become animated instead of just heard. Because we are asleep we're not actually controlling our thoughts. They become jumbled up, so the characters and places change and dreams don't usually make sense. If you're thinking about something, or excited, then you dream that because you're thinking about it so much.*

1 In a small group, talk about why you think that *you* dream and which of these suggestions you agree or disagree with. Can you remember examples from your own dreams which would support any of these ideas?

What do we dream about?

What are the things you dream about most? Brenda Mallon's survey suggested that people are most likely to dream about major events in their lives, and changes in the ways they view the world or feel that it views them. Becoming an adult is a time of great physical and mental change and social upheaval and this is reflected in teenagers' dreams. According to her survey, 14–16 year olds are likely to dream about some or all of the following things:

School: especially examinations, school uniform and getting into trouble.

Responsibility: having to look after parents, brothers and sisters, losing things and forgetting to do jobs.

Independence: being left alone or ignored in dangerous situations, feeling rejected by friends, murdering or attacking other people.

Violence: being attacked or fighting to defend family and friends and being chased, often through corridors and up staircases. Sometimes being paralysed and powerless to resist.

Sexuality: romantic dreams about stars, partners and having babies, or about sexual relationships – very often with people you would not normally be attracted to – and sexual attacks and violence.

Good and evil: devils, creatures, grandparents who have died and heaven or hell.

Wishes and worries: winning at sport, meeting pop stars, being in the street with no clothes on, car crashes or other accidents and wars or the end of the world.

2 With your group, talk about your own dreams. Then, each keep a dream diary for a week. Put a notepad and pen by your bed and try to write about your dreams if you wake in the night or as soon as you wake in the morning. Just a few scribbled notes on waking will help you to remember a dream later.

What do dreams mean?

For centuries people have believed that their dreams are significant and that it is possible to dream about the future or about places you have never visited. When you have the experience of *déjà vu* – being in a situation and suddenly having the feeling that you have been there before – some people would suggest that you may have dreamed it previously.

Of course, there is a clear relationship in some ways between dreams and people's lives. Sick children often dream of being fit and well and Brenda Mallon's research showed that children in Northern Ireland were more likely to dream about violence, guns and bombs than children in the rest of the United Kingdom. You will know that a frightening film or video can often trigger off a dream, or nightmare.

Dream analysts believe that our subconscious minds work in similar ways and that there is a kind of dream language which we all share. Water, snakes, knives, tunnels and corridors are typical dream features which a dream psychologist would see as *symbols* relating to, and saying something about, our attitudes to life, sexuality and death. For example, dreaming that you can fly might symbolise your level of self-confidence. So, if you dream of flying across the sea it means you are over-confident and conceited while flying close to the ground is supposed to indicate a setback in your life. If you dream of growing taller, then that shows that your self-respect is growing but if someone else is growing taller in your dream that indicates that you are worried about what the future has in store for you. Because the snake is a symbol of evil, if you kill one in a dream you are supposed to prevent someone from harming you.

3 How well do you understand the language of dreams? With a partner, look at this list of actions you might carry out in a dream and their mixed up interpretations and see if you can agree how to pair them together.

IF YOU ARE . . .		IT MEANS YOU . . .	
1	DRIVING A CAR	A	are willing to get involved in life
2	SWEEPING A PATH	B	have hopes which will never be realised
3	DANCING ON YOUR OWN	C	are in control of your own destiny
4	GETTING INTO A BATH	D	are getting into debt
5	WRAPPING A PRESENT	E	know that you have made a mistake
6	OPENING A SAFE	F	are facing up to difficulties in life
7	DIGGING A HOLE	G	are not getting on as well as you might
8	WASHING HAIR	H	are no longer keeping a secret from your family
9	TELEPHONING A FRIEND	I	have a surprise awaiting you
10	THROWING THINGS	J	keeping your feelings under control

Compare your matchings with those of other pairs. If you tend to agree with each other, then that suggests that there is a language of dreams.

Dreams and writing

Somewhere between waking and sleeping, is the world of the imagination and daydreams. Daydreams are fantasies about what life might be like or about what the future holds for us. Ambitions and anxieties are both kinds of daydream where we imagine how things might turn out, well or badly.

Writers use dreams, daydreams and their imaginations to help them think of ideas and images. Some poets have claimed to dream complete poems and have written them down on awaking and film-makers have dreamed images which are so startling that they are inspired to make a whole film around them. Dreams or nightmares may have given you ideas for stories or poems in the past.

The extracts here show how dreams and nightmares have inspired two different writers:

NIGHTMARE

WHEN you're lying awake with a dismal headache,
    and repose is taboo'd by anxiety,
I conceive you may use any language you choose to
    indulge in, without impropriety;
For your brain is on fire – the bedclothes conspire of usual
    slumber to plunder you:
First your counterpane goes, and uncovers your toes, and
    your sheet slips demurely from under you;
Then the blanketing tickles – you feel like mixed pickles –
    so terribly sharp is the pricking,
And you're hot, and you're cross, and you tumble and toss
    till there's nothing 'twixt you and the ticking.
Then the bedclothes all creep to the ground in a heap, and
    you pick 'em all up in a tangle;
Next your pillow resigns and politely declines to remain at
    its usual angle!
Well, you get some repose in the form of a doze, with hot
    eye-balls and head ever aching,
But your slumbering teems with such horrible dreams that
    you'd very much better be waking;
For you dream you are crossing the Channel, and tossing
    about in a steamer from Harwich –
Which is something between a large bathing machine and
    a very small second-class carriage –
And you're giving a treat (penny ice and cold meat) to a
    party of friends and relations –
They're a ravenous horde – and they all came on board at
    Sloane Square and South Kensington Stations.
And bound on that journey you find your attorney (who
    started that morning from Devon);
He's a bit undersized, and you don't feel surprised when
    he tells you he's only eleven.
Well, you're driving like mad with this singular lad (by-
    the-bye the ship's now a four-wheeler),
And you're playing round games, and he calls you bad
    names when you tell him that 'ties pay the dealer';

But this you can't stand, so you throw up your hand, and
    you find you're as cold as an icicle,
In your shirt and your socks (the black silk with gold
    clocks), crossing Salisbury Plain on a bicycle:
And he and the crew are on bicycles too – which they've
    somehow or other invested in –
And he's telling the tars, all the particulars of a company
    he's interested in –
It's a scheme of devices, to get at low prices, all goods
    from cough mixtures to cables
(Which tickled the sailors) by treating retailers, as though
    they were all vegetables –
You get a good spadesman to plant a small tradesman,
    (first take off his boots with a boot-tree),
And his legs will take root, and his fingers will shoot, and
    they'll blossom and bud like a fruit-tree –
From the greengrocer tree you get grapes and green pea,
    cauliflower, pineapple, and cranberries,
While the pastrycook plant, cherry brandy will grant,
    apple puffs, and three-corners, and banberries –
The shares are a penny, and ever so many are taken by
    Rothschild and Baring,
And just as a few are allotted to you, you awake with a
    shudder despairing –
You're a regular wreck, with a crick in your neck, and no
    wonder you snore, for your head's on the floor, and
    you've needles and pins from your soles to your shins
    and your flesh is a-creep for your left leg's asleep, and
    you've cramp in your toes, and a fly on your nose,
    and some fluff in your lung, and a feverish tongue,
    and a thirst that's intense, and a general sense that
    you haven't been sleeping in clover;
But the darkness has passed, and it's daylight at last, and
    the night has been long – ditto ditto my song – and
    thank goodness they're both of them over!

William Schwenck Gilbert

THE DAY I ONCE DREAMED

This is the day I first thought of
in my closed eyes,
deep in my eyes,
the day I first thought of;
with the sun strands weaving,
sun drops sparkling
in the high streams,
on the high seas —
the day I once dreamed.

This is the day I first saw
down in my mind,
deep in my brain,
the day I first saw;
with the wild gulls calling,
barley sheen swishing
in the high wind,
on the high hill —
the day I once dreamed.

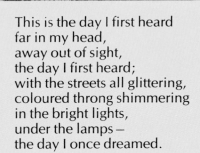

This is the day I first heard
far in my head,
away out of sight,
the day I first heard;
with the streets all glittering,
coloured throng shimmering
in the bright lights,
under the lamps —
the day I once dreamed.

That was the day I then saw,
the day I then heard,
when I opened my eyes,
when I unblocked my ears;
the day I then knew
when I focused my mind,
the day I then knew.

With the huge cloud thundering,
thick sky asphyxiating
right overhead,
night overhead,
all over the land —
that was the day I then knew;
the terrible night,
the night of the doom.
That was the night I then knew —
the night of the end of the world.

Pat Arrowsmith

4 Write your own dream or nightmare poem. Use startling images
and description to convey the confusion of a dream and the way
that events and people merge or come in and out of a dream at
random.

Now, read this story by Jade Eves. It is about daydreams and the way they connect to reality. Read it on your own or with your group.

D R E A M S

My life has been the same as long as I can remember and now I'm bored. But I'm trapped and all I can do is dream. I spread out luxuriously, face down, like a starfish, on the king-size bed in the hotel suite, stroking the silk-satin surface of the counterpane with both hands. It's scarlet and is a perfect match for my newly painted nails. I stretch my legs until I can feel my silk-stockinged toes pressed against the quilted leather headboard. Life's a dream, I think.

Thousands of miles away, in a cramped bedsit on the outskirts of London, I sit, legs stretched out in front of me, on my narrow bed. The grey overblanket is rough to the touch and moth-eaten in places. A good match for my socks, I think. I poke a finger through one of the holes in the blanket, making it bigger. I study my fingernails absently – they are bitten to the quick – and lean back against the cold, bare wall. The gas fire has gone out and I put another 50-pence in the meter. I am bored: there's nothing to do but dream . . .

Back in the plush hotel suite, I smile to myself and turn my head to one side. Beyond the tall French windows, the orange Antiguan twilight casts long shadows of wrought iron railings across the marble slabbed floor of the balcony, into the room and over the bed. Sighing, I lift my head to look at the clock on the wall: seven o'clock, it says. But the time doesn't matter, I'm not in a hurry. I pick up one of the many glossy magazines I am featured in and, rolling onto my back, I flick idly through the pages.

There I am, swathed in summer silks . . . There I am again, dressed from head to toe in winter furs. Back home, my face is everywhere – on posters at underground stations, smiling down on the bustling crowds from huge bill-boards. Truly beautiful. I would never say that out loud, never drop my shield of fake modesty (because that very modesty is part of my appeal), but I know it's true. I am beautiful. Sometimes, I wish I wasn't.

Back in my colourless bedsit world, I sigh and walk over to the window. Outside, the sky is heavy with thick, grey cloud and the streets are damp from fog. Opposite the building is a huge billboard. A model girl with a crimson smile beams out at me. She's jumping up in the air against a Caribbean background, full of the joys of spring, unaware that it's always winter where I live.

I drop the glossy magazine onto the soft silver shag-pile. There's singing coming from the bathroom – one of my favourite songs, one of your songs – not quite as tuneful as on the album, but melodious nonetheless.

I smile as you emerge from the bathroom in a cloud of steam, your dark hair damp against your head. A fluffy white towel is tucked around your slim waist and your suntan looks perfect against the whiteness.

'You look sexy,' you say, coming towards the bed.

'I was just about to say the same thing,' I laugh, pulling you onto the bed and close to me. As you run your fingers through my hair, I wonder if you'd still want me if I wasn't sexy.

I see you trudging down the street, your fists thrust into your coat pockets. Your eyebrows are knitted in concentration. You look like you're singing, the way you usually do – one of the pop songs you heard on the radio at the factory, most probably. Your hair is damp from the fog. You look beautiful.

I smooth down my skirt as I hear the front door open; then you are inside, unbuttoning your shabby tweed coat, shivering.

'It's colder in here than it is out there,' you remark.

'Come here and I'll warm you up,' I say moving towards you and sliding my hands inside your coat.

Outside the window, the billboard girl continues to grin. I wonder what it would be like to be her.

The Antiguan sun has well and truly set but the air is still warm as we lie together on the red bed. I glance over at you in the violet half-light: your eyes are closed but I know you're not sleeping, because your breathing is irregular and your eyelids are fluttering, as if you're thinking.

I run a feather-light finger along the bridge of your nose, and you open your eyes and smile.

'Shall we get ready?' you ask.

'OK,' I reply, swinging my long legs off the edge of the bed and sitting up. I pick my clothes up from the floor and head for the bathroom. I don't really want to get dressed again – I'd be quite happy to stay in bed for the rest of the night – but the restaurant and night-club await.

The mirror in the bathroom confirms what I already know – that I am beautiful and that that is the real reason you chose me. From a glossy magazine, you made your choice. One call to the model agency and I was yours. But you can do things like that: you believe that fame and fortune can buy you almost anything. And you're almost right. Like a purchase from a catalogue, I delivered myself to you, gift-wrapped.

The grey clouds have darkened over the silent streets and the sky is now bruise-coloured. We are in bed because there's nothing good on the telly and because you're on the early shift tomorrow morning. The air around us is still cold but, under the covers, we are warm. It's dark in the room, but I can see your profile silhouetted against the purple light. I snuggle up close to you.

'Are you asleep?' I whisper.

'No,' you whisper back.

'Why are you whispering then?' I laugh.

You smile, I can't see it but I know it is there. Your smile is like the sun to me: when you smile, I automatically feel warm. I'm sure I'd die without it. I love you for your smile. I love you for yourself.

'I love you,' you say.

'Good,' I reply.

The curtains are drawn on the girl with the lipstick grin.

I watch you coming across the dance-floor from the night-club bar. You are carrying two drinks – Buck's Fizz, most probably. That's what we start on, then we move onto straight champagne as the night progresses. You place the glasses on the table and smile at me.

We haven't spoken for over an hour – the music is too loud. But I'm good at sitting pretty, looking good. I'm wearing a simple black vest-dress and diamonds. My fair hair is slicked back. My lips are deepest carmine.

Movement on the stage on the opposite side of the dance-floor causes me to look up. A cabaret act bounces into view and starts singing and dancing, all sparkly sequins and fuchsia feathers. It makes a change you not being on stage. It makes a change us being able to go out without you being recognised. But, although your records are on sale in the shops here, you're not as famous as you are at home, where we can never have a normal night out. That really gets to me sometimes.

I sit back, knock back my fourth Buck's Fizz, and start to dream . . .

In a dark, still bedsit room on the outskirts of London, an unknown girl and the boy she loves sleep peacefully, because in spite of small problems, they are happy. Beyond the curtains, the sky is now the colour of Indian ink. Outside, the billboard girl still smiles.

On a king-size bed in a lavish hotel suite in Antigua, a beautiful model girl has collapsed in a drunken stupor. She has staggered home on her own, while her pop star boyfriend dances the night away in the arms of yet another adoring fan. She hates it when he does that, but she can't leave him.

As she closes her eyes, she begins to dream – the same dream she always has, night after night after night. A dream of life in a small flat back home in London, an ordinary life, a quiet life, with a boy who really loves her. But for her, that is never to be. This is her reality; the rest – the girl in the bedsit, the girl she longs to be – is the fantasy.

'Life's a dream,' she whispers as she drifts off to sleep.

5. This story brings the worlds of dream and reality very close together. With your group discuss:

— when you realised what was happening in the story
— how far your expectations and predictions led you to read the story in the wrong way
— how the writer conceals the truth from the reader
— how the writer links the two threads of the story
— whether, when you look back, there were any clues in the story which you missed
— the style of the writing and how it conveys the sense of being a dream.

6. Now, write your own story which mixes dreams and reality in this way. You may get some ideas from your discussion of dreams and their meanings at the beginning of this unit. Try to create a dream world and a real world which reflect one another in some way and where, perhaps, there is some confusion for the reader.

As you redraft, ask your partner to read it through and to assess how successfully you are managing to do this before you write your final version.

7. Collect together the dream diaries, poems and stories from the group, as a display. First, survey and analyse the dreams contained in the diaries. How often, and how much, do the group report dreaming? Do the dreams have anything in common in terms of their content?

Mix up the dream reports and each suggest an analysis of one of them without knowing whose dream it was. As you try to analyse a dream, consider what the dreamer is doing in the dream. Think about what he or she is trying to achieve or failing to achieve, is trying to show or to conceal and how the dreamer relates to other people in the dream. Put your analysis with the dream report as part of your display.

Tips for Success

◆ Talking about one dream will often help you to remember another, just as you remember more and more details once you start retelling a dream.

◆ Remember that the meaning of the dream is not its literal meaning, e.g. driving a car does not have anything to do with being a driver but says something about a person's direction in life, his or her confidence or anxiety and so on

◆ When you write your story try to build an element of surprise into it as you link the threads of the real world and the dream.

The future in your hands

Can you discover the hidden secrets of someone's personality by analysing their hands? This unit lets you find out what you can say about your friends – their personalities and their futures – by doing just that. Here, Lori Reid, a well-known hand analyst, talks about her work.

you will be . . . .

- Locating and selecting information
- Following instructions
- Presenting a performance
- Presenting non-literary material

Reading a hand is like reading a detective story. Clues, scattered all over the palms and fingers, can be collected and sifted and built up into an identikit picture of the individual.

Our hands are remarkable indicators of our characters and personalities. They mirror our physical condition and our states of mind. Based on an age-old system of observation and deduction, hand analysis has shown over the centuries, that people with particular shapes to their hands behave in particular ways. Those with long fingers see the world in quite a different way to those with short fingers!

A good analysis of the hand, therefore, can give valuable insight into every aspect of a person's life. It can describe character and personality in minute detail. It can throw light on emotional issues and help to smooth relationship problems. It can pinpoint latent gifts and talents. Invaluable in career guidance at every age, it can point the direction, whether selecting GCSE courses at school or finding oneself at a crossroads in later life.

But whether an individual who consults me wants a general analysis or has a specific query in mind, my method follows a strict procedure. First, I write down some basic personal details for my records – name, date of birth, whether right- or left-handed, that sort of thing. Then I closely examine the hands, noting the shape and bone construction, the look and direction of the lines in the palms, and the general colour and feel of the skin. Whilst making these observations, I mentally piece together all the clues that I can pick up from their hands. I need to construct a picture of the individual and his or her life in my own mind, before I begin to speak. This helps me to know how to couch what I say. Different people see life differently and by formulating that initial picture, I feel I can get onto their wavelength, see things from their point of view, and so express myself in their terms.

However, I always begin my reading by making two crucial points very clear. The first is that hands and lines can, and do, change. And the second is that we all have free-will. This means that if a negative trend shows up for the future, that individual may have time to prevent it.

Then, the actual analysis of the hand begins. Here, I slowly unravel, in minute detail, the psychological intricacies that make up the individual and outline the trends and possible events that might take place in the future. I hope that by the end of it, my clients will be better able to make their own decisions as to how, and where, they want their lives to go.

How to read your palm

The following section describes how you can read your own palm or a friend's. Read through it with a partner. As you are reading, put both hands out in front of you so that you can compare your own hands with what the article says. Do not stretch your hands out flat but allow them to relax and curl slightly – that way the lines will show more clearly.

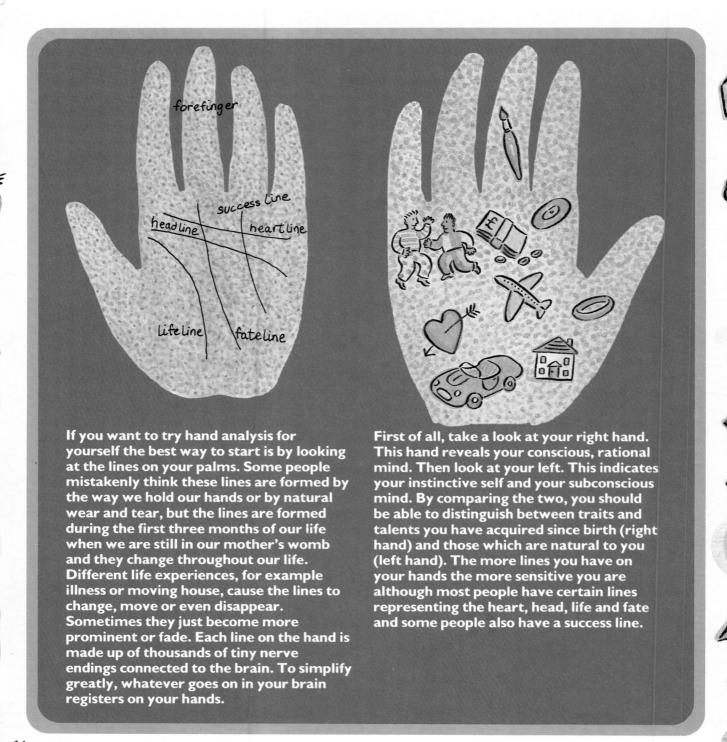

forefinger

success line

head line

heart line

life line

fate line

If you want to try hand analysis for yourself the best way to start is by looking at the lines on your palms. Some people mistakenly think these lines are formed by the way we hold our hands or by natural wear and tear, but the lines are formed during the first three months of our life when we are still in our mother's womb and they change throughout our life. Different life experiences, for example illness or moving house, cause the lines to change, move or even disappear. Sometimes they just become more prominent or fade. Each line on the hand is made up of thousands of tiny nerve endings connected to the brain. To simplify greatly, whatever goes on in your brain registers on your hands.

First of all, take a look at your right hand. This hand reveals your conscious, rational mind. Then look at your left. This indicates your instinctive self and your subconscious mind. By comparing the two, you should be able to distinguish between traits and talents you have acquired since birth (right hand) and those which are natural to you (left hand). The more lines you have on your hands the more sensitive you are although most people have certain lines representing the heart, head, life and fate and some people also have a success line.

Your *head line*

reveals your thought patterns and intellectual powers. A short head line does not indicate a lack of intellect, but can show the specialist who likes to concentrate on a specific sphere of interest. A long head line shows someone with foresight, who can see the implications of their actions. If it is very straight and clearly defined you have a logical, calculating mind. This type of head line is often found in accountants or people who have a head for figures or are good at mathematics and science.

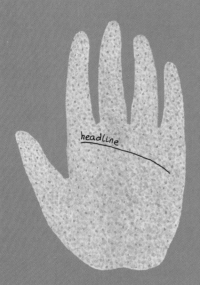

headline

However, if your head line curves down onto your palm you are very imaginative and likely to be drawn to the arts. You are also emotional and can be more easily upset by others. If the line forks at the end this indicates duality. In other words, you can see both sides of any situation. This is a useful ability in helping other people to overcome their problems, but in your own life it can cause trouble as you may have difficulty in making up your mind about things.

Sometimes your head line will be curved on the left hand but straight on the right. This means you react emotionally in certain situations but decide on practical solutions.

Your *heart line*

shows your emotional and sexual nature. A deeply curved line indicates a very physical and emotional personality. You are more likely to talk to people you meet and approach new friends rather than wait for them to make the first move. If the heart line is long and deeply set you have a

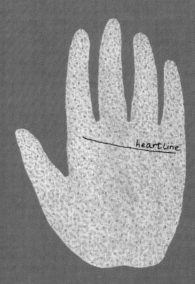

heart line

great capacity to give and receive affection. You are also likely to need a partner who is physically appealing, whereas for those with a straight heart line, a mentally stimulating relationship is most important.

A straight line indicates a quieter, more passive nature, and a short heart line indicates an explosive temper. If there is a line running above, and parallel to the heart line, you have acting ability. But if this and the other lines are broad and deep, you are very much influenced by the moods of those around you.

If your heart line curves up towards your little finger you will choose a partner with money as you need financial security. The head and heart line are joined as one line in around five per cent of people. This is known as the simian line and indicates that you are very determined and will see problems through to the end.

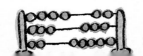

Your *life line*

does not, as some people believe, denote length of life. Rather it indicates vitality and satisfaction with your environment. A short life line means you probably have intense bursts of physical energy with breaks in between exertions. The longer the life line the greater your physical energy.

If your life line curves right round it is likely you are a person who will settle in your home country. However, if there is a branch from the line down towards the ulna section of your palm (the side of the palm opposite to your thumb joint) then you are extremely restless and have a desire to travel. If a section of the line is faint, this is a sure sign you will be

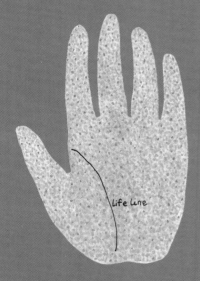

Life line

dissatisfied with your environment at that point in your life. Also, look out for an 'island' on your life line as this indicates indecision about where to live. An island is where the line splits up and then rejoins and its presence often tells palmists about changes and disturbance in people's lives.

The *fate line*

shows the drive within a person to improve their position in life. It indicates a sense of direction and responsibility. However, not everybody has a fate line – the absence of one tends to indicate someone with no sense of direction, a drifter.

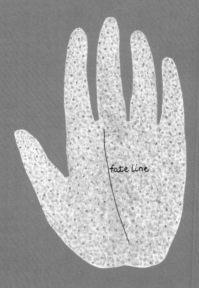

fate line

If the fate line on your left hand is not very clear, and that on your right is, you have overcome initial uncertainty. If the right one is faint, you are not using your potential. Sometimes it is joined to your life line which means that you are close to your family and have probably felt over-protected or restricted. Conversely, if it is separate from your life line you are independent.

Lines running parallel indicate you have various interests but an island clearly indicates you will face a difficult decision. Many small lines running into your fate line mean you will probably have many relationships.

The **success line** is sometimes known as the sun line, but not everyone has this. It indicates a happy magnetic personality who appreciates beauty. Anyone with this line has the ability to get on in life. Sometimes there are three success lines. These indicate you have talents and are lucky with money. If there are islands in the line there may be some kind of scandal in your life and a break with an overlap shows a change of residence.

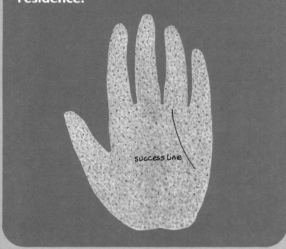

success line

1 Now make sure that you can find these five lines on your own hands. Compare your hands with your partner's. Help each other to trace round your hands (palm facing up) and draw an outline of them. On the outline mark your head, heart, life and fate lines. Mark your success line if you have one. Look back at the article and try to decide with your partner what each line says about you.

2 Together, study the hands below which belong to two 17 year olds. Look at the major lines on them and see what you can say about the personalities of the people whose hands they are. What jobs might they do in the future? What kinds of people might they be?

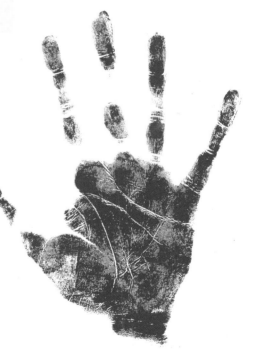

The *branch lines*

on your hands are a further source of interesting clues. Looking closely at your palms will probably have shown you that there are many other lines, crosses and intersections, apart from the major lines. These branch lines can also be interpreted. For example, lines sloping from your life line towards the bottom left of the hand indicate restlessness.

It is possible here to see details of possible relationships and children. Underneath your little finger there may be one or more small horizontal lines. These represent potential relationships. Very close parallel lines can mean you will have two romances in progress at the same time! Jutting vertically upwards out of this marriage/relationship line there may be one or more faint lines. These are supposed to represent the children you will have. Round the base of your thumb is the family circle. If this is very clearly defined you have a strong relationship with your family but if it is faint and unclear you are more distant from them.

Are you intuitive and able to make quick judgements? Your hands will certainly reveal whether or not you are. A semi-circular line in the ulna section of your hand shows you must learn to trust your instincts. It is easy to dismiss feelings such as an instant mistrust of someone. But you have probably realised by now that your early instincts are usually correct. Another sign of an intuitive person is a triangle formed between the head, life and fate lines.

Are you ambitious? If you have lines extending up from the life line towards the forefinger you certainly are. A line pointing towards your middle finger from the life line indicates you will soon enjoy a positive change, for example, a new home or examination success. If you can see an island in your fate line you are unsure about what lies ahead and you are allowing emotional problems to interfere with material progress. Islands in your heart line mean emotional uncertainty and sometimes difficulty in committing yourself to a relationship. Criss crosses where the head and life lines join are a sign of shyness.

Here is a typical hand reading by Lori Reid. The print belongs to Christina, a 32 year old architect.

The first point to notice is its long sloping *head line* which is a sign of a creative and imaginative mind. The forked ending is the mark of the writer or artist. The long slender fingers suggest a sense of refinement and the long lean thumb shows elegance of thought. This means that Christina's ideas will be fresh, imaginative and sophisticated. The space between the second and third fingers indicates that she is a deep thinker. The whorl pattern on the fingertips highlights individualism but also adds a sense of isolation. The strong fate line, swerving towards the ring finger, and the series of branches rising up out of the *head line,* confirm that she will fulfill a good many of her ambitions in life.

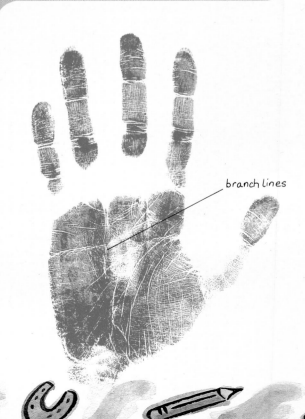

branch lines

Finally, studying

hand shape

is another key indicator to a person's character and life trends. Six basic hand types are recognisable, but in reality most people's hands are a mixture of two or more types. The six types are:

SQUARE HAND   This hand has square-tipped fingers, a square palm and square thumb. It reveals a practical, level-headed person who rarely takes risks.

CONIC HAND   This hand is soft and pliable with flexible thumbs and pointed fingers. Someone with a conic hand is lively and changeable and is certainly not one for the quiet life.

SPATULATE HAND   This hand is fairly firm but flexible, with fingers that broaden slightly towards the tips. This person is alert, perceptive and extremely individualistic.

PSYCHIC HAND   This hand has very fine skin with long rounded nails and belongs to someone more at home on a spiritual plane than a practical one. His or her sense of intuition is strong and communication skills are good.

PHILOSOPHIC HAND   This hand is very bony and angular with pronounced joints, obvious veins and finely lined skin. He or she is a complex and sensitive person, who is often difficult to understand but who is good at understanding others.

ELEMENTARY HAND   This hand is thick-set, strong and heavy with short broad lines, revealing a physically strong person with lots of drive. Capable of hard work, he or she is also extremely materialistic.

3. Use what you have found out to write an analysis of your partner's personality based on your reading of their hand. Write a separate comment for each major line and say something about any clear branch lines you can see. Take into account the overall shape and feel of the hand. At the end of your analysis, say whether or not you agree with what the reading suggests. You may notice that you have used other facts and information you already knew about your partner's interests to fill out your analysis.

4. Try reading the hand of someone else in the group. Study both of their hands and tell them what you can say about them from the reading. Trace each major line and describe your interpretation of it. As you talk, watch the subject's face for clues and listen to whether they appear to be agreeing with you. Do not be too definite in what you say. Talk about what the lines 'suggest' and 'indicate' about the person rather than saying what kind of person they are. Use them as the starting point for your analysis.

Try your new skill out at home, or on teachers and friends. Remember, the fun in analysing people's hands lies as much in what you do not say as in what you do. Reading palms well means developing the language of ambiguity (saying things which might have more than one meaning) and suggestion in order to catch and hold your listener's interest. And, it means responding to the non-verbal clues the listener gives you, to help you decide what ideas to develop – and when to move on to a new point.

Tips for Success

◆ When you are reading someone's hand, speak confidently and keep referring to your subject's hand as you analyse its features.
◆ Remember that the key to involving your subject when you are reading or analysing the lines in someone's palm, is to hint at what is there rather than being too specific.

PHOTO POEMS

Ideas for poems can come from all sorts of sources. This unit explores a series of poems based on newspaper articles and photographs. They were written by Edwin Morgan.

What's news?

With a partner, look at the photographs on these pages which have all appeared on newspaper front pages. Describe what you can see in each of them. What can you tell about what has happened in each of them? Can you recognise, or guess at, the news stories they are connected with?

you will be . . . .

 Sharing ideas

 Responding to a writer

 Responding to literature

Writing a poem

snap

snap

1 Join with another pair and share your ideas. Now each pick one photograph and note down your ideas about:

— What made this news?
— What do you think is happening?
— What are the people in it doing and thinking?

Get together with the people from other groups who looked at the same photograph. Share your ideas with them. You will probably find that you agree quite closely on what is taking place but that some of you have noticed different details. Appoint one person from this group to report back to the class.

POET TALKING

Edwin Morgan is a poet who has used newspaper articles and, occasionally, photographs as the starting point for poetry.

Below, he talks about his poetry collections, *Instamatic Poems* and *Takes*, and how he uses news stories.

poetry

'I first started collecting newspaper cuttings in the late 1960s. My idea was to use the unusual, bizarre, surprising, violent, yet human stories which we encounter every day in newspapers and magazines, as material for poems. The name 'instamatic poetry' comes from one of the small fully automatic cameras which were produced then.

The idea for gathering the material grew from my fascination with the short-lived nature of these human dramas, frozen in time, yet forgotten almost immediately as the news rushes past us day by day. For my particular style, I struck on the idea of the image of an imaginary photograph, a word-picture poem to freeze the actual event more firmly in reality. By using this same form, the events, facts, and actions which took place in different places and at different times could be brought together into a unified book. Although I had not been present at any of these events, they could be seen and described in detail in my mind's eye and commented on.

I often found – and some people have criticised this – that the stories which caught my eye were shocking or highly dramatic or apparently morbid, even though true. But actually, if you go through the poems, only about a third of them are concerned with violent events and many of the rest are humorous or quizzical, or merely strange. Of course the poems reflect the newspapers they're taken from and purely happy events are often not seen as newsworthy.

In choosing subjects to turn into poems, I think the chief motivation was to record the extraordinary variety of human experience. I tried to pick out vital facts, blend these into a workable poetic style or framework and give this the overall impression of a freshly taken photograph that tells all.

The style I decided on could be said to be more blunt and straightforward than lengthily descriptive; I wanted it to be intense and concentrated. I took a lot of care over line-endings and rhythm, emphasised a list-like style of presenting the details, in a sentence-based approach, with occasional tight metaphor or simple repetition and rhyme to remind readers that these are poems and not pictures.

Mostly the poems are in the present tense, for the fresh – just happened – effect I was hoping for. I also tried to remain a detached observer or narrator of the event, as far as the tone of the poem was concerned.

Some of these articles and poems are also, of course, mere snippets, brief attempts to record or capture some bizarre event from around the world. I tried to add a touch of wry humour or irony to these little examples of our human failings, triumphs and eccentricities. Even the shortest of the stories and poems can reveal something unexpected about life.'

Look at the four poems below and on page 24 and the stories and photograph which go with them:

Cleaning up on wasps

VIENNA: Baker Peter Hoeffer, 54, is recovering in hospital after trying to rid his shop in Innsbruck of a plague of wasps with a vacuum cleaner.

He sucked the wasps up into the cleaner's bag and then connected it to a gas pipe. The bag burst and the wasps, still very much alive, swarmed all over him.

Sunday Express

INNSBRUCK JULY 1971

A furious baker with wasps in his pastry
has sucked a swarm of them into the bag
of a vacuum cleaner and fixed the bag
to a gas pipe. But in this picture
the bag has just burst, and the man is falling
backwards black with clouds of stings.
The furious wasps have a baker in their pastry.

Tattooed body found in reservoir

A TATTOOED man, believed to be a Scot, found strangled and weighted down in a sleeping bag in a reservoir in New York state was identified yesterday as a British Army deserter.

Dental records and tattoos positively identified James Scott, 23.

Mr Scott, whose home-town was not disclosed, deserted the 1st Battalion of the Royal Green Jackets in Germany in April, along with another soldier.

His body was found by a fisherman on Saturday.

He had a flag tattooed on his upper right arm, with the words 'Scotland the Brave'. A thistle was tattooed on his right breast and a jester on his right leg.

Cashier used LSD for revenge

Vivien Bagge (17), a cashier, was annoyed when she was dismissed from the jeweller's shop where she worked.

Her revenge was to send her boss on an LSD trip by lacing his afternoon cup of tea with the hallucinatory drug, a court heard yesterday. After sipping the tea, the shop manager, Mr David Henderson, felt like throwing himself out of a window.

He felt sick, numb and light-headed, so he went to the local Labour Exchange for help.

When he was being taken to hospital he thought the ambulancemen were from the North Sea gas conversion teams. The hallucinations continued. When he was about to leave hospital he had another urge to throw himself out of a window.

Bagge, of Poplar Road, Merton Park, pleaded guilty at South-West London Quarter Sessions to unlawfully and maliciously causing poison or other obnoxious things to be taken by Mr Henderson with intent to injure, annoy or aggrieve, and to stealing four rings from the shop.

She was remanded for reports until July 20 on bail of £20 with £100 surety.

Glasgow Herald

NEW YORK STATE JULY 1990

A man fishing an upstate reservoir
has caught a sleeping bag, opened it,
starts back in horror, stared at
by a livid body with strangle-marks.
Young, stocky, lapped by waters
that did not need to drown him,
he has come thousands of miles to die.
The American fisherman tries to piece together
three tattoos, right arm, right breast, right leg:
a Scotland The Brave flag,
a spiky thistle,
a jester.

LONDON JUNE 1971

**The manager of a jeweller's shop
has with difficulty climbed onto the sill
and is measuring the window-breadth
against his wings.
He is eager to fly out over the traffic.
His secretary, Miss Bagge,
whom he sacked that morning for pocketing four rings,
is standing behind him. She fails to see the wings.
Having laced his afternoon tea with LSD
she watches his shoulders heave, and grins.**

Shots welcome frigate to Glasgow

THE veteran Falklands frigate *HMS Plymouth* came under fire again last night when shots were fired as she made her way to her new home alongside Plantation Quay in Glasgow.

An official of the Warship Preservation Trust, which has brought the vessel to Glasgow from Plymouth, said four or five shots appeared to have been fired from the river bank, possibly from an air gun, while the frigate moved up the Clyde.

Mr Brian Jarvis, a volunteer who had joined the *Plymouth* at Greenock, was struck as he stood on the bridge.

The official said: 'He is not seriously hurt but has a large red blotch on his stomach. It is not the welcome to Glasgow we anticipated.'

The trust will operate the ship as a tourist attraction, but still requires to raise about £15,000 to develop the ship and the site.

HMS Plymouth was bought by the trust after Ministry of Defence moves to use her as a missile target. She was hit by four bombs during the Falklands war although none exploded and she was the first vessel to enter Stanley Harbour.

Glasgow Herald

GLASGOW 15 JUNE 1990

Nosing greyly up the Clyde on a calm
summer evening
a frigate and its tug make a faint skein of rippl
and are reflected
(like trees on the bank and clouds above)
in lazy estuary pewter.
Unlazily, a man with an air gun
has fired at *HMS Plymouth* to give her
a Scottish welcome; on the bridge
a figure clutches his stomach. The frigate,
having survived four bombs in the Falklands,
finds out not everyone loved that war.

2   Look back at the four poems. As a group of four or five, read the poems aloud to one another and then analyse how Edwin Morgan achieves his 'instamatic' effects.

▬ List the facts from the news articles that Edwin Morgan chooses to use.

▬ Talk about the ways language is used in the poems. Remember what Edwin Morgan says about photographic effects, line structure, lists, rhythm, rhyme and repetition to help you do this.

▬ Say why you think the article might have appealed to Edwin Morgan in terms of its human characters or the message in the events it describes.

▬ Say what you liked about the poems or which poem you liked most. Is there anything you dislike? Say why.

3   Working on your own, pick two or three poems and write your own appreciation of them. Use quotations and examples to support the points you make.

4   Now, look at the two news stories printed opposite and choose one of them or one of the pictures on pages 20-21 as the basis for writing your own instamatic poem. Try to convey the idea that your reader is looking at a photograph and, if you can, allow your reader a brief glimpse into your own feelings about the event. Try to visualise the story as a picture and then think about the kind of detail which will make your poem authentic. It may help you to draw the scene before you write.

Mad dog puts bite on poor Wilbur

Report by TONY SMITH

WILBUR, a small black mongrel out for exercise with his owner in the Parkland Walk on Sunday, was savagely attacked by a pit bull terrier.

Nicola Nahal and her friend Martin James were taking photographs and the popular nature trail was full of people and dogs.

They were in the Hornsey Rise area when a couple with a child and a pit bull approached them. Without warning the terrier viciously lunged at Wilbur, grabbed him by the throat and savagely shook him. The owner tried in vain to free Wilbur from the terrier's grasp.

Nicola said Wilbur was saved by his collar. Without it the terrier would have bitten straight through his throat.

Poor Wilbur was in the grasp of the terrier for over five minutes.

Three joggers and another passer-by attempted to assist the owner but to no avail. The pit bull finally let go of its own accord. Wilbur was rushed to a vet and treated for shock and bandaged around the affected area.

Nicola, who works for the BBC, said 'I actually like American pit bull terriers – they are beautiful dogs – but after this I can see there is no way they should be allowed to walk in public.'

Nicola has reported the case to the police and intends to write to her MP, Sir Hugh Rossi.

Hornsey and Muswell Hill Journal

GUN RAIDERS DEFIED BY BRAVE EXAM GIRL

Brutal thieves beat up family

SCHOOLGIRL Anna Holmes had a sleepless night before her vital GCSE exams yesterday — she had four armed raiders sitting on her bed.

Anna, 16, hid in a tiny cupboard when the brutal thugs broke into her home and beat up her family before searching for cash.

But the cupboard was so cramped she decided to get out, seconds after the men entered her room. Anna said yesterday, after coming home 'reasonably pleased' with her exams: 'They were all slouching on my bed smoking cigarettes and didn't even bother to get up.

'I told them: "Don't you dare burn my duvet. I'm going downstairs to make a cup of tea. I hope that's all right by you."'

Anna's ordeal began after the men burst into her father George's post office at Mildenhall, Wilts.

Ransack

They punched Mr Holmes, 65, beat up his wife Wendy, 48, and broke their son Michael's arm as he tried to fight them off.

Then they tied up the family before ransacking the house.

But the Holmes's lodger, Michael Baggs, 22, managed to tip-toe out of the house to raise the alarm.

Fifteen minutes later, police raced up and the men were held. A shotgun and pistol were found.

Postmaster Mr Holmes said: 'We were woken by the doorbell and like a fool I went to answer it.

'I thought it might be a neighbour in trouble. I asked the man what he wanted and he smacked me across the face and they all piled in.'

Four men were still being questioned by police last night.

Daily Mirror

Write your poem alone but share your first draft with your group and listen to their suggestions as to how it might be improved. When you have produced a final version, keep both drafts to show the changes you have made.

In this unit you are going to look closely at the world of television 'soap operas' and explore the ways that they present their characters and stories.

- **Relating personal experience**
- **Giving an opinion**
- **Recognising non-literary material**
- **Responding to a range of texts**
- **Commenting on language use**
- **Reporting on group discussion**

It was in the early years of broadcasting that programme-planners first realised the appeal of soap operas – long-running stories which presented the interwoven lives of a range of characters. Unlike a play which has a clear beginning and ending, a soap is a continually unfolding drama which follows the lives of a range of characters. Instead of one main plot, a soap is made up of many storylines which can be connected, recur at intervals or finish completely after a number of episodes. New characters are introduced, and old ones get written out, as the actors who play them move on.

The label 'soap opera' is thought to have come from the early daytime television serials shown in the United States. These were so popular that they attracted a host of advertisements directed at housewives. Many of these were for soap powder, hence the name 'soap opera'.

People often try to explain the popularity of soaps. One suggestion is that watching television, unlike going to a film in the cinema, is a casual family activity so that the television in most homes is part of the family circle. The characters in the soaps become an extension of people's lives and achieve the status almost of friends. Outside the home, knowledge about these 'friends' can be shared with other friends and relatives.

BROOKSIDE

HOME

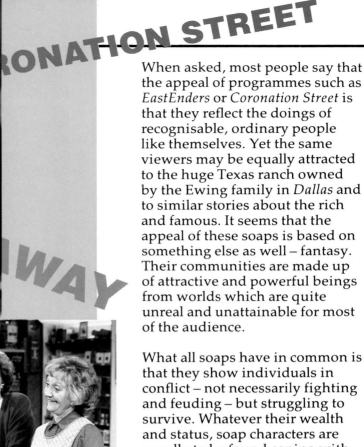

When asked, most people say that the appeal of programmes such as *EastEnders* or *Coronation Street* is that they reflect the doings of recognisable, ordinary people like themselves. Yet the same viewers may be equally attracted to the huge Texas ranch owned by the Ewing family in *Dallas* and to similar stories about the rich and famous. It seems that the appeal of these soaps is based on something else as well – fantasy. Their communities are made up of attractive and powerful beings from worlds which are quite unreal and unattainable for most of the audience.

What all soaps have in common is that they show individuals in conflict – not necessarily fighting and feuding – but struggling to survive. Whatever their wealth and status, soap characters are usually to be found coping with the stresses and strains of life while trying to make, and hold on to, relationships of all kinds.

1 Working as a small group, discuss the soaps you watch regularly. Think about your answers to these questions:

▪ How regularly and how often do you watch soaps? To what extent do you organise your life around the programmes you watch regularly?

▪ If you are a regular watcher, try to say what it is that particularly appeals to you in the soap, or soaps, that you follow. If you do not watch regularly, try to explain what you do not like about them. Why do you think they are so popular?

▪ What storyline have you most enjoyed watching, or found most compelling? Are there any themes or issues that particularly attract you?

▪ Have you heard or read criticisms of soaps, and the people who watch them? If so, what do you think about these views?

Soaps usually feature a community of characters like the people who live in an area or work together. The choice of these characters and their personalities is crucial to the popularity of the programme.

It is important to remember that almost nothing in a soap happens by accident. Every aspect of the characters, the settings and the storyline has been carefully considered and planned to achieve a particular effect.

So, who do the programme-makers choose to include in their soap communities? And, when they have chosen certain categories of people, what kind of image do they present of them? Questions like these are to do with *representation* – the way in which groups of people (old people, ethnic groups , business people or police men and women) are shown through the images created on the screen.

One way to understand how representation works is to look at how one typical group of people – teenagers – is represented in soaps, and in the media generally.

2 In your group, look at the images on these pages and collect together, or think of, other examples for yourselves. These could include television programmes, films, pop music, radio or film, and television advertising. Discuss what they reveal about how teenagers are *represented* in the media. As you talk, think about your answers to the questions opposite:

MOUNTAIN BIKES

It's wild, it's wicked, the Lizard rocks – Tune it if you can. Lizard is his bike, from Raleigh. ATBs and Mountain Bikes from £175 to £1300 and more. Ring 0898 106 712* for your free colour brochure.

BEST MATES
You can't beat them!
(But can you match them?)

...the secrets of friendships.

YOUNGSTER

Comical capers boost charity

For youngsters from Waterbeach Barracks, "beanz meanz" a big boost for charity.

Two brave teenagers — Michelle McPeak and Sarah Dickson — sat in a bath and got showered with baked beans to raise about £80 for the Red Nose appeal.

Michelle and Sarah, both 15, were doing their bit in a bumper day of fund-raising at the barracks youth club.

Sarah's father Sgt "Geordie" Dickson was sponsored as a disc jockey to the tune of £40 and all the other club members took part in a marathon dance session from midday to midnight.

They raised about £300 in total.

Said Sgt Dickson: "Many of the children's fathers are still out in the Gulf so they feel they are doing their bit back home while their fathers are doing their bit out there."

Cover-up ... Michelle McPeak and Sarah Dickson get a show
baked beans.

Picture: Chris

How varied and realistic are the representations of teenagers in the media? How broad a picture is given in terms of age, race, class or sex, where teenagers live, or what their interests are?

Can you find any stereotypes (very common or typical representations of teenagers) among these images? Are any of the representations *caricatures* rather than stereotypes? A caricature is a comic (but often insulting) image in which one or two of a character's features are greatly exaggerated.

Are there any unusual, or unexpected, images which you have not met before?

What are the main messages about teenagers being offered by the 'evidence' as a whole? Is the overall picture positive or negative, offensive or flattering?

Who do you think created or chose to use these images of teenagers in the media? Who are they aimed at and what do you think is their message?

3. Use your discussion and your own research to write a commentary on how young people are represented in a number of soap operas. Describe two or three characters and then comment on the way they are presented in the programme.

Think about the kinds of things they do, the consequences of their actions and how other people in the programme react to them. How far is the audience intended to sympathise with them? Try to identify any contrasts or similarities between the characters you have chosen.

29

If you switch on a soap opera you have not seen before, it does not take long before you understand the characters and their stories. The conventions that are used to create this very accessible world are part of the 'language' of soap operas.

4 Now, split the group into pairs to look in more detail at the way soap people are presented. Each pair should choose a different soap opera and make a list of all the major characters.

Then, use a chart like the one below to show how these characters are represented. Briefly describe their representation – the kind of person they are meant to be – and then note down the features which the programme-makers use to build up that image. It may help you to concentrate on a single scene or shot, rather than on different storylines here. Think about the settings and places where the characters are seen, the way they speak, their habits, clothes, possessions and body language. Think, as well, about their relationships with other people and how they are referred to by others.

Settings, clothes and possessions all help to build up a character's image.

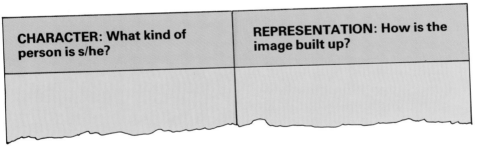

CHARACTER: What kind of person is s/he?	REPRESENTATION: How is the image built up?

Try to describe all the characters on your list under each heading. Afterwards, explain your findings and conclusions to the rest of the group.

Now, look closely at your completed charts and the range of characters you have covered.

- What categories of people are featured most? What kinds of people feature little or not at all?

- What patterns can you find in the kinds of relationships and lifestyles the different categories of people have?

- Are there some characters you are meant to sympathise with or approve of more than others? How do you know this? How much is left to you to decide?

- Are new or unexpected images to be found more in some soaps than others?

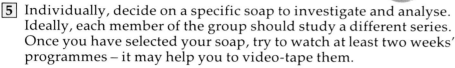

5 Individually, decide on a specific soap to investigate and analyse. Ideally, each member of the group should study a different series. Once you have selected your soap, try to watch at least two weeks' programmes – it may help you to video-tape them.

As you watch, think about what the programme-makers have chosen to show you – and how the message is put over. Jot down your comments. Here are some of the things you might mention:

— the current storylines and how they are developing
— the settings
— themes which are being explored from particular points of view
— the way episodes begin and end, and maintain our interest
— character groupings (especially families), stereotypes and new images.

As your viewing goes on, you should be able to comment on some of the issues which the programme raises. These might be concerned with:

— gender issues – the way the sexes are portrayed
— race – the way different races or minorities are shown
— class – the different features which 'tell' the viewer about a character's social class
— social issues – things like drug abuse, work and unemployment, law and order, alcoholism, violence, politics and infidelity.

These are only examples. Be sure to include your own thoughts and knowledge of that particular soap. Compare your notes with those made by others in the class who are working on the same series. Then, draft your analysis. You could take as your title 'SOAP COMMUNITIES: REAL OR FANTASY? .

FIRST give a brief outline of the programme you have chosen and why you chose it. Say something about the overall setting and the main characters in the soap community.

THEN work through your analysis point by point. In each paragraph, put forward a separate point evaluating the representation of characters and issues. Aim to develop your comments about the messages which the programme conveys to its viewers.

END with your own point of view and conclusions. Say what you found effective and convincing and where you think the soap succeeded or failed.

YOUR OWN

soap

Now, use what you have found out about to write your own episode for your favourite soap.

6 Choose one of the storylines below and a soap that you know quite well. Decide on which characters might be involved in it and the roles they might play.

— A character is trapped in an embarrassing or awkward situation.
— An act of betrayal is revealed by one character to another.
— Someone discovers a letter, not addressed to them, which nonetheless has drastic implications for them.
— Over-confidence leads to disaster, but an older person helps out.
— Someone desperately needs money – at the last moment some turns up from an unexpected quarter.
— An unexpected treat cheers someone up.
— A misunderstanding almost ends up in a public fight.

As a group, try improvising the scenes you have thought of to help develop your ideas. Then, individually or in pairs, write a section of the script from the episode where these events take place.

Introduce one or two new teenage characters, using what you have learned about the way teenagers are represented in soaps. Incorporate them into your scene or script.

Finally, *either*, individually complete a revised version of your script *or*, as a group, present a polished version of your improvisation to the rest of the class.

SOAP UPDATE

WHO'S WHO AND WHAT'S HAPPENING

Keep up to date with what's been going on in all your favour soaps — including, of course, the BBC's EastEnders and Neigh

Pippa (Vanessa Downing) faced up to bereavement

Home and Away
Monday to Friday, twice daily, **ITV**
Bridget made trouble for Ailsa. Steven realised the effect Tom's death had on him. And Pippa came to terms with the loss of her husband.

Beverly (Shaunna O'Grady) was annoyed with Jim

Neighbours
Monday to Friday, twice daily, **BBC1**
Beverly blamed Jim for threatening her future. Two spies discovered unusual goings-on in the Ramsay backyard.

Geoff (Kevin Carson) led an erratic love life

Brookside
Monday, Wednesday, Friday, omnibus Saturday, **Channel 4**
Josie's job was put in jeopardy when she did some moonlighting. Geoff discovered that the course of true love doesn't always run smoothly. Sammy confronted her parents with some disturbing news. Tony xe nr plans to 'welcome' Max am back home.

Elizabeth (Kat solved a pr

Emmerdale
Tuesday, Thursday, Michael and Eliza cepted Turner's off manent home. Wilk the Woolpack was ged into the Nineti was pleased to fin working at Emmerda

Sue (Morag Hood) found her secret was out

Families
Monday, Tuesday, **ITV**
Lisa became suspicious of a colleague. Sue and John had some explaining to do when their secret was discovered.

Bet (Julie Goodyear) — has Alex upset her?

Coronation Street
Monday, Wednesday and Friday, **ITV**
Vera made a startling discovery. There were doubts over how Bet would feel about Alec dealing with Phil Jenning

Davie (Derek Lord), a tough-talking crofter

Take the High Road
Days vary, twice a week, **ITV**
The dramas continued at Glendarroch as some previously strained relationships med to be nea re ng poin

Mark (Todd Ca had a roving e

EastEnders
Tuesday, Thursday, Sunday, **BBC1**
Ethel celebrated he birthday. Disa's mothe in Albert Square to try her back to Sunderlan Phil received a cour shock! And Mark had be timing Di

Tips for Success

◆ As you talk about soaps, do not assume that you all know what is being discussed. Give examples, elaborate your points and develop your ideas for effective communication.

◆ When you watch a soap or analyse the characters, remember that you are watching a representation that could have been very different. Ask yourself why it is like it is.

◆ When you write your own analysis make sure that you do not retell the story of the episodes you have studied. Make separate points and back them up with examples.

Home ground

This unit explores how, if you only look closely, you can see your own local environment in unexpected new ways.

Your neighbourhood

Sometimes, living in the same area for a period of time can stop you from seeing it properly. Can you remember what colour the front door of your neighbour's house is painted, whether there are white lines down the centre of your road, what shape the nearest street lamps are and which homes in your street have had windows or doors replaced? And, if you are not sure of those details, think what else you might be missing.

1 In a group of four or five, think of some of the landmarks or special places in the area where you live now or where you used to live. Are there any distinctive buildings or natural features? Try telling one another about them as if the people in your group do not know the area you are describing. Then, talk about any events or incidents you particularly remember which are associated with them.

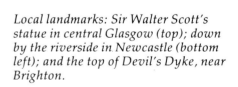

you will be . . . .

- Recounting events
- Responding to a writer
- Responding to literature
- Writing a narrative
- Arguing a point of view

Local landmarks: Sir Walter Scott's statue in central Glasgow (top); down by the riverside in Newcastle (bottom left); and the top of Devil's Dyke, near Brighton.

True stories . . .

Sometimes places are not what they seem on the surface. For years, teacher and writer Alan Combes dreamed of living in a cottage with a stream at the end of the garden. But, when he found his dream home he discovered that there was more to the river than he had expected. Read about what happened one summer:

NASTY TALES OF A CUTE LITTLE COTTAGE BY THE RIVER BANK

LIVING by the river took some getting used to. It didn't matter having only a small cottage garden for we were fronted by the weir and a miniature green. A privileged view devoid of the responsibility for maintenance; but a place which drew the village children like butterflies to buddleia both in the depth of summer and when snow was on the ground.

There was another unforeseen consequence. Sleep became fractured time and again through the necessity of paying dues to nature. It took a while to catch on to the link between the flow within and the flow without. And the constant fizz of the water as it bubbled over the weir frequently woke us in fear that the noise was fire hungrily eating the house beneath us. These things took some getting used to.

Last summer the river became a source of personal shame. For many years there had been rumours that the waters were haunted by a huge pike which not only feasted off the trout managing to get this far upstream, but also pulled down ducklings.

I was buttering toast at the kitchen window when I saw a teenage boy, later to be fêted in the media for his derring-do, fighting with his rod and line after the manner of shark anglers. By the time I got to him, he had hauled the 22-pound pike out of the water and bodies appeared from all directions, intent on admiring his catch.

I know nothing about angling or river fish, but it was plain that here was an immense, evil, magnificent creature. I also remembered Ted Hughes's superb poem about pike – 'killers from the egg'. The teenage fisherman could only stare at the legend he had landed as it writhed on the grass, flashing its vile jaws.

I like to think it was because I could no longer bear the sight of the pike going through its death throes that I ran indoors to fetch the axe. I also cannot evade the fact that in my ignorance I reckoned I was acting for the best – for the sake of the wildlife on this stretch of the river. I thought, the pike should die. A visitor to the nearby pub, who claimed to know what he was doing, bludgeoned it to death with the axe's blunt end.

As it lay there in death, it occurred to me that for all its malevolence it was undoubtedly the finest creature in the river. And we had killed it. Another poem came to mind, the one Lawrence wrote about a deadly snake visiting him in Sicily. 'If you were not afraid, you would kill him!' the voice of his accursed human education had said to him.

The consequence of the pike's death has been a growth in the duck population to plague proportions. Take away the quacking chorus and return the silent, gliding menace any day.

But this year the river, apparently at its most innocuous, has proved a wolf in sheep's clothing. By the end of May, its susurrations had virtually ceased as the rainfall stuttered to a halt. No one in the village could recall a time when the river had dried up so completely in its course. The level dropped six inches, a foot, 18 inches below the weir. Kids came from miles around, now able to explore parts of the Derwent which had never been exposed to view.

The first tragedy occurred as we were sitting down to Sunday lunch. An inhuman caterwauling came from next door's garden and we rushed out to find Celia, our much loved Siamese, sitting on a bird table in acute distress. The lower half of her body appeared to be covered in sleek, oily water.

We rushed her to the vet and he tried desperately to administer oxygen and to make her vomit. He was unsuccessful and she died an hour later, choked by the mud which had invaded her lungs.

'Daddy, I hate the river,' my four-year-old daughter spat.

She was to hate it even more before the rain returned the river to its proper level this autumn.

On a Thursday afternoon towards the end of August, Lizzie, six years old and bubbling with life, went for a paddle in the water at the foot of the weir. Although only six inches deep, the normally swirling water had become stagnant since the flow dried up. In her wellingtons, Lizzie stumbled and fell on to a jagged bottle. Made brittle by years of immersion, the glass shattered and scrunched into Lizzie's knee, driving right through to the bone. Fortunately, the local doctor was home for lunch in his riverside house and after dressing the wound, ordered that she be taken to hospital.

So heavy was the flow of blood that the wound was lightly stitched in hospital so that X-Rays could be taken to ascertain where the glass had lodged. Bacteria were present and moved quickly into the bloodstream. One tiny glass fragment had got behind the knee and the surgeon decided to leave it there as the alternative was major bone surgery. The hope was that the body could fight any impurity from such a splinter and that it would be no more than a benign presence for the rest of Lizzie's life.

For two weeks the little girl's body fought the threat of serious infection. Each time her temperature rose worryingly high, she was whisked down to theatre for cleansing of the wound. By now she was in almost permanent agony.

Meanwhile, Lizzie's dad set about cleaning up the river at the offending point. With the help of children present at the time of the accident, he located the actual bottle and it now holds a place of dishonour in the house. Imagine his anger when he caught his neighbour, a kind and generous man, lovely with children, throwing an old car headlight into the river at the bottom of his garden. 'What do you think you're doing with that? Don't you realise our daughter cut her leg open because someone dumped glass in the river?'

'But no kids ever play in the water here.'

'No, but it's going to float downstream to where they do play in the river, isn't it?'

We turn a blind eye to so much in life until someone or something forces us to look. Then we are furious at the voluntary blindness of others, cursing their stupidity and unaware of our own hypocrisy.

At Scarborough hospital the fight for Lizzie's leg continued and lab tests were carried out on a sample taken from the wound. By now the little girl and her mum had spent three weeks in hospital and were itching to go home. 'Not until we're one hundred per cent in the clear,' the specialist told them. 'There's something nasty lurking in that river.'

The culture grown showed that our 22-pound pike had been succeeded as the Darth Vader of the Derwent by a more terrible presence – raw sewage. Drowning wasn't the cause of our cat's death: toxicity was.

One day some of the teenage hoodlums who have pummelled the river bank all summer long, discovered the delights of sucking the river water with their bicycle pumps and spraying it into each other's faces. Conscience beat about me with great wings before I decided to let nature be the teacher.

Dreams prompted by childhood story books of cute cottages with rivers at the bottom of the garden have been banished. If such a dream home ever existed, it was before my time. Nor is a thing of beauty necessarily a joy forever. That aphorism lost its credibility when teenagers discovered how to be clubbable.

Living by the river remains a source of pleasure, but tempered now by thoughts of pike and cat and broken bottle. The river has emerged from the picture book and taken its place as a holder, carrier, creator and destroyer of life.

Finding a style

The writing you have just read is of a very particular kind. It is not a story, though it has a strong narrative thread running through it. It is not autobiography: it focuses more on the place than a single incident or person Alan Combes remembers. It is not primarily a persuasive piece of writing, though it does communicate opinions that the writer would like his reader to share.

To try to understand how this kind of writing works, you have to consider how its purpose (why it was written) and its audience (who it was written for) have influenced both its content and the style in which it is written.

For Alan Combes, it was a combination of unexpected events that made him suddenly view the local area in another way. Below, he writes about how he came to write his article:

'As a youngster it was my burning ambition to be a newspaper reporter. That ambition never materialised because of a long conversation with a newspaper editor; he convinced me that journalism wasn't half as exciting as it appeared and the strong chance was that I would finish up reporting on Parish Council meetings in some sleepy rural backwater.

There were other factors too. Journalism was the reporting of factual data, with no room for imagination. It was writing in the third person, keeping 'me' and 'I' right out of things. In short, the message I got all those years ago was that writing for a newspaper was dealing with the humdrum in a dispassionate way. No wonder I said 'No thanks'.

Although my chosen profession is teaching, I have been fortunate enough to sell my writing to newspapers and magazines too. I've also discovered one or two things about what I thought I'd learned all those years ago. Reporting facts doesn't have to be humdrum; you can employ your imagination even when telling a true story; and you can put bits of yourself into factual data.

But there are important differences between the imagination used to write newspaper articles and that used to create fiction.

Telling Lizzie's *story* I would have had to set the scene by contrasting her innocent charm with the river's lurking peril. If I had made a short story about the killing of the pike, I might have chosen to write it as though I was the boy who caught it. But no, these are facts I'm dealing with so I cannot enter his head.

The piece of writing you've just read was written for the 'Grassroots' page in *The Guardian* newspaper. Many of the articles in 'Grassroots' are about the environment, but not in the conventional meaning of the word. We need to ask what we mean by the term environment. To a dentist, his surgery is the most important environment. To a pilot, the sky matters most. To me, a cottage with a river at the bottom of the garden was a lifetime dream, so it assumed great importance.

As a result of my feelings about living in a 'cute little cottage', I built up a storybook picture of what life would be like. I made the environment into a kind of Garden of Eden and completely forgot that nature can be terribly cruel and also that it was an environment which had to accommodate human beings. And everyone knows that human beings can be terrible spoilers; this planet certainly does!'

2 In your group, discuss what you have read so far. Try to bring the following questions into your discussion:

■ Why do you think Alan Combes might have chosen, or wanted, to write about the river and what happened?

■ How does his view of the pike change?

■ How far are people, rather than nature, responsible for the events he describes?

■ How would his account have been different if it was written as a story? Would it have been as effective?

■ How would his account have been different if written as a news report on the dangers of river pollution?

3 Now, go on to talk about the main characteristics of this kind of writing. Discuss which of the following features are most important in giving it a particular style.

First person narrative	The way it is written in the first person and the 'I' is the writer – unlike in a story where a writer can imagine himself or herself as another character.
Local detail	The way it is based on detailed personal knowledge of a place the writer knows well and on his experience of events that happened there.
Atmospheric description	The way it includes some powerful description. Look back at the article and identify details that appeal to your sense of sight, hearing, touch and smell. Pick out well-chosen adjectives and thought-provoking comparisons.
Literary style	The way the style of writing is literary rather than journalistic, so that the writer tells a story rather than reports what happened. Pick out the references to poems. Can you identify any other literary **idioms** like 'a wolf in sheep's clothing' where comparison or description is used to make the description of real events more vivid.
Linking of events	The way it relates several incidents, only connected in that they happened at the same place.
Comparisons and contrasts	The way the writing presents **analogies** by showing the similarities between different elements of the writing such as the pike and the sewage.
Environmental themes	The way the writer stresses the links between the people and their natural environment, and the way people alter the natural balance – usually by spoiling it.
Personal comment	The way the writer makes it clear that the article has a message and leaves his audience in no doubt as to the point which the writing is trying to make.

Made up stories . . .

As you have read and discussed Alan Combes's account of what happened, you may have noticed that how he describes what happened is quite like a story. The river could be the central character, and the bad things that happen gradually get worse. Then there is a disaster but everything is finally all right. Many stories are structured like that.

If it was another kind of story – one with an obvious moral like a fable – then the killing of the pike could be a crime against nature and the writer could suggest that the river was 'hurt' and was trying to take its revenge.

4 Graham Swift is a novelist who was born and brought up in the Norfolk fenlands. In the extract below, he uses what he remembers about the place and his own childhood there as part of the opening to his novel, *Waterland*. Read it in your group and talk about how this **fictional** story compares with Alan Combes's true account. Make your own list of the characteristics of this writing.

WE lived in a lock-keeper's cottage by the River Leem, which flows out of Norfolk into the Great Ouse. And no one needs telling that the land in that part of the world is flat. Flat, with an unrelieved and monotonous flatness, enough of itself, some might say, to drive a man to unquiet and sleep-defeating thoughts. From the raised banks of the Leem, it stretched away to the horizon, its uniform colour, peat-black, varied only by the crops that grew upon it – grey-green potato leaves, blue-green beet leaves, yellow-green wheat; its uniform levelness broken only by the furrowed and dead-straight lines of ditches and drains, which, depending on the state of the sky and the angle of the sun, ran like silver, copper or golden wires across the fields and which, when you stood and looked at them, made you shut one eye and fall prey to fruitless meditations on the laws of perspective.

And yet this land, so regular, so prostrate, so tamed and cultivated, would transform itself, in my five- or six-year-old mind, into an empty wilderness. On those nights when my mother would be forced to tell me stories, it would seem that in our lock-keeper's cottage we were in the middle of nowhere; and the noise of the trains passing on the lines to King's Lynn, Gildsey and Ely was like the baying of a monster closing in on us in our isolation.

A fairy-tale land, after all.

My father kept the lock on the River Leem, two miles from where it empties into the Ouse. But because a lock-keeper's duties are irregular and his pay, set against the rent-free cottage in which he lives, is scant, and because, in any case, by the nineteen-thirties, the river-traffic on the Leem had dwindled, my father also grew vegetables, kept chickens and trapped eels. It was only in times of heavy rain or thaw that these secondary occupations were abandoned. Then he would have to watch and anticipate the water-level. Then he would have to raise the sluice which cut across the far side of the stream like a giant guillotine.

For the river in front of our cottage divided into two channels, the nearer containing the navigation lock, the farther the sluice, with, in between, a solidly built brick-faced pier, a tiny island, on which stood the cabin housing the sluice engine. And even before the river had visibly risen, even before its colour had changed and it began to show the milky brown of the Norfolk chalk hills from which it flowed, Dad would know when to cross the lock-gates to the cabin and begin – with a groaning of metal and throbbing of released water – to crank up the sluice.

But under normal conditions the sluice remained lowered, almost to the river bottom, its firm blade holding back the slow-flowing Leem, making it fit for the passage of boats. Then the water in the enclosure above it, like the water in the lock-pen, would be smooth and placid and it would give off that smell which is characteristic of places where fresh water and human ingenuity meet, and which is smelt over and over again in the Fens. A cool, slimy but strangely poignant and nostalgic smell. A smell which is half man and half fish. And at such times Dad would have plenty of leisure for his eel traps and vegetables, and little to do with the sluice, save to combat rust, grease the cog-wheels and clear away from the water the accumulations of flotsam.

For, flood or no flood, the Leem brought down its unceasing booty of debris. Willow branches; alder branches; sedge; fencing; crates; old clothes; dead sheep; bottles; potato sacks; straw bales; fruit boxes; fertiliser bags. All floated down on the westerly current, lodged against the sluice-gate and had to be cleared away with boat-hooks and weed-rakes.

And thus it was that one night, in midsummer, when God's withheld benedictions were shining in the sky, though this was several years after Dad told us about the stars, but only two or three since he began to speak of hearts and mother's milk, and the tump-tump of the pumps was drowned now, in the evening, by the roar of ascending bombers – it was, to be precise, July, 1943 – that something floated down the Leem, struck the ironwork of the sluice and, tugged by the eddies, continued to knock and scrape against it till morning. Something extraordinary and unprecedented, and not to be disposed of like a branch or potato sack or even a dead sheep. For this something was a body. And the body belonged to Freddie Parr, who lived less than a mile away and was my age, give or take a month.

Now, write . . .

5 Think about beginning some writing of your own which is connected to events in your own local environment. It can be a true account of something which happened, or your 'added to' version of something which you have heard about.

▦ First, think of a setting and a place. It may help you to draw a detailed map of the area you intend to write about and mark on it the names you use for the places of importance to you.

▦ Then, decide on the incident you will use as a starting point. Can you think of another incident which relates to it in any way? What order should they come in as you write?

▦ Start writing by describing the place in detail. Build up the atmosphere. It might well be in direct contrast with what follows: shock tactics can be very effective.

▦ Tell of the incident or incidents as vividly as possible. Keep the place in mind and describe relevant details as you write. Remember to describe your feelings about the events you portray.

▦ Finish by sharing with your reader your insights about the 'message' your writing contains. This is not just a story or a piece of description: you are aiming to make a point.

On home ground

Alan Combes's English class talked about their local environment in this way and about bringing personal feelings into this kind of writing. Below are three examples. Like you, they were given the freedom to blend fact and fiction, so long as they were honest about their feelings for the chosen environment.

A HANDY HOUSE

Our house is practically on the edge of the woods: a little cottage with bay windows and a thatched roof. I have been taking my dog Toby for a walk in the woods ever since we got him as a pup and that was seven years ago. I've never got lost, lost Toby or been afraid even when we go under a canopy of branches and it goes all dark. Toby seems to love searching in all the holes trying to smell out rabbits and barking up trees at squirrels and birds.

But today was different. We set off for our early walk at 7 a.m. before I had to go to school. I let Toby off the lead and threw his ball for him. He went chasing after it and brought it back and then the whining began. I thought he had something in his paw so I checked. Nothing. I threw his ball again, but he didn't do anything, just trotted along beside me looking all around him. I wondered what was wrong with him, but I just kept throwing the ball, trying to get him interested.

A rabbit went hopping by behind us. Normally he would have chased it and barked but he did nothing. I was beginning to feel a bit uneasy as the squirrels started rushing about in the trees and the birds all flew from their resting places. Rabbits scurried into their burrows. Now this was really strange and in a way, scary. At every little noise I turned round and now my stomach had butterflies.

What was this thing that terrified the animals, gobsmacked Toby and made me feel so scared? I got out of that wood so fast my feet hardly touched the ground.

Next morning I went back with Toby and everything was the same. Toby rabbiting and barking up the trees and squirrels who were collecting nuts. Rabbits were playing together and the birds were once again flitting through the trees.

RUBBISH

It must be nice to live by the sea. A constant fresh supply of fish, nice walks along the beach, and an occasional dip. But then I spoke to Mr Jenkinson, a former fisherman turned lighthouse watchman.

There are three main problems polluting the North Sea, he told me. First, is the raw sewage pumped into the sea. At Scarborough we have outfall which will just dump raw sewage straight into the sea.

The next problem is nuclear waste such as cadmium. This is being pumped into the North and Irish Sea. Mr Jenkinson said he would never eat a fish from the North or Irish Sea as it is so bad. They have found sea birds with so much cadmium in them that the same level in humans would kill them.

Then there is a toxic waste being burned about 100 miles off Scarborough by the Vulcanus II. They burn such things as arsenic from Europe. This is where Dogger Bank is a breeding ground for fish. Fishermen have caught fish with severe deformities and growths.

How can I eat fish and chips and go for a swim in the sea without thinking of these things? Mr Jenkinson has changed my thoughts on the seaside forever.

The beach

The sand looked dark brown today. My dog was still splashing in the sea. As I crossed the beach, I saw two little children destroying sandcastles. It was getting darker and the beach seemed deserted. I looked towards the sea, I saw the surfers coming in and a tremendous amount of rubbish and litter. Funny how I never notice the rubbish when it's light.

I'd walked for about four miles and it was very dark so I whistled the dog and changed direction. When I got onto the road I noticed a van pulling up. A man jumped out of the van, opened his side doors and started to get boxes out. He went over the pavement with them and threw them over the railings onto the sand. I was shocked. I didn't know whether to call the police, but I thought the man would be gone by then. So I decided I would confront him.

He was still running about, throwing rubbish out. So I got my dog by the collar and started to cross the road. Just as I got near him, he jumped back in the van and drove off.

I saw the rubbish on the beach and thought myself a coward for not having enough guts to say something to him earlier.

THE STRUGGLE

We live in a free country. This unit asks you to consider the situation in other parts of the world where personal freedom is virtually unknown.

The patterns of history

A sad and recurring theme throughout history, and throughout the world, has been the way groups of people have conquered and gained control over others. Having done so, the new rulers have frequently maintained their position of advantage by denying the conquered people equal rights and opportunities. They are often given poorer education, limited health services, the worst housing and few job opportunities. Their culture and traditional ways may be looked down on as inferior. They may even be forbidden to speak their own language.

There is often much resistance to the new rulers. Such resistance may, at times, be put down in a very brutal way. Nevertheless, it often continues for a very long time.

Although the language, religion, and ways of the new rulers may dominate, those of other groups may secretly be kept alive and survive.

Sometimes, over time, the difference between those who have conquered and taken power and other groups becomes blurred. In most cases, however, the group who have gained power maintain for themselves a special position.

As you work through this unit, you will be asked to explore some situations, past and present, where one group, either through conquest or by passing laws, has gained complete control over another.

Sometimes, when you live in a relatively free society like ours, it is hard to imagine a situation like this and what it would mean. In the second part of this unit you are asked to do just that – to imagine your thoughts and actions if your country was taken over by another group, the Alphas.

Struggles – past and present

AD43: The Roman conquest of Britain

WHEN the Romans invaded Britain in AD43, the country was ruled by a number of separate Celtic kingdoms. Celtic languages, beliefs, customs, manners, values and the ways they organised themselves were very different from those of the Romans. In their 400 years of rule in Britain, the Romans changed these greatly. The traditional separate Celtic kingdoms disappeared. Wealthy Celtic families adopted Roman ways; poorer Celts worked for the Romans. Latin became the official language of Britain and the language which had status – although people continued to speak the Celtic languages. Britain became a province of the Roman Empire – its cornfields bringing much wealth to Rome.

Under the Romans, Latin was imposed as the official langauge in Britain, and Celtic customs declined. This Celtic decoration (below) was found on a bucket, at Aylesford.

❛ You are the builders of coursed stone walls, the makers of straight roads and ordered justice and disciplined troops. We know that, we know it all too well. We know that your justice is more sure than ours, and when we rise against you, we see our hosts break against the discipline of your troops, as the sea breaks against a rock. And we do not understand, because all these things are of the ordered pattern, and only the free curves of the shield-boss are real to us. We do not understand. And when the time comes that we begin to understand your world, too often we lose the understanding of our own. ❜

Esca, the Celtic warrior who has been taken as a slave by the Romans, talking to Marcus, his Roman master in *The Eagle of the Ninth* by Rosemary Sutcliff.

43

AD1519: The Spanish conquest of the Aztecs of Mexico

THROUGHOUT the fifteenth and sixteenth centuries, Spanish explorers became increasingly drawn to the wealth of central and southern America.

In 1519, Hernando Cortes landed on the American mainland. Moving inland, he discovered in the mountains of Mexico, the Aztec people. Aztec culture, language and ways of organisation were very rich – as was their gold. Aztec society was based on tribes. Each tribe was more or less independent, looking after its own fields, city planning and religious functions.

When news reached the Aztecs that Cortes and his army were approaching, there was some confusion. Cortes was welcomed at first as a god by the leader of the Aztecs. Thinking of this as a sign of weakness and seeing that the Aztecs were virtually defenceless, Cortes arrested their leader, seized their gold and put the town under his control. However, the Aztec people now counterattacked forcing Cortes to leave without the gold he had melted down to take with him. He vowed to return some day.

In 1521, Cortes returned, taking terrible vengeance against the Aztecs. Two hundred thousand Aztecs died. The city was ruined.

The Spanish conquerors introduced a new religion – Christianity – to the remaining Aztec people. From 1522 onwards, the Spanish began to settle in Mexico, taking over the best land. The Aztecs were forced into slave labour and their culture disappeared.

Spanish invaders completely wiped out the Aztec way of life. This pottery figure (below left) is an Aztec model of a priest.

> Tell me, by what right and justice do you keep these people in such cruel and humble servitude? Why do you keep them so oppressed and weary, not giving them enough to eat nor taking care of them in their illness? For with the excessive work you demand of them they fall ill and die, or rather you kill them with your desire to extract and acquire gold every day. Are these not men?

Montesinos, a Spanish monk, arguing with Spanish settlers about the exploitation of the Aztecs.

AD1800: The colonisation of Australia

BEFORE colonisation by Europeans, Australia was inhabited by 300,000 or so Aborigine people, scattered widely across the land.

It is believed that Aborigine people had inhabited the land for at least 40,000 years. They were divided into about 600 tribes, each with their own language. Each group had their own collection of sacred stories and ceremonies. The Aborigines saw themselves linked to the land through the stories and places of Dreamtime – a time when the land was flat and about to burst into life. They believed that the land owned them, rather than them owning the land.

The first meeting between the Aborigines and the Europeans took place in 1770 when Captain Cook landed in Australia. Cook did not stay, however, and Australia was not colonised by Europeans for another 20 years.

Europeans first settled in Eastern Australia, declaring the land and all the people theirs. Similar white settlements grew up across Australia. Even though the Aborigines saved the lives of the Europeans by sharing their skills and their food, still their lands were taken from them.

Well into this century, Aborigine people suffered all kinds of discrimination. Since 1967, there have been laws guaranteeing greater equality, but the Aborigine people's struggle to regain and hold areas of land which once belonged to them, continues.

I am a child of the dreamtime people,
Part of this land like the gnarled gum tree,
I am the river softly singing,
Chanting our Songs on the way to the sea.
My spirit is the dust devils,
Mirages that dance on the plains,
I'm the snow, the wind and the falling rain,
I'm part of the rocks and the red desert earth,
Red as the blood that flows in my veins,
I am eagle, crow and the snake that glides,
Through the rain forests that cling to the
   mountainside.
I awakened here when the earth was new . . .
There was emu, wombat, kangaroo.
No other man of a different hue!
I am this land and this land is me.
I am Australia.

Hyllus Maris (an aborigine poet)

Ayers Rock has been an important sacred site for the Aboriginal peoples for thousands of years. After the Europeans arrived 200 years ago, they claimed this land as theirs and stopped the Aborigines using it. After years of protest the Aborigines reclaimed their rights.

45

AD1948: The apartheid system in South Africa

IN South Africa, under the apartheid system, the white and black populations were forced apart by complex laws which aimed to keep political, economic and military power in the hands of white people.

The laws of apartheid were introduced in 1948. They separated the population into different racial groups and stated where each group could live. Eighty six per cent of the land went to 15 per cent of the people – the white population. Fourteen per cent of the land was set aside for the black population – 80 per cent of the people. These areas were known as the tribal 'homelands'. Work, however, was in the cities. The black people who needed to work in the cities had to live in townships outside the main cities where conditions were extremely poor. Above all, no black person was allowed to vote.

Education was separate in South Africa. Education was not free for black students and the resources provided for them were far worse than those for white students.

In 1976, the Minister of Education announced that half the subjects in the schools for black students were to be taught in Afrikaans – the language of the original Dutch settlers and still the language of the ruling Afrikaaner government. To black people, as Afrikaans was spoken nowhere else in the world, it was very limiting as a means of communication. It was also considered to be the language of their oppressors.

Black students decided to boycott their schools. The protest spread rapidly and became increasingly violent after the police attacked the striking students with batons and tear gas. On 16 June 1976, Hector Peterson, a school student from Soweto, was shot dead by the police. He was the first of many students who died in the protests.

The governments of many countries refused to trade with South Africa until the basic human rights of the black population were recognised. Partly in response to such pressure, some changes began to be made, and in 1990, after 27 years, Nelson Mandela of the African National Congress was released from prison. However, the struggle for political and economic equality continues.

Under the system of apartheid, black students struggled in dismal conditions to gain an education.

Hector P.

It could have been anywhere
but it was here
It could have been anybody
but it was you
It could have happened anyway
but it was this way
It could have been due to anything
but it was this
It could have stopped anything
but it was you
Maybe it could not be helped
by us unwary mortals
It was never planned
but by the jittery hands
of a few . . .

We remembered you again
yesterday.

Tembeka Mbobo

I began school in Evaton, a village 20 miles south of Johannesburg. When I went to school, white education was compulsory and virtually free – and still is today. Yet, I, like other black students, had to pay school fees to the government. If your parents could afford the fees you could get an education. But, if your parents could afford the fees but not the uniform, you couldn't get an education. If your parents could afford a uniform and school fees but no books, you still couldn't get an education. And then, even if all fees were paid, you couldn't go to school if you didn't have a 'Christian' name – meaning a name that whites could pronounce. We would often lead dual lives. At home I was Dumisani. At school I became Shadrack. Every so often, the government inspectors would come and check the school register for Christian names and if we had paid our school fees. Those that hadn't paid were sent away.

In spite of the fees paid to the government, black education was often left up to the community. In other words, the government didn't build schools for black students, so my parents had to help build mine. They had to buy the furniture; they had to buy the books, the chalk and help to pay the teacher's salary.

The school I went to was just four mud walls and a corrugated iron roof. During the summer the school was like an oven because there were only little holes for windows. When it rained – or hailed – we couldn't hear each other speak because of the corrugated iron roof. We had to wear uniforms . . . We had one teacher for a class of 120. All the grades were mixed up together. The teacher divided us into two shifts, one from 7 in the morning to 1 and the next from 1 to 5 . . .

From an article by Dumisani Kumalo, an exiled South African student now living in America.

The Aliens

How would you feel if your country was invaded by aliens and the freedoms that you thought were part of normal life were suddenly taken away? Now, working in a group of five or six, go on to explore these feelings through role-play, improvisation and writing.

WEEK 6 INVASION

OUR country has been taken over by the 'aliens' who landed six weeks ago from somewhere in space. They resemble humans but are perhaps slightly taller. They tend to look very similar to one another and have a pinkish looking sheen on their skin. They dress in similar clothes made from a grey artificial fabric.

They announced in the first week that they wished to trade with the Earth and had chosen our country as a base for geographical reasons. They indicated that they posed no threat to any other country on the globe but that they possessed great weapons of destruction should the need arise. After some initial panic, the American, European and Soviet governments recognised the new rulers and accepted their assurances that the people of our country would be fairly treated and would prosper under the new regime.

There was some opposition to the arrival of the aliens, or Alphas as they preferred to be called, and a few people were killed but the takeover was so sudden that there was little chance to think about what was going on. Since then, there has been a lot of disagreement and argument.

Some people argue that our country has lost its standing in the world and that the Alphas, 'Big As' as they call them, will restore that position. There will be many business opportunities, and jobs will be available for all as the rest of the world comes to our shores to trade.

Others believe that these aliens, 'Plasties' as they call them, will force us to become their slaves. They will take the best homes and jobs for themselves and make us into workers, or even, treat us as little better than farm animals.

1 In your group, improvise some of the discussions which might take place in workplaces or your college. Decide whether you are in favour of, or opposed to, the aliens. Begin your improvisation with one person saying how an alien came into their place of work to discuss their future.

WEEK **8** O P P R E S S I O N

THERE has been a formal announcement that from this point onwards all school lessons will be conducted in the Alphean language. In the last two weeks, the Alphas have shown that they are quite likely to use violence to enforce their commands and a strike by miners — the Alphas value coal highly — was put down very brutally. Because none of you know more than very basic Alpean, there will not be much opportunity to learn anything.

2 In your groups, consider what to do. Each group has to discuss and plan a course of action to be taken in response to this announcement. You might think about:

▪ **Demonstrations:** What would the advantages and disadvantages be?

▪ **Protest letters:** Who to? What could they say?

▪ **Strikes/boycotts:** What are the pros and cons?

▪ **Organising and informing other students:** How could this be done?

Each group should take notes of their proposals and try to agree on the course of action to be taken.

3 Now, select one member of the group to report to the class (renamed as the Student Council). As you listen to the reports from each group, consider why certain actions have been recommended and others rejected. Try to decide on the position that you wish to adopt and get together with other groups you agree with. Eventually, there will be a majority view in the Student Council although you may need to vote on some issues before you come to any conclusions. It may help you to elect a chairperson and/or a secretary.

4 After the Student Council meeting, each of you should write something. Choose one of these:

▪ A protest letter to someone – perhaps a newspaper, the Education Minister or a foreign country's rulers.

▪ A report for the student newsletter, outlining the Student Council's proposals and expressing their opposition and resistance to the Alphean language in their school.

▪ A leaflet or a poster giving details of a demonstration against the new ruling and encouraging people to attend it. Make sure to include the date, time and place as well as a lively heading.

▪ A letter to a pen-friend in another country expressing your fears and anxieties about what is happening to your country.

▪ Slogans for the banners which will be carried at the demonstration. Remember that they need to be short and punchy.

WEEK **10** R E S I S T A N C E

READ each other's writing to share your feelings and responses. Are there ways in which people have reacted which surprise you?

The demonstration takes place. It is violently broken up by the police. Bullets and tear gas are used. There are casualties.

5 Imagine that you were one of the students who was on the demonstration. With a friend to interview you, role-play a news interview describing your feelings from the peaceful beginning, through the police intervention, and the casualties.

6 Imagine you are a reporter who has the job of covering the demonstration. Write the report as it might have appeared in one of the newspapers described below. Make sure that, within your group, you write newspaper reports of the demonstration from each newspaper.

Typical phrases of the type used by each newspaper are provided to give you a feel for their style and the ways they use words:

THE NEW WORLD
A PRO-ALPHEAN NEWSPAPER

A small gang . . . yobbish youths . . . disturbed the peace . . . hoodlums . . . law-abiding citizens looked on in horror . . . noisy slogan-shouting . . . unruly . . . undisciplined . . . hurled stones . . . innocent passers-by . . . orgy of violence . . . need for firmer police treatment . . . law and order . . . severely punished . . . outrage.

The Daily Correspondent
A MIDDLE-OF-THE-ROAD NEWSPAPER

Demonstration . . . Central London . . . 10,000 school students . . . protesting against alien language . . . marched in rows . . . carrying banners . . . 3 p.m. police intervened . . . tear gas . . . plastic bullets . . . casualties . . . fleeing students . . . panic . . . threw stones at Alphean Central Government Offices . . . quiet restored by evening.

PATRIOT
A STUDENT COUNCIL NEWSLETTER

Comrade students . . . fascist alien government . . . our schools threatened . . . our language . . . thought-police . . . injustice . . . brutality . . . victims . . . fight back . . . brutal police aggression . . . student bravery . . . martyrs.

WEEK **12** **T R A G E D Y**

THINGS HAVE GOT WORSE! THERE HAS BEEN ANOTHER DEMONSTRATION. THE ALPHAS WERE READY. THEIR POWER HAS BEEN BROUGHT HOME TO YOU IN THE WORST POSSIBLE WAY.

7 Your friend was shot down and killed on the demonstration. The Student Council is organising the funeral and you have been asked to write a poem in memory of your friend. It will be read aloud at the funeral. As you write, think about including some of the following:

■ Specific references to your friend – what he or she hoped for from life and what their death means to others – and to his or her friends, parents and the student cause.

■ A suggestion that their death was not in vain, or that it will strengthen the students' determination to win.

Read your poem aloud to the class or your group.

8 Improvise a family mealtime where the family, including three school-age children, discuss whether to obey the latest decree. Try to bring out the differing attitudes of the parents and of the older and younger children to the situation.

There has been an announcement from the Alpha Government that anyone not attending school will be fined first time, and then imprisoned.

9 *Either* write a diary of ten days in prison, including arrest, from a student's point of view *or* write a diary written by a student's mother for ten days. This should include the student not turning up at home, looking for them at police stations, having difficulty in obtaining information, locating them at last, anxiety about their treatment in prison, and so on.

WEEK **20** ESCAPE AND EXILE

AS THE Alphas' grip on your country has increased, you manage to escape to another country. There you are surprised to find that, while some people oppose the Alphas' rule, others are in favour of it and are happy to trade with the aliens. The majority are simply apathetic and do not care about what is happening in another country. You have the chance to go around making speeches and describing what has happened to a variety of audiences. Your job is to make them realise what the Alphas have done and that it is the duty of other nations to oppose them.

10 Write the speech you make to a group of students in your country of exile. Remember, that you must make them realise what is happening and persuade them to join the opposition to the Alpha rulers.

If you fail, you can never return to your home and country. It will never be free.

DREAMS OF BETTER DAYS

In the last section, you imagined what life might be like under alien rule and what you might do to resist. For many people, past and present, the struggle for justice and equal rights has been, and is, a real-life struggle.

Much of the work you have done was based on real events in South Africa where white people imposed their rule on a black majority and where the Afrikaans language was forced onto Bantu schools and a schools' boycott resulted.

Below and on the next two pages are the thoughts of some of the people who were, or still are, involved in that struggle for freedom. Many of the extracts have a message of hope; some are testaments to the courage of others. Read them in a small group.

FOR A DEAD AFRICAN

We have no heroes and no wars
only victims of a sickly state
succumbing to the variegated sores
that flower under lashing rains of hate.

We have no battles and no fights
for history to record with trite remark
only captives killed on eyeless nights
and accidental dyings in the dark.

Yet when the roll of those who died
to free our land is called, without surprise
these nameless unarmed ones will stand beside
the warriors who secured the final prize.

Dennis Brutus

The Sounds Begin Again

The sounds begin again;
The siren in
the night
The thunder at the door
The shriek of nerves in
pain.

Then the keening crescendo
Of faces split by pain
The
wordless, endless wail
Only the unfree know.

Importunate as
rain
The wraiths exhale their woe
Over the sirens, knuckles,
boots;
My sounds begin again.

Dennis Brutus

'How I pray that Our Lord would open our eyes so that we would see the real, the true identity of each one of us, that this is not a so-called 'coloured', or white, or black or Indian, but a brother, a sister – and treat each other as such. Basically, I long for a South Africa that is more open and more just, where people count and where they will have equal access to the good things of life, with equal opportunities to live, work and learn.'

Desmond Tutu, Archbishop of Capetown, South Africa

A Dry White Season

It is a dry white season
dark leaves don't last, their brief lives dry out
and with a broken heart they dive down gently headed
    for the earth
not even bleeding.
It is a dry white season brother, only the trees know the
    pain as they
still stand erect
dry like steel, their branches dry like wire,
indeed, it is a dry white season
but seasons come to pass.

Mongane Wally Serote

'During my lifetime I have dedicated myself to this struggle of the African people. I have fought against white domination, and I have fought against black domination. I have cherished the ideal of a democratic and free society in which all persons live together in harmony and with equal opportunities. It is an ideal which I hope to live for and to achieve. But if needs be it is an ideal for which I am prepared to die.'

Nelson Mandela

Dedication

you can bind my hands in chains
my feet in shackles
you can put me in detention without trial
subject me to solitary confinement
you won't enslave my heart
till the last drop of my blood
and the last pulse in my veins
i shall resist

Mzwandile Mguba

Your message

Clearly many of the writers of the poems and extracts on the previous pages believed very strongly in the cause they were fighting for.

11 Many groups and individuals continue to struggle for freedom and justice in parts of the world today. Choose a different country which has been involved in a similar struggle and compile your own short anthology around this theme. Finally, write a short tribute to their struggle. You could write a poem or a short piece of prose.

Put all your work together in your folder or mount it as a display.

Tips for Success

◆ Think hard to imagine what life would be like under alien domination. Imagine a typical day and the things that would be different. As you role-play, concentrate on making your character as genuine as possible and react to what others in the group are saying.
◆ As you read these extracts and poems, remember that they are one outcome of years of suffering and oppression and contain powerful feelings. Try to bring this across as you read them aloud.
◆ Think carefully before you write. This kind of empathic writing, where you imagine yourself to be in a different situation, takes a lot of concentration so work where you will not be disturbed.

LIFE STORY

In this unit you are going to be telling part of your life story and writing about events which really happened. A book or a piece of writing where someone recounts events from his or her own life in this way is called an **autobiography** and this kind of writing is called **autobiographical**. A **biography** is a similar kind of writing, where the writer tells the story of another person.

Fiction and reality

Before you begin your own stories it is worth spending some time talking about the difference between real-life experience and fiction.

1. In small groups, look at the photographs and extracts on these pages. Decide which you think describe, or show, real events and which are fictional.

   Discuss whether you *view* a photograph differently when you believe it to be real. How does knowing that a piece of writing describes a real situation influence a person's reaction to it?

you will be . . . .

- Offering explanations
- Responding to a writer
- Recounting events
- Commenting on language use
- Relating personal experience
- Editing and redrafting

Vida smiled at him, then his arms were round her and he pulled her close against him.

For a moment he looked down at her face as if he was engraving it on his memory.

The first time he asked me out to lunch he said he knew a really great sushi bar. To be honest, I didn't know what sushi was but I wasn't about to let on about that.

I had never seen anything so beautiful in my life — tall, slim, auburn hair, uptilted nose, lovely mouth and the most enormous grey eyes I had ever seen.
   It really happened the way it does when written by the worst lady novelists . . . I goggled, I had difficulty swallowing and I had champagne in my knees.

2. In your groups, make a list of any novels, poems, plays, films or television programmes you remember that you know are based on something that really happened. Then, discuss your answers to these questions:

■ Why do writers and producers often tell their audiences that their stories, poems and films are based on true stories?

■ What is the effect on you personally of knowing that something you are reading or watching is true?

■ Were the things you remembered mostly happy or mostly tragic? Which category does your group tend to remember most vividly?

'You want a soda?'
'No thanks.' I turned and went back to the steam table, sweat nibbling above my top lip and under my arms. I wished him away but could feel his gaze on my back.

Real-life fiction

When you read a biography or autobiography all of what you read is based on fact. Below, Andy Tricker describes the background to how he came to write his autobiography and the methods he used to write it.

Dear New Dimensions,

When and why you choose to write your autobiography is a good place to start it. It's your life you are writing about and the story you are telling is what you've seen your life to be. The characters in your writing will be loved ones, family, friends, and even old enemies from years past. They will be instantly recognisable to you and, as you write about them, their faces and characteristics will be there in your mind. The way the story is to go will already be set out. You will always know what comes next, the high points and the low, the good times and the bad.

At this point, I'd like to explain a little about myself. At 17, which is not a lot older than you are now, I had a motorbike accident on the way home from college which left me paralysed and in a wheelchair. I spent several months in Stoke Mandeville Hospital and was then sent home and told to get on with my life. I was also told that I'd never walk again. You can try to imagine how I felt. There I was, 17 years old and being told my life was over.

Having always rebelled throughout my life, I could not accept what I had been told and, over the following years, kept trying to prove the doctors wrong. Five years later, I found myself sitting in my bedroom and just decided to have a go at writing about how I felt and what I'd been through. In a way, it was like a release to put it down on paper and to finally get it out of my system. And this was how I came to write my first book *Accidents Will Happen*.

Some examples from the book may explain how and why I wrote about some episodes in particular. You must bear in mind that, like you, I had no previous professional writing experience and no pre-fixed ideas on how a book should be written. Also, before I get into showing you different extracts from the book, I think you have to be aware that writing your autobiography is a very soul-searching thing to do. You will be revealing, or will have to show your friends, family, and anyone who reads your work, things you have kept hidden from even your closest friends. You've got to be able to give part of yourself for the writing to be any good. I know it sounds a bit over the top, but I'm afraid it is true – perhaps it is this act of giving which makes a good autobiography.

When you write about your family and friends, some of them (having read what you have written) won't be as pleased as others. The most important thing here is to be honest with yourself. Write as *you* see things were, or are, and then what you have written will always seem right.

My book starts off on the day of the accident:

'Andy, it's twenty to eight!'

'Uhm, O.K!'

I rolled onto my back and looked up at the ceiling. Little did I know then that this view would become compulsory for me in the coming months. I threw back the covers and climbed out of bed. I stood for a minute, rubbing the sleep from my eyes, bent down to pick up my working clothes, then suddenly realised that it was Friday and day release. I worked for a large garage in the nearby town of Ipswich as an apprentice mechanic, and on Fridays attended the Civic College to work towards getting my City and Guilds.

In those first few lines, I wanted to show I was just an ordinary lad, able to stand, bend and go out to work. But I also wanted to hint at what was to happen to me in the coming months. As well, at the beginning of the first chapter, I introduce you to my mum and sister and at the end to my girlfriend Kate. I explain how Kate and I first met at school. My mother and Kate are probably the two strongest characters throughout the book.

In Chapter Two, I wanted to explain how the accident happened one wet April afternoon and describe the sudden realisation that I couldn't move as I lay there underneath a lorry, with lines such as 'Kim, I can't feel my legs', 'Hello, I'm a doctor, how do you feel then?', 'I can't move, I can't feel anything except for some pain in my arms'. I wanted to show my complete helplessness as I lay there on that road.

East Anglian Daily Times, Monday, October 12, 1987

Crash victim's fight to succeed

WHEN Andy Tricker was 17 he came off his motorcycle and broke his neck.

Now ten years later he has written a book about his accident, about his treatment in the spinal unit at Stoke Mandeville Hospital, and about coming to terms with the fact that he could not walk or do many other things that he had always taken for granted.

Andy, 27, who lives with his parents Roy and Joan at Brantham, was an apprentice motor mechanic before his accident. He never expected to become an author.

He wrote Accidents Will Happen about five years ago.

'I sat down at my typewriter and didn't stop.'

Andy types literally with two fingers. His injury affected his arms as well as his legs.

'My fingers are not too good,' he says. 'They don't stop me doing anything, really. It takes longer, obviously.'

'People say life's not that great. You realise how precious it is when you can't do things any more. You don't want to give up. You don't want to lose it'. . . . Andy Tricker.

'A release'

Simply writing the book was a considerable feat. He never expected to get it published.

'I didn't write it for that reason,' he says. 'It was a release, really.'

But a chance conversation led to a local publisher accepting his manuscript. Unfortunately the company went out of business before the book appeared.

But then a national publisher heard of Andy's story, read it, loved it, and now, at last, the book is available. And Andy is thinking about a follow-up.

'I am hoping to get a council flat and live on my own. Most people have left home by my age. I am ready for my independence.'

Andy's quest for independence will be the subject of the next book.

'I would like to think I can write something else. It is nice to see it in print, even if nothing else happens.'

He thinks the book has been valuable for his friends and family.

'They all went through it with me, but didn't realise what I went through mentally, until they read the book.'

The book should also be an eye-opener for motorcycle crazy teenagers, and for members of the medical profession.

Accidents Will Happen describes Andy's mental and physical progress through long weeks lying in bed, graduating eventually to a wheelchair, and leaving hospital to pick up the threads of his old life.

Reluctant to accept that he would never walk again, he devoted himself to a rigorous exercise programme to keep himself fit, to be ready for the breakthrough when it came.

Since writing the book he has made further progress, taking part in the Pinner-based Walk Fund scheme, learning to walk in a brace.

'I can walk around indoors. I am getting better. I get stronger and stronger. I have got a choice: using the chair or the brace.

'It is a step further to help keep me fit and well until something comes along.'

Andy says that if he had a job he would not have time for the exercise he needs. It takes him an hour and a half to get dressed. He hopes that perhaps writing may become a career.

Nerve-wracking

He has written a novel since finishing Accidents Will Happen.

He has also experienced publicising a book, being interviewed by national, as well as East Anglian journalists, and, most nerve-wracking of all, giving a talk to Ipswich School sixth-formers.

'They were ever so nice. I was shaking like a leaf. It was the first time I had ever done anything like that.'

Andy was flown by helicopter from Ipswich School playing field (just across the road from the old Ipswich casualty department) to Stoke Mandeville but did not realise the connection until he went to talk to the boys.

Andy received no financial compensation for his injuries.

'It would have made life easier. It would be no compensation in itself.'

He lives on disability pension and Social Security payments, but does not complain.

'It is quite good really.' He has managed to save and invest in independence.

He has had to find a lot of money for his treatment at Pinner, but thinks that

The book is not just about what *I* went through but what my family and friends had to go through as well, watching me day in day out, wondering if I was going to improve. When I first had the accident, I was taken to my local hospital and, after the doctor had had a look at the X-Rays, he called my parents into the sister's office. I describe in the book the way he told them the news and the manner in which he told them, bearing in mind they had no idea of the severity of my injuries.

'I've looked at your son's X-Rays, and I've got to tell you he has broken his neck and will never walk again.'

I remember my Mum telling me months later that she had looked at Dad: the colour had drained from his face and he tried to lean against the wall for support. Then he spoke, 'Are you sure, Doctor?'

'Yes. Well you parents will buy your children these bloody motorbikes.'

My Mum took hold of my Dad's arm, 'Don't worry, dear, something will work out,' she said, and both their eyes welled with tears.

As the doctor walked to the door, he turned to my parents and said, 'I'm trying to arrange for your son to be airlifted by helicopter to Stoke Mandeville in the next couple of days. It is world famous for its spinal unit,' and with that, he left my parents in the sister's office.

Now, if you compare that to the way the doctor at Stoke Mandeville Hospital explained my injuries to my parents, you can see how I tried to show what the difference in a person's manner can sometimes make.

'Mr and Mrs Tricker, I wonder, would you step into my office for a few moments.'

They got up from their chairs and walked into his office; a sliding door was pulled across to prevent me from hearing their conversation, but months later, Mum told me what he had said.

'Sit down, please, Mr and Mrs Tricker. Andrew has had a very serious accident and has damaged the sixth vertebra in his neck, and also damaged his spinal cord – to what extent, at the moment, we cannot say. I must tell you that your son could die at any time in the next two weeks. Now, you can stay at a hostel just over the road if you want, or have you got other people to think about back home?' The news that I could die had not crossed their minds until that moment and was another terrible shock to them. They knew it was impossible to stay at the hostel as there was no one at home to look after Lou: they decided that they would travel back and forth each day.

My parents returned to their seats beside my bed and began to chat again. I asked what the Doctor had said. 'Oh, he was just telling us what damage you had done to your neck, and why they had to put those callipers in you.' I remember they sat talking to me for quite a while. The time had crept on when at last Dad said they had better make a move for home, as it would be half-past nine before they got back. They promised to come again in the morning.

As they got up my eyes began to fill with tears, but I bit my tongue to stop myself from crying in front of them. Mum leant over and kissed me and Dad squeezed my hand. As they turned, I knew they too were close to tears. Although there were other people in the ward, in that bed I seemed to be cut off from everything around me, and I could not stop the tears from creeping out from the corners of my eyes and running down my cheeks. 'God help me, please,' I cried out in my mind. 'Please make me well.'

In that extract, I tried to show what my parents went through at that particular time, the heartache they had to bear in those first few days of my accident, the coldness of one doctor, and then the terrible possibility that I could die. I wanted to put across how they kept so strong in front of me, coming back and sitting and talking to me as if nothing was up, having just been told I could die. And then leaving that hospital wondering if I would still be there the following day. That is what I tried to communicate.

And then, at the end, I tried to express how I felt – the loneliness and despair and how I cried and even prayed as I lay there unable to move. It might not seem much to you, but to write about the way I cried and prayed was hard for me because if the book ever got published all my mates would read it. Having been a bit of a tearaway in my teenage years, I didn't want to come across as being, well ... soft, you know, a Mummy's boy. But, on the other hand, I had to show exactly how I was feeling at that desperate point in my life where I was so scared and frightened at what tomorrow might bring.

3 Talk about what you have read so far in your group. What impression have you formed of Andy Tricker and his approach to writing his autobiography?

Now, each think of an incident which involved you and your family or friends and tell your group about it. It can be amusing or serious, but try to hold the attention of your listeners by making your description lively and interesting.

You may see that you are starting to 'tell' a story in which you are the central character.

Now, read on . . .

Below, is Andy Tricker's advice on how to write part of your own autobiography.

In showing you different extracts from the book and explaining how they came about, I hope this letter may have helped you in some small way with your writing about your own past.

There will be times when you are writing something and you'll think, maybe I shouldn't say that. But do say it, put it down on paper anyway. That way you can read it back and then, if you're still not happy with it, you can rub it out. But you might be pleasantly surprised and it might look and sound really good.

I hope I'm not giving you the impression that *Accidents Will Happen* is all doom and gloom – it isn't. Someone wrote to me the other day saying how much they had enjoyed the book and how it had made them laugh *and* cry, and I thought what a lovely compliment that was. The thing was, lying flat on your back with a broken neck didn't split your sides with laughter, so to get over this I would lie there remembering things that had happened before the accident occurred. At the same time, this gave me the opportunity to show the reader what my life was like when I was a few years younger.

I found, by recalling memories as I lay there in bed, that they helped to break up my story, so the reader wasn't only reading about my struggle to overcome my injuries but was also seeing glimpses of my life before the accident as well as during it.

For example, I had special memories of a mate of mine by the name of Terry. We had been friends a long time now, from playing football on the local playing field, to going to secondary school and so on. One of the evenings I recalled with Terry was when he was going out with a girl called Lucy.

She had just packed him up for another bloke, and he was feeling pretty miserable, so when he heard she was going to be at a disco we were going to, he decided to get a little bit the worse for wear – that's a bit of an understatement. Anyway, we never managed even to get to the disco! After drinking almost a full bottle of wine on his own, we spent the rest of the night walking him around the local housing estate, stopping at every appropriate drain so that he could throw up. After that, I had to get him home on his bike and remind him that he had to pedal a bike to make it move. We eventually got home after a couple of somersaults onto the bank at the side of the road but the biggest laugh occurred the following morning. When Terry was drunk, we had arranged to go pea picking the next day at seven o'clock in the morning. So, there I stood knocking at his back door. His dad stuck his head out of the bedroom window, and I asked whether Terry was coming pea picking. His dad said that he hadn't come home last night at all. At that moment, the door of the garden shed opened and who should appear but Terry! He hadn't been able to make anybody hear the night before and so he'd had to sleep on the bench in the shed. We still went pea picking, but had to come away just after lunch as Terry was still feeling the effects of the night before.

To finish, I want to say something about the techniques I used when writing my autobiography. First of all, I would make some general headings and then arrange them in the sequence they were to come. As I said earlier, with an autobiography these are already pre-determined to a certain degree once you have chosen where you wish to start your story from. Once I had the main headings, it was a matter of taking the first one and writing beside it other little things of interest to do with that time in my life; a name of someone who I was close to; a particular day around that time which I recalled because of something sad, or equally of something funny. I'd try and remember conversations on the type of things we would be talking about at that time of my life. Then, having taken two, maybe three, major headings and embroidered on them, I'd start to write. The reason I say only take two or three headings at one time is that otherwise you will start to think of things that should come much later, and you must be careful not to either make the work too short, or too long.

Another thing that adds variety to an autobiography is to use the words people say. I tend to use a lot of speech, not 'he says', and then 'she says' but actual conversation. I think it helps you, the reader, feel as if you are there listening to what is being said.

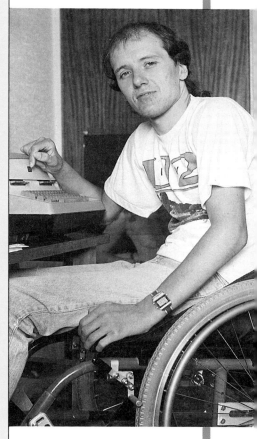

I said earlier on that the characters in your book will be instantly recognisable as they will be friends or loved ones but you don't have to physically describe them as being six feet tall with blue eyes and blonde hair, as if they are in an identity parade for the police. Instead, try to describe what part they played or play in your life. Having put something down on paper, I'd read through it correcting spellings, and also changing the odd word or sentence here and there. The golden rule I tend to follow here is, having read through it twice, if it still sounds good then leave well alone. But if you're still not happy with the odd sentence or word don't be afraid to change it.

I hope that I've helped you think you might like to have a go at writing your autobiography. I wish you all the luck in the future with your writing and one little thought to leave you with. It sometimes helps to read the odd autobiography for yourself in order to get some hints, and someone did tell me the name of a book called, what was it now? . . . *Accidents* . . . something or other, which they said wasn't too bad a read.

Good luck and good reading

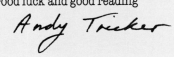

[4] In your group, skim back over Andy Tricker's letter and locate the information to answer these questions:

- How does Andy Tricker suggest you might portray a character in writing?

- What advice does he give on structuring autobiographical writing?

- What is Andy Tricker's method of drafting his work? What does he warn against doing?

- What suggestion does he make about how to use dialogue in writing?

As a group, decide how you would describe the style of Andy Tricker's writing. Is it formal or informal, comic or serious, personal or objective? Finally, discuss how far you agree with Andy Tricker's comments about the need for honesty in one's writing.

Finding a voice

Andy Tricker's final piece of advice is to read some different autobiographies. The two extracts below are written by two very different writers – Maya Angelou, a black woman writer brought up in the Caribbean and Bob Geldof, a pop star, who spent his early days in a small Catholic school in Ireland.

I WAS mortified. A silly white woman who probably counted on her toes looked me in the face and said I had not passed. The examination had been constructed by morons for idiots. Of course I breezed through without thinking much about it.

Rearrange these letters: A C T – A R T – A S T

Okay. CAT. RAT. SAT. Now what?

She stood behind her make-up and coiffed hair and manicured nails and dresser-drawers of scented angora sweaters and years of white ignorance and said that I had not passed.

'The telephone company spends thousands of dollars training operators. We simply cannot risk employing anyone who made the marks you made. I'm sorry.'

She was sorry? I was stunned. In a stupor I considered that maybe my outsized intellectual conceit had led me to take the test for granted. And maybe I deserved this high-handed witch's remarks.

'May I take it again?' That was painful to ask.

'No, I'm sorry.' If she said she was sorry one more time, I was going to take her by her sorry shoulders and shake a job out of her.

'There is an opening, though' – she might have sensed my unspoken threat – 'for a bus girl in the cafeteria.'

'What does a bus girl do?' I wasn't sure I could do it.

'The boy in the kitchen will tell you.'

After I filled out forms and was found uninfected by a doctor, I reported to the cafeteria. There the boy, who was a grandfather, informed me, 'Collect the dishes, wipe the tables, make sure the salt and pepper shakers are clean, and here's your uniform.'

The coarse white dress and apron had been starched with concrete and was too long. I stood at the side of the room, the dress hem scratching my calves, waiting for the tables to clear. Many of the trainee operators had been my classmates. Now they stood over laden tables waiting for me or one of the other dumb bus girls to remove the used dishes so that they could set down their trays.

I lasted at the job a week, and so hated the salary that I spent it all the afternoon I quit.

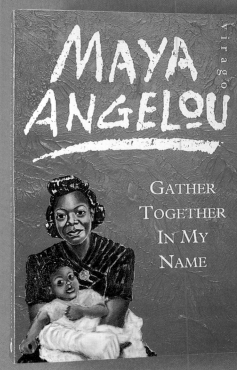

Gather Together in My Name
by Maya Angelou, published by Virago Press

EVERY week before he went on his travels around Ireland my father would give me my school fees money in an envelope. It was nice to have some money so I opened the envelope myself instead of handing it in to the school office. It was a few pounds. You could buy cream buns from The Nook or use it to go to the pictures on Saturday afternoon at the Adelphi. No one seemed to mind. But then, at the end of that term, a bill came. He rang the school without telling me.

'Good morning, Father Stanley,' said the boys in chorus. He did not enter the class during lessons except for some serious reason.

'Robert Geldof. Will you please leave the classroom.'

Everyone looked at me. I moved my books to the corner of my desk and straightened my pencil – half wanting to impress the Dean with my neatness, half wanting to put off, even if only for a few seconds, the awful moment when I would discover why he wanted me. I had no idea. But I felt in my stomach that it must be bad.

I stood in the corridor in silence as the story of my wrong-doing was recounted. Somehow from his lips the whole thing sounded far worse than it had ever seemed to me. '. . . It is not simply the amount, though that is grave of itself; your father is by no means a wealthy man, he makes sacrifices to send you here. He will now have to find the amount which you owe to the school. But it is more than that. It is the deceit and dishonesty it embodied. Such behaviour is sinful. Your father and I have talked about the whole matter. He is going to beat you and so am I.'

Father Stanley had what the boys called a 'biffer'. The word was a joke, but the implement was not. A thick, flexible rubber strap, it hurt unbearably. I was outraged and shamed by this terrible injustice. But what happened at home was much worse. There was no one to plead for me. I was utterly alone. On the bus home, in panic, I prayed to my mother. I was in pain from the beating at school and in terror of what lay ahead.

First there was the silence and the sobbing.

'Why did you do it?' Lynn asked me. Lynn was supposed to be my friend.

'I don't know. It didn't seem that important. I'm sorry.'

'Don't you know that since Mammy died the house has had to run on trust while Daddy is away all week? We are all on our honour to behave ourselves,' said Cleo. Cleo was a grown-up, more than twenty now, but she was only my sister. Why should she be allowed to speak to me like this? 'I'm on my honour to be in by ten o'clock every night and I don't break the trust. Lynn is on her honour to do her schoolwork for her Intermediates and she doesn't break the trust. But you, you can't even be trusted to take in your dinner money. Why did you do it?'

'I don't know. I'm sorry, I'll pay it back.'

'Go upstairs, Robert,' said my father.

There was a sofa in the room where he hit me. He spoke to me first. 'This will hurt me more than it hurts you.' He actually said that. It did not seem real, it was like some schoolboy novel. What was most horrible was that he had got a bamboo cane to hit me with. Had he gone out and bought it? The cold-blooded calculation of that simple act is the thing that still bothers me. He had decided to inflict as much pain as he could. He had thought about that as he chose it: 'No, that one won't be as painful as this cane.'

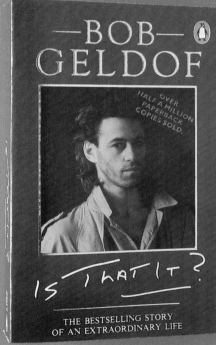

Is That It? *by Bob Geldof, published by Penguin Books*

'I am going to hit you six times.' His voice was cold. 'You are never going to do this again. Hold onto the back of the sofa and bend over.'

'No, Da. Please don't hit me. I'll be good now.' I still didn't really grasp what had been so bad. I ran around the sofa.

'Come back.'

I went to the sofa and held fast to it. My knuckles were white with the gripping, but they did not seem like my own. I felt as though I was watching someone else's hands. The cane swished and a hot line of pain cut across my buttocks. It burned like the pain you get when your hand brushed by accident against the kitchen stove. I howled, but I did not move. The second would be easier, I told myself. But it wasn't, it was a hurt on top of the hurt. My whole body was now entirely concentrated in those few inches of flesh. The third set my entire being into a contortion of agony. I screamed and ran away.

'Come back.'

'No.'

'Come back.'

'Please, Da. Please, no more, please.'

He chased me around the room, grabbed me and hit out again and again. I could not believe he would do this. Then, at the end, the bastard tried to hug me. How dare he salve his own pathetic conscience with that act of hypocrisy? If you're going to hurt someone, hurt them, but don't pretend it's love. That's perversion. I was filled with disgust and I hated him. The hurt, the rage, the shame and the bewilderment were too deep. From that day on, my father and I were at loggerheads. He would pay.

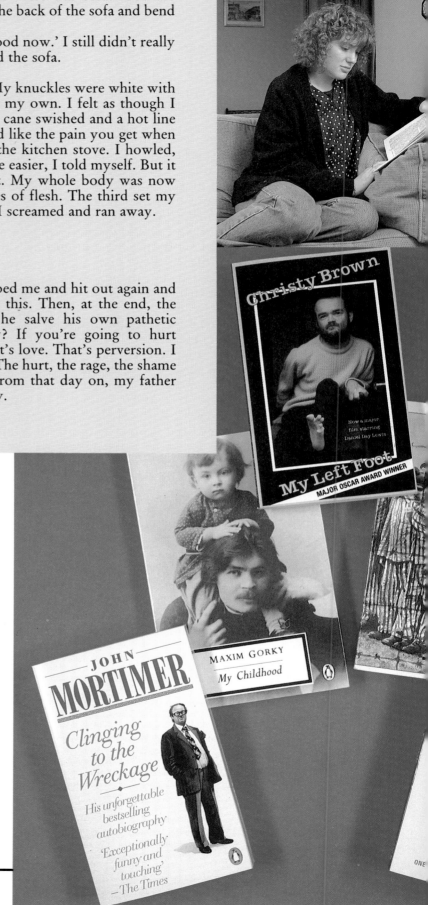

5 In your group, discuss your answers to these questions:

- In what ways do these selections from Maya Angelou's and Bob Geldof's autobiographies differ from the extracts Andy Tricker included?

- In what ways are all three pieces similar?

- Do you think Maya Angelou and Bob Geldof would offer their readers similar advice to that given by Andy Tricker? What might they disagree with? What might they add?

Telling your own story

Now, start work on some autobiographical writing of your own. The reading and talking you have done so far should help you to think about writing your own autobiography. All you need now is a place to start.

Gathering your ideas

Not everyone has a grand story of suffering or achievement to tell, but everyone has some memories of strong emotions which can be communicated effectively. One way of getting started is to share ideas within your group. Try talking about some of the following things:

— the happiest and the worst times of your life so far
— your most thrilling and embarrassing moments
— your favourite possession and why it is special to you
— people you no longer see regularly who once made a strong impact on you.

Once you have begun to reminisce on these or other topics you will probably find that there is a particular memory that stands out. Do not try to be too ambitious, to start right from the beginning of your life or to describe everything that ever happened to you. It is better to begin by writing about one particular episode in your life, so pick a time when things happened that you would like to focus on.

Planning

Andy Tricker describes how he plans his writing using headings and jotting down key points of interest to do with each of them. Look back at his comments and then start to plan your own piece. You could make a list of headings as he does, or draw a spidergram or a bubbleplan to help you decide what to include. As you do this, think about how you can use each aspect in your telling of the story.

Happy or sad times?

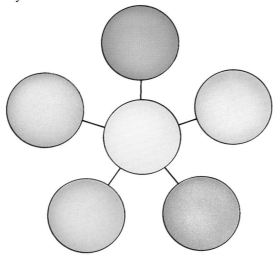

Drafting and redrafting

As you begin your first draft, think about your answers to these questions:

◼ How has the episode, or person, you are going to write about influenced your life or your personality?

◼ What will be the best way of making sure that your readers can understand the character or situation you have chosen?

◼ How much 'background' detail will you need to add?

◼ What methods will you use to bring the events or characters you are describing to life?

Remember Andy Tricker's advice about redrafting and revising your autobiography section by section rather than leaving it all to the end. You may find that it helps to show your work to a partner or to your group so that they can ask questions about things they do not understand in your writing or suggest ways in which it might be improved.

In responding to each other's work, listen especially to see if the main point of the section is clear. Ask yourself whether everything adds to the point of the story or could some details be left out to give the writing more impact? See what you can tell about the personality of the writer – could they show more of their inner thoughts and feelings?

Remember that autobiography is one way of looking at your own life and episodes from it. In writing it, you are presenting your version, your 'story', of the events in which you were involved.

Presenting your autobiography

Present your final version neatly and carefully. Check through and correct your punctuation and spelling. If possible, use a word processor to produce your final version. Try to include photographs and drawings to add interest to your story. Think of a strong title and design a cover which will draw people's attention to, and make them want to read, your autobiography.

Front cover and opening page of an autobiography by a GCSE student

Tips for Success

◆ As you talk about the past remember what Andy Tricker says about giving something of yourself in an autobiography. But, if you have memories which you do not want to discuss, feel free to keep them to yourself.

◆ As you read other autobiographical writing see how far the writer succeeds in taking you into his or her own world and lets you share past experiences.

◆ Aim to do the same in your own writing. Recreate a time and a place as vividly as you can. Using your characters' ways of speaking and their conversation is as important as description in doing this.

The World Turned Upside Down

An Autobiography by

Phillip Taylor

The World Turned Upside Down

Chapter One - Bye. Bye Big Sister.

I couldn't wait till my sister Sara left home. I planned to move into her room and take over her Hi-Fi as soon as she was out of the door. The trouble was she never seemed to get round to leaving. I'd been back at school for ages whilst she was still swanning around going to parties and pretending to work on her "Reading List." People say that students waste tax-payers money but I didn't see how she was going to have time to even spend all the money she'd earned on her holiday job let alone her grant.

When she finally went there were some pretty embarrassing scenes at the door before Dad drove her off to the station with her suitcase and about nine million plastic bags. These contained things like: food for the journey; food for when she arrived; some snacks for when she was studying; a years supply of *Mars Bars*; some fruit cake in case she needed to celebrate anything and a really rancid piece of soft cheese that Mum wanted to get out of the house. As you will learn if you carry on reading my Mum thinks that you shouldn't plan a journey of more than about ten yards without taking some food along with you.

VOICE PLAYS

This unit explores the attraction of listening to voices and the way that listening to a voice, or voices, can give a vivid impression of a situation or a character. It shows you some of the different ways of projecting your own voice in presenting your own plays for voices, and radio plays.

The power of the human voice

From the start of national radio broadcasting, and up until the coming of television into most homes, radio plays were as popular a form of entertainment as, for example, videos are today. One famous American radio play was an adaptation of the novel *War of the Worlds* which was broadcast in 1939. Police switchboards were jammed and there was near panic as huge numbers of listeners believed that they were hearing a genuine news bulletin about a Martian invasion!

A play for voices is not quite the same as a radio play. It is usually performed in front of a live audience and the emphasis is on the use of the voice to evoke a place or situation and the people in it.

Perhaps the most famous play for voices ever written was *Under Milk Wood* by Dylan Thomas. The play is about a day in the life of a small Welsh fishing village and the stories in it are all told by past and present village people. It was first performed in New York in 1953 where a small cast of six actors, including Dylan Thomas, played 54 characters.

It was an enormous success and, soon after, the play was recorded for BBC Radio. It has been repeated many times since, as well as being adapted as a stage play, as a television film and has been released on record.

you will be....

- Sharing ideas
- Presenting a performance
- Responding to a writer
- Writing a playscript

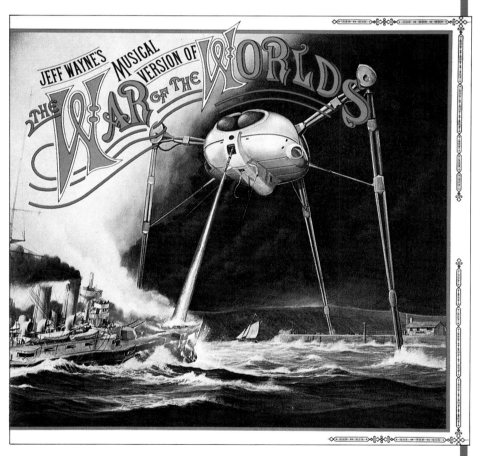

The first radio broadcast of War of the Worlds *panicked US listeners into thinking the Martians had landed.*

A play for voices

The short play that you are about to read and listen to uses the same techniques as *Under Milk Wood* in the way that it describes a single day through the voices of many characters. The play is *I Cried At Your Wedding* by Madeline Sotheby. The characters are as follows:

Mum	An old man
Tom	The Butcher
Dad	Megan Jones
Susan	Bert
Ted	A woman and man
Miss Plum	Hazel
Mrs Hobbs	Percy Jones
Sam	**Gossips** – two male
Sid	and two female

THE FIRST READING

To start with, read the play through quietly to yourself. As you read, do not worry too much about such details as the division of scenes, or their location; you know what the subject of the play is from the title. Simply build up a picture of the situation and the characters for yourself.

The numbering of each speech is designed to help performers and producers to identify them quickly.

I Cried At Your Wedding

(THERE IS TO BE A WEDDING — IT COULD BE ALMOST ANYWHERE)

1 **Gossip** Goodmorning.

2 **Gossip** Morning.

3 **Gossip** Morning.

4 **Gossip** Sun's coming up. Going to be a scorcher. Morning.

5 **Gossip** Morning.

6 **Gossip** That's the Wilkins' clock. Striking seven.

7 **Gossip** There's young Tom Wilkins. Creeping crafty down the passage.

8 **Gossip** Susie Wilkins getting married. Twelve o'clock this morning.

9 **Miss Plum** That boy's up to something. Something mischievous.

10 **Gossip** Marrying Ted Packer. Him whose Dad what has the garage.

11 **Miss Plum** Scarified my cat he did. Master Thomas Wilkins.

12 **Old man** Boys will be boys Miss Plum.

13 **Miss Plum** Throwing pebbles at it. Never been the same, my cat, since.

14 **Tom** Dear God. Keep them sleeping. Me Mum and Dad and that cow Susan.

15 **Gossip** Where's he going eh? Where's Tom Wilkins off to?

16 **Tom** Keep them sleeping till I'm clear of the house. Open the door . . . Gentle does it . . .

17 **Mum** Tom!

18 **Tom** Blast!

19 **Gossip** His Mum's caught him!

20 **Miss Plum** Caught him red handed. That'll teach

him. That'll learn him.

1 **Mum** Where are you sneaking off to? On the day of your sister's wedding?

2 **Tom** Felt like some fresh air. Thought I'd take a walk Mum.

3 **Mum** Oh yes. You'll take a walk my lad. Shopping.

4 **Tom** Shopping!

5 **Mum** Shopping.

6 **Miss Plum** That'll teach him! That'll learn him.

7 **Tom** It's Susan's wedding. She can do her own shopping.

8 **Mum** Don't argue. Do your shoes up. Fred and Sylvie's stopping over. They'll be having your bedroom.

9 **Tom** Where'll I be sleeping?

10 **Mum** The camp bed. In the hall.

11 **Tom** Mum!

12 **Mum** Like it or lump it. Plug me in the hoover.

13 **Tom** Where's me breakfast then?

14 **Mum** There ain't no breakfast. Not on the day of your sister's wedding.

15 **Tom** Oooh Mum.

16 **Mum** And I want that coal scuttle filled before you fetch the shopping.

17 **Gossip** Susie Wilkins. Fancy. And just seventeen last birthday.

18 **Gossip** Only yesterday. All pigtails and pimples.

19 **Gossip** She's something different now.

20 **All** Yes. Yes.

21 **Gossip** Ted's Mum's got varicose. Had the operation.

22 **Gossip** Ted's done alright. She's alright Susie Wilkins.

23 **Mum** Susan!

24 **Gossip** Yeah. She ain't plaits and pimples now.

25 **Tom** Here comes the bride, fair, fat and wide.

26 **Susan** Shut up you.

27 **Tom** See how she waddles from side to side.

28 **Mum** That's enough Tom. And do them shoes up. Alright love?

29 **Susan** I got a headache.

30 **Tom** I need me breakfast. I'm growing.

31 **Mum** Out of my way. Where's your Dad?

32 **Susan** Mum. I feel sick.

33 **Mum** I heard love. I told Aunt Sal to bring her own blankets . . . if she remembers . . . Bert!

34 **Gossip** Big Bert Wilkins. Never round when he's wanted.

35 **Gossip** Lazy good for nothing.

36 **Gossip** Big boozee belly. All mouth and no doing.

37 **Gossip** Ted Packer now. He's a worker.

38 **Gossip** Bert's alright.

39 **Miss Plum** That boy's no good neither.

40 **Old man** Boys will be boys Miss Plum.

41 **Miss Plum** Good for nothing.

42 **Mum** Bert!

43 **Miss Plum** And he's got a vicious nature.

44 **Mum** Your Dad's going deaf.

45 **Susan** Mum. I got a headache.

46 **Dad** I'm in the bath Jeannie.

47 **Mum** Then get on out. There's things as need doing. I hope Lucy ain't grown. She'll have to curl up on the sofa.

48 **Susan** Mum . . .

49 **Mum** Got a headache. Course you have love. Run along and have your bath.

50 **Susan** I can't. Dad's in it.

51 **Mum** I'll hurry him out. Mrs Hobbs is coming later. Said she'd lend a hand. Bert! More trouble than she's worth. Tom, that duster. Old nosey parker.

52 **Mrs Hobbs** I'd said I'd pop round later. Someone had to lend a hand.

53 **Gossip** Her Bert. He's a hindrance.

54 **Gossip** They're having a buf-fet. A help yourself buf-fet in their lounge cum diner.

55 **Gossip** When my Sandra were wed, it was a sit down reception. Had it at the George in their banquet hall.

56 **Gossip** Make a lovely bride Susie Wilkins. That blonde hair.

57 **Gossip** You know where she gets it.

58 **Gossip** Gets it from her mother. I remember her mother.

59 **Gossip** From her mother nothing. From a chemist from a bottle. Ted'll discover.

60 **Gossip** Ted's done alright.

61 **Gossip** He's a good lad Ted Packer. Not like her father.

62 **Mum** Bert! How many times.

63 **Dad** She's getting married in the morning. Ding dong the bells are going to chime. Morning! Set up a whopper, pull out the stopper, and we'll get her to the church in time.

64 **Susan** Oooh. Leave me alone. Leave me alone.

65 **Dad** What's the matter with her?

66 **Mum** Never you mind. Tom. That shopping. Won't take a minute. It's only round the corner. Bert. You start on that boiler.

67 **Dad** I'll want me breakfast Jeannie.

68 **Mum** I ain't getting no breakfast.

69 **Tom/Mum** Not on the day of our Susan's wedding.

70 **Mum** Saucey monkey.

71 **Susan** Mum!

72 **Mum** Yes love. The boiler Bert.

73 **Susan** Dad's used up all the soap.

74 **Dad** I never.

75 **Mum** You gone and wrapped it in your flannel. How many times . . .

76 **Dad** I never. I left it in the plug hole.

77 **Tom** You want that shopping or don't you?

1 **Mum** I can't find me list.

2 **Dad** What's that in your hand?

3 **Susan** Mum . . . Oh what's it matter.

4 **Mum** Do you think I'll have enough trifle? Yes love.

5 **Susan** I made a mistake. I don't think I love him Mum.

6 **Mum** We'll sort it out later. Just have your bath. You got those messages straight Tom?

7 **Tom** Sausages and the crisps.

8 **Mum** You're to get them from the butcher. They're already ordered, nothing more to pay. And then there's the cake.

9 **Dad** Yes. The cake.

10 **Tom** What cake?

11 **Mum** The wedding cake.

12 **Tom** I ain't carrying that. Not in the street.

13 **Mum** It'll be in a box.

14 **Tom** With silver bells on.

15 **Mum** I've no time to argue. Just get that cake home. Or there won't be a wedding.

16 **Dad/Tom** There won't be a wedding.

17 **Mum** Well. You can't have a wedding. Not without a cake. Go on. Get a move on. And if I catch you loitering . . .

18 **Dad** Go on. Get a move on.

19 **Tom** If you'd both stop yattering.

20 **Dad/Mum** Cheek!

21 **Gossip** Goodmorning.

22 **Tom** Morning.

23 **Gossip** Goodmorning.

24 **Tom** Goodmorning.

25 **Gossip** Morning Tom. Lovely day for it.

26 **Tom** Lovely day for what?

27 **Gossip** Your sister's wedding.

28 **Gossip** Susie Wilkins' wearing white. All white.

29 **Gossip** Lovely dress. Her Mum made it.

30 **Gossip** When my Sandra were wed, we had hers made professional.

31 **Gossip** Professional was it?

32 **Gossip** Professional. None of your home mades with curvey crooked hems.

33 **Voice** Any old iron, any old iron.

34 **Boy 1** Coming to the match Tom?

35 **Boy 2** Yeah. Coming to the match?

36 **Tom** Can't. Sister's getting hitched.

37 **Gossip** Hello Tom. Tell your Dad, I'm looking forward to his beer. Bert makes it himself.

38 **Gossip** Has to do something.

39 **Gossip** There's an art to brewing.

40 **Gossip** Does nothing else I know of.

41 **Gossip** Makes it with natural hops he does.

42 **Gossip** She's having two bridesmaids. Bridesmaids in lavender.

43 **Gossip** When my Sandra were wed, it was pageboys *and* bridesmaids.

44 **Miss Plum** Look at that. Tom Wilkins. Hands in his pockets. Scuffing up his shoes his Mum cleaned special for the wedding.

45 **Old man** Boys will be boys Miss Plum. Morning.

46 **Gossip** Good morning Tom.

47 **Tom** I don't know what's so good about this morning. It's a rotten morning.

48 **Sam** Ahoy there Tom.

49 **Tom** Hullo sailor Sam.

50 **Sam** Shopping eh? Shopping and weddings. Usually find them hand in hand.

51 **Gossip** Old sailor Sam . . . It's a shame. Ain't been the same since his parrot died.

52 **Sam** Talking of weddings. I ever tell you about my Great Uncle Bell.

53 **Gossip** I heard Ted Packer sent her a whole dozen orchids. Morning Sam. Tom.

1 **Sam** Morning. Yes. Runs off to sea to get away from women. Gets himself shipwrecked. And blow me, if a mermaid don't nab him.

2 **Tom** Go on.

3 **Sam** True as I stand here. He gets hooked by a mermaid bride. As for what happened after . . . Morning.

4 **Gossip** Morning Sam.

5 **Sam** That'll make you laugh Tom. Sit down lad. If you ain't in a hurry.

6 **Tom** No. Not really.

7 **Gossips** Thomas Wilkins! What an outright, barefaced, downright liar.

8 **Voice** Any old iron. Any old iron . . .

9 **Voice** Any old iron. Any old iron.

10 **Dad** Any old iron, Jeannie.

11 **Mum** Not unless it's your head. Where's that boy Bert?

12 **Dad** Give him time Jeannie. Where'll I put the budgie?

13 **Mum** Leave him where he is. That boiler's smoking.

14 **Dad** He don't like crowds.

15 **Mum** In the cupboard then. Under the stairs.

16 **Dad** He don't like the dark.

17 **Mrs Hobbs** Ooohoo! It's me!

18 **Mum** That'll be Mrs Hobbs. Bert, stop wandering. In here Mrs Hobbs.

19 **Susan** Mum!

20 **Mrs Hobbs** How are we this morning? Everything hunky dorey?

21 **Mum** Coming along.

22 **Mrs Hobbs** Well I'm here to help. Hullo Bert. And where's our happy bride?

23 **Susan** Mum!

24 **Mum** Alright love. Mrs Hobbs just come.

25 **Dad** Put the budgie outside shall I?

26 **Mum** Miss Plum's cat'll get him.

27 **Susan** Mum. Tell Ted from me. I ain't marrying him! I don't love him! I hate him! I hate him!

28 **Mrs Hobbs** Ted Packer. What's he done!

29 **Dad** Nothing. Yet.

30 **Mum** Bert! Mrs Hobbs if you could wash over me salads.

31 **Mrs Hobbs** Oh. The salads. I thought I'd do the flowers.

32 **Mum** Kitchen's in here. Bert, where's that boy got to?

33 **Susan** And he can send back all the presents. And tell him – I dropped that vase his Gran gave us accidentally on purpose.

34 **Mum** Bert! Where's that Tom got to? Where's he blooming got to?

35 **Gossip** Morning Mr Bones.

36 **Gossip** Morning.

37 **Butcher** Morning! Morning! Who's next? Who's next? What's it to be then? Bacon for the beach?

38 **Gossip** I'll have something for a curry. Fancy something hot.

39 **Various** Oi! Oi!

40 **Butcher** Watch it! Watch it! Something nice! Something hot! Bit of rump? Bit of skirt?

41 **Various** Oi! Oi!

42 **Gossip** I'll have the curried skirt.

43 **Various** Oi! Oi!

44 **Butcher** Skirt coming up! Wrap it up Hazel!

45 **Hazel** Yes Mr Bones.

46 **Butcher** Who's next! Who's next? Morning Tom.

47 **Tom** Morning.

48 **Butcher** All set then for the doings.

49 **Various** Oi! Oi!

50 **Butcher** Watch it! Watch it!

51 **Miss Plum** Got here have you? Tom Wilkins.

52 **Tom** What do you mean?

53 **Miss Plum** I saw you gassing to old Sailor Sam.

54 **Old man** Boys will be boys Miss Plum.

55 **Gossip** Old Sam. It's a shame. A man on his own.

56 **Gossip** Still he keeps himself tidy.

57 **Gossip** Well he would wouldn't he? It's the sailors' habit.

58 **Gossip** A woman's touch though. Makes all the difference.

59 **Butcher** Who's next? Who's next?

60 **Gossip** How's Susie, Tom?

61 **Tom** I dunno.

62 **Gossip** Looking forward to it is she?

63 **Gossip** I'll have a roast.

64 **Megan** Just a moment. It was me that was next.

65 **Gossip** It never was Megan Jones.

66 **Megan** Percy! Was it me that was next or wasn't it? Percy!

67 **Percy** Eh? Oh? Yes Megan.

68 **Megan** Then why didn't you say so? What kind of man are you?

69 **Gossip** Typical! Megan Jones. Pushing her way to the top of the queue.

70 **Megan** Now you've gone and dropped the umbrella – Pick it up Percy.

71 **Percy** Yes Megan.

72 **Gossip** She's got a front.

73 **Gossip** She's got a front alright.

74 **Gossip** All bosom in front and husband behind!

75 **Megan** I heard that. Percy, are you going to stand there and let your wife be insulted?

76 **Gossip** Poor Percy Jones. What a life!

77 **Megan** What kind of man are you?

78 **Gossip** What a wife! He's a bit of a mouse.

79 **Megan** Just a mouse a mouse a mouse of a man.

80 **Gossip** Yes. Wouldn't say no to a goose with no feather.

1 **Megan**   I've married a goose. Is that what I've married!

2 **Percy**   I know what they're whispering behind my back. A goose. A mouse is it? How do they know? Bionic eyes is it all of a sudden to see through the flesh to the man inside! To the man that I am! To the real Percy Jones. And the things he could do if he had a mind to!

3 **Megan**   I'm ashamed. Ashamed of a man that I've married.

4 **Percy**   I'm glad of that Megan Jones! I'd go to the Devil rather than give her a pleasurable pride in the man that she's married!

5 **Butcher**   Here you are Tom. Sausages and crisps. All wrapped and paid for.

6 **Megan**   It was me before him!

7 **Gossip**   Tom's in a hurry. His sister's getting married.

8 **Butcher**   See you Tom at the doings. Who's next? Who's next?

9 **Miss Plum**   I seen you Tom Wilkins.

10 **Tom**   Eh? What?

11 **Miss Plum**   Eh? What? I were taught 'beg pardon'. I seen you loitering.

12 **Old man**   Boys will be boys, Miss Plum.

13 **Miss Plum**   And your mum no doubt waiting desperate for her shopping.

14 **Tom**   I've been as quick as I could.

15 **Miss Plum**   Oh yes? Gassing to old Sailor Sam . . . I'll tell his Mum. That'll teach him . . . That'll learn him.

16 **Mum**   Bert! Where is he? Where's that boy got to? He's had himself an accident!

17 **Dad**   Now Jeannie.

18 **Mum**   It'd be just like him on the day of Susan's wedding. You should have gone.

19 **Dad**   You never asked me.

20 **Mum**   You should have offered. Oh, Mrs Hobbs. You never laid out the jellies.

21 **Mrs Hobbs**   Sorry I'm sure.

22 **Mum**   They've all gone and melted. Bert, do up me fastener. Careful! Oh! That salmon!

23 **Bert**   I done like you told me. Put it on the table.

24 **Mum**   You might have troubled first to take it from the tin.

25 **Susan**   Mum!

26 **Mum**   Get those glasses polished. They're all sticky fingers. And I hope you changed your socks. Coming love.

27 **Mrs Hobbs**   Shall I do the flowers now?

28 **Mum**   If Tom ain't back soon . . . I've got to cook the sausages.

29 **Mum**   The hospital . . . Tom's been run over.

30 **Susan**   It's Ted! I know it's Ted!

31 **Bert**   Hullo.

32 **Susan**   He's calling it off. He's changed his mind.

33 **Mum**   I knew I shouldn't have sent him.

34 **Susan**   He don't want to marry me.

35 **Mum**   ⎤ Bert!

36 **Susan**   ⎦ Mum!

37 **Bert**   It's Sid.

38 **Mum**   Sid?

39 **Bert**   He wants to stop over. Put his caravan in the garden.

40 **Mum**   It's only Sid love. Giving people frights.

41 **Mrs Hobbs**   These the only vases Jeannie.

42 **Mum**   Yes. No. Jim's got his tent in it.

43 **Bert**   Alright Sid. You'll have to share it with a tent.

44 **Mum**   I got those volley vonts. Bert. Those glasses.

45 **Bert**   See you later Sid.

46 **Mrs Hobbs**   I'll need another vase Jeannie.

47 **Bert**   I've been laying out the bottles.

48 **Mum**   As long as they ain't laying out you. Though I dare say that'll come later.

49 **Mum**   The police. Our Tom.

50 **Susan**   It's him. Ted!

51 **Mrs Hobbs**   Run up dear. The groom mustn't see you.

52 **Susan**   He can't call it off. Tell him I love him.

53 **Mum**   Our Tom run over.

54 **Susan**   I've got me veil on. I'm all set to be married.

55 **Mum**   The cake, run over. Ruined.

56 **Susan**   I'll kill myself. Tell him I'll kill myself. Then he'll think twice.

57 **Mrs Hobbs**   Now now now now.

58 **Bert**   It's Miss Plum.

59 **Miss Plum**   I just popped in.

60 **Mum**   Eh? Oh?

61 **Miss Plum**   Thought I'd let you know Jeannie.

62 **Bert**   She's seen our Tom.

63 **Miss Plum**   Gassing to old Sailor Sam. Then hanging about at the butchers. Thought you might have been wondering.

64 **Mum**   Yes. Well, thank you.

65 **Miss Plum**   Wondering where he'd got to. See you at the wedding. That'll teach him. That'll learn him.

66 **Dad**   Old bat.

67 **Mum**   I'll do him.

68 **Susan**   If he ain't back in time and messes up my wedding, I'll kill him. I'll have his guts for garters!

69 **Dad**   Susan! On your wedding!

70 **Mum**   Look at the time. If he ain't here in a minute, there won't be a wedding.

71 **Dad/Susan**   There won't be a wedding?

72 **Mum**   You can't have a wedding. Not without a cake!

1 **Tom**   Morning.
2 **Woman**   Hullo dear. It's Tom dear. For the cake.
3 **Man**   Hullo Tom. I can save you a trip. Van's
       mended. We'll deliver you and the cake.
4 **Woman**   I'll just get my hat.
5 **Man**   She got a new hat. Fifty years we've been
       married.
6 **Woman**   Fifty years today. And no regrets.
7 **Man**   No regrets. She lets me be. I lets her be.
8 **Woman**   It was a day like this. Do you remember?
9 **Man**   Aye. Let's be off then. I remember. Like it
       was yesterday.
10 **Gossip**   Speech . . . speech.
11 **Mum**   Go on Bert.
12 **Dad**   I ain't one for speeches. So. All I got to say
       is, I'm a proud and happy man. I ain't losing
       a daughter. I'm gaining a son.
13 **Gossip**   Very original.
14 **Dad**   And may all their troubles be little ones.
15 **All**   Ooooh!
16 **Mum**   Cut the cake now love.
17 **Gossip**   Lovely do Jeannie. Lovely cake.
18 **Gossip**   When my Sandra were wed, her cake
       were three layers. Had a bridal iced
       couple on top.
19 **Tom**   Sausages, crisps anyone?
20 **Mum**   Not now Tom.
21 **Tom**   You told me to pass things round.
22 **Mum**   There's a time and place. Susan's cutting
       her cake. Don't forget to wish love.
23 **Susan**   What'll I wish for Ted?
24 **Ted**   I dunno.
25 **Susan**   I dunno neither.
26 **Ted**   They seem to be enjoying themselves.
27 **Susan**   Yes. I feel all funny.
28 **Voice**   Makes it himself he does. Soil-grown hops.
29 **Ted**   Come on Mrs Packer. Let's scarper.
30 **Miss Plum**   Done yourself up Tom Wilkins.
31 **Tom**   We do our best you know. Have a crisp Miss
       Plum.
32 **Miss Plum**   Well. Seeing you asked.
33 **Tom**   And a sausage for the cat.
34 **Miss Plum**   Cheek.
35 **Old man**   Boys will be boys.
36 **Gossip**   Looked lovely didn't she.
37 **Gossip**   Ted done alright. Lucky old Ted.
38 **Gossip**   I manures mine in winter and prunes
       them in the autumn.
39 **Gossip**   Fancy.
40 **Mum**   Over here Bert. Mrs Hobbs want filling. All
       right Gran?
41 **Gran**   I dunno Jeannie, seems just yesterday I
       cried at your wedding.
42 **Sid**   Hey Bert.
43 **Bert**   Give us your glass Sid. Fill 'em up everyone.

44 **Sid**   Talking of glass. Your greenhouse Bert. Took
       a knock.
45 **Bert**   Eh? Me greenhouse.
46 **Sid**   I were parking the caravan and accidents will
       happen.
47 **Megan**   When I were married, the whole village
       turned up to see it. Didn't they Percy?
48 **Percy**   Yes Megan.
49 **Gossip**   It was her popped the question. He'd
       never the nerve.
50 **Gossip**   Nor the inclination. Coerced he was.
       Coerced into wedlock.
51 **Gossip**   Deathlock more like. Poor old Percy.
52 **Megan**   Drunk Percy Jones. Drunk as a brute.
53 **Percy**   Yes Megan.
54 **Megan**   What kind of man have I married?
55 **Percy**   That's the question eh Megan Jones. What
       kind of man *have* you married?
56 **Bert**   Fill 'em up. Everybody happy? You done a
       grand job Jeannie.
57 **Mum**   She looked lovely Bert.
58 **Dad**   She's a good girl. Like her Mum.
59 **Mum**   Bert Wilkins! We'll want some more
       glasses.

1	**Gossip**	They'll be rolling up the carpet. Having a knees up.
2	**Sam**	Ahoy there Tom. This is a do eh?
3	**Tom**	Not bad.
4	**Sam**	Your turn next.
5	**Tom**	Me? Never?
6	**Gossip**	Your turn'll come Tom.
7	**Gossip**	You'll see.
8	**Miss Plum**	His turn'll come alright.
9	**Old man**	Boys will be boys, Miss Plum.
10	**Miss Plum**	His turn'll come. That'll teach him. That'll learn him.
11	**Mum**	Bert. Our Susan's gone. She run off with Ted Packer.
12	**Dad**	She married him ain't she.
13	**Susan**	Bye. Bye Mum. Thanks for everything.
14	**Mum**	Bye love.
15	**Bert**	Look after her Ted.
16	**Gossip**	Ted's done alright.

1 When you have finished, talk about the reading with a partner. There is a lot to sort out from this first reading. Check with each other that you have understood the details of the play by agreeing on these details:

— What relation is Tom to Susan?
— What is their surname?
— Who is Bert?
— What does he do wrong?
— What does he make?
— Who is Susan marrying?
— What was Sam once?
— Who owns a budgie, a cat, and used to own a parrot?
— Who is staying overnight?
— What is Mum's Christian name?

THE SECOND READING

2 Now, join with another pair and get ready to read the play aloud – this time as a group, allocating characters to individuals. Before you begin, you will need to think about:

Who will read each part?

With 20 parts this will take some serious planning, but to begin with decide who will read the major parts – highlighted on the list of characters on page 70. Then, share out the other parts as you go along.

Playing more than one part is called **doubling**. It is quite a test for each member of the group to read a number of characters and make a clear distinction between the personalities and voices of two or more characters.

How will you read the gossips?

The identification of the separate 'gossips' has been omitted and it is part of your task to decide which gossip is saying which lines. It is only when you read their words carefully, and see how each character fits into the shape of each small scene, that you will be able to decide.

■ Read the play as a group for the first time. Do not worry if your reading moves in fits and starts as you keep checking on who is reading which part.

Now meet a producer

David Griffiths works on plays like these as both a writer and producer. Below, he gives some hints on how to present a play for voices.

A play for voices requires a particular skill and much practice on the part of the performers to be able to make the characters of the play 'live' in the minds of the audience, when they are restricted to the use of their voices only.

The performers in a play for voices *engage* their live audience in the same way that they would for a conventional play, feeling their presence, and adjusting and responding to their mood and responses. However, they have to do this with their voices only. It is a special skill, and requires a lot of practice.

Although the audience can physically see the actors reading their scripts, the focus has to be directed on their vocal qualities at the expense of their bodies. It is the agility and colour of their voices which must demand attention. The audience should be able to close their eyes, and feel and hear the presence of the characters.

To achieve this, the actor or actress must learn to *place* the voice in the space of the audience's listening so that they can identify a particular voice at once. Whatever else happens, each *voice* has to be clearly heard by all the audience.

At the same time, the performers must avoid making their characters sound as though they are being read off the page. The words and thoughts of their characters must seem to live naturally and easily in their minds and then they will sound convincing to an audience.

For some people this is very difficult. Many professional actors find the first read-through of plays a harrowing and sometimes humiliating experience. It is only after a long process of discovery, and especially absorbing the *feel* of their character, that they begin to make the language of their character, their own; they speak with the same voice and the written words begin to come alive.

Others seem to be able to instinctively associate with the mind and personality of their character and find a convincing performance very quickly with apparently little effort. So don't become despondent if you seem to need more time than others to prepare a convincing performance.

THE THIRD READING

Before you read the play for a third time, spend some time exploring the way it develops and the way it achieves some of its effects. On your own, jot down some notes in response to the following points suggesting how you could make use of them in your reading of particular characters:

THE WAY THE STORY IS TOLD

When writers tell stories, they use many dramatic devices to help them do this. Madeline Sotheby is no exception. She tells the audience where the characters are and what they are doing by letting us overhear their conversation and thoughts.

How will that affect the way you read different lines from the play?

THE USE OF DESCRIPTION

Madeline Sotheby does not spoon-feed her audience with descriptive detail. She engages their interest by dropping in occasional clues in the script, so they become engaged in the story.

How can you make sure your audience picks up these hints and suggestions in your reading?

THE STYLE

The kind of language used in the play is intended to suggest real speech but, at times, it is more like poetry or is made up of questions and answers which are deliberately in the same rhythm.

How many examples of **alliteration** can you find in this play? What effect does alliteration have upon the sounds and rhythm of the language of the play? How will you treat it in your presentation?

Where is **repetition** used? Look at how the sense of the old man's line 'Boys will be boys, Miss Plum' changes according to where it is spoken. How can you vary the way the line sounds?

Why is **abbreviation** so important? Notice how the speeches include many abbreviations such as 'there's, 'they'll', 'I'm', 'he's, 'Ted's, and so on.

DRAMATIC FOCUS

On whom or what is the play focused? Is it a play about a wedding, a community, a family wedding in a particular community, or one person or persons?

Which characters are most important to the overall shape and movement of the story? How can you make them stand out?

THE GOSSIPS

Many older and traditional plays, as well as some musicals, have what is called a **chorus** as part of the cast. This group of characters comment on what is happening to change the mood and emphasis of a scene and also describe new locations or note the passing of time.

What do you think is the function of the gossips in this play? How can you show this in the way they speak?

MOVEMENT

In the play, there is a clear impression of people moving to and fro within and outside the household.

People seem to pass each other or to stop for a chat before moving on.

How will your reading put across this sense of bustle and pace?

HUMOUR

The play is written in a light and frothy style. Do you think there are any amusing moments? What comic devices are used by Madeline Sotheby when she is only able to convey comedy through words and sounds? How can you present the comedy to best effect or highlight the comic elements in your presentation?

VOICEBOX

Points to watch when you are
reading or speaking aloud.

VOLUME
Make sure that your voice can be heard – and heard at
the back. That means looking upwards and outwards
and *projecting* your voice to the back row of your
audience. If the person sitting there cannot hear you, all
your efforts will be pointless. To make your character
speak quietly, try to soften your voice without losing
volume.

TONE-COLOUR
Give your voice a warm or cold
feeling as your presentation
requires. Try speaking a few lines
with a smile on your face – you
will find it much more difficult to
sound cold if you are smiling.

PACE AND PITCH
Pitch is the level (high or low) at
which you speak and pace is the
rate (fast or slow). Raise the voice
and speak faster to convey
excitement, anger or tension. Use
a lower, slower delivery to show
depression, worry or boredom.
Varying the pitch and pace of your
voice continually, helps to give
feeling to your words.

PAUSE
A pause is the lack of sound when you stop speaking. It
can be very effective as a way of highlighting the words
you are speaking. Remember that what seems like a
long pause to you will seem shorter for the audience.
Use pauses before or after words you particularly want
the audience to notice.

STRESS AND INFLEXION
Stress is another way of highlighting a word or syllable,
while inflexion describes the way the voice can be
continuously distorted slightly. Changing the stress and
inflexion of speech can change its meaning completely
to show admiration, disbelief or shock. A simple
sentence, like 'Marion passed her driving test', could be
read in any of these ways.

3 Now, re-read the play in your group. This time use David
Griffiths's advice and what you have discovered about the play to
make your reading come to life. After practising your reading,
perform your play for voices in front of another group or class.

Radio plays

Turning a play for voices into a radio play makes you think about different aspects of using your voice to maximum effect. Below, David Griffiths identifies some of the key techniques employed in making a radio recording from a playscript:

The main difference between the presentation of a play for voices and a radio play, is that the first is essentially a *live* performance presented to an assembled audience, whereas the second is recorded in a sound studio on tape and then broadcast. It is likely to be listened to by an individual rather than a group. Radio creates pictures in the imagination of the listener, in sound. This sound is projected directly to the centre of the head of the listener. In this sense it is a very personal and absorbing medium.

Radio plays are made in a sound studio. The essential equipment consists of a microphone, a tape-machine to record and play back the recording and a room which has the simple facility to alter the sound quality of the recording.

While a professional sound studio will have a very sophisticated assembly of high-technology recording machines, it is worth remembering that some classic radio drama was broadcast live and in front of an audience using little more than the basic equipment described above.

The first consideration is the location of the microphone because the microphone becomes like the individual ear of the listener. For every scene, the first question which has to be asked is where should the microphone be situated?

Once you realise this, it is quite easy to think about where you wish to place the listener in each scene. You have to decide from whose point of view, or which **perspective**, is each scene being overheard. Film-makers have a similar decision to make in deciding whose eyes they want to show a scene through.

The second consideration is the texture and depth of sound you hope to achieve. It is fascinating to play with perspective and space in sound. For example, it is quite easy to create the illusion of a person walking towards or away from the listener. This can be done by actually walking round the studio, or by using a microphone which has a 'dead' and a 'live' side to it. This allows an actress to remain virtually in the same space and show distance by simply moving herself slightly from the live side, which picks up sound, to the dead side, which does not.

It is also quite simple to create a quality of sound which recreates the illusion of being inside or outside. The sound of being inside, **interior sound**, comes from the nature of the surfaces surrounding the speaker. A room with hard plastered, stone, brick, or wooden walls, is likely to produce a quality of sound which has a sharp, reverberating echo to it. That's why, if you sing in the bathroom it seems sharp and full of life. Outside, in an enclosed yard or entry, surrounded by hard, non-absorbent surfaces, the same echo effect is created naturally.

If, however, the room is carpeted and heavily draped with curtains and soft furnishings, the sound quality is **muted**, as the sound is absorbed by the assortment of fabrics. In the countryside, despite the bird song or rural sounds, the voice reverberates little and has no echo, as the sound **dissembles** in the open-air space.

It is possible to create a small sound booth in a room around which drapes, such as old curtains or blankets, can be added and removed according to the sound qualities required to record a scene.

Sometimes a character is saying things in his or her head, thinking aloud. To create this, the sound booth can simulate a tiny telephone cubicle where all sound is blanketed out. Then, the microphone is set very close to the actor's mouth, and he speaks very quietly. In this way, the voice appears to come from inside the character's head. Sometimes, the director wants to hear these thoughts over the conversations of others. This is called a **voice-over** (VO) where the audience hears what is said against a background of other talk or sounds.

One of the most exciting and exacting elements of sound recording is to experiment with the design of a simple booth to find the exact 'environment' in sound quality, which makes a scene seem authentically located and real.

In the studio, the voices for radio dramas are recorded first. Then, the **sound effects** (FX) are added – **dubbed** or **mixed** – from special effects recordings. Often a sound effect like milk bottles clattering or birds singing is used to show the passing of time in a recording or a change of scene. Finally, any errors in recording are **edited** from the original tape.

One important technical point in recording voices and other effects is known as **cueing**. In order that the actors start to speak at the right time, a system of visual (noiseless) signals is required. Flashing lights are often used. Coming in *on cue* means beginning a sequence of dialogue at exactly the right time.

Write your own play

4 Use what you have learned about plays for voices to write your own play. Work in pairs or small groups for this. Make the subject of your play an event where your audience will have some expectations of what may happen and what may go wrong or, eventually, be all right. For example:

my birthday party

Christmas lunch

Speech Day

last day of term

Sports Day

Drafting and redrafting

Think and talk before you begin to write. Identify your central characters and give them names. Talk about how old they are and what they are like. Relating them to people you all know can help with this. Jot down the kinds of things they might say on such an occasion. Then, on separate sheets of paper, each write a short scene or pieces of dialogue and conversation in which they are involved. Read these out loud to one another and begin to link the sheets of paper together into your play.

Add characters as you do this, and then link your new characters so that they turn up in more than one scene. Add more scenes as well and remember the features of Madeline Sotheby's play – her style, the language and the idea of giving clues and brief suggestions as to what is happening.

Keep on doing this until you have a rough draft of your script. Go on to write your final version either individually or in your group.

Revising

When you write your scripts indicate any movements, instructions or sound effects as **directions**. These are normally written in capital letters and placed in brackets to help the performers and director to understand clearly what action is being indicated.

There is one other technical detail to include when you have completed your script. Put numbers on the left-hand side of the page to identify each speech – as they are used in the script for *I Cried At Your Wedding*. These numbers provide a quick reference between actor and director when rehearsing.

Performing

5 Having written your play, direct it as a play for voices or produce it as a radio play. One way to do this is to mix the two ways and to record a live presentation of the script for an invited audience. Much actual radio drama is produced in this way.

If you rehearse your script thoroughly, with all the effects added in their proper place as they are needed, the recording should be improved by the special discipline of a live performance. But, unlike a live performance, you can always repeat and re-record sections in the event of mistakes being made.

Tips for Success

◆ As you read for the second and third time, concentrate on projecting what the character is feeling or thinking through. Work hard to communicate that in your reading.
◆ Experiment with some different ways of using your voice – changing tone, pace and pitch or using pauses, stress and inflexions – to communicate different feelings and emotions.
◆ As you write your own play, bear in mind that a script will be studied closely by actors who will not be able to ask you what you meant. Be clear and precise and present the script carefully.

Sugar & Snails

All four of these babies are British. All four will be growing up in the twenty-first century. Yet, unless things change very rapidly during the next ten years, we can already predict certain facts that will make their expectations in life quite different.

you will be . . . .

- Offering explanations
- Giving an opinion
- Reporting on group discussion
- Responding to literature
- Writing a narrative

1 Working with a partner, discuss these questions. Which two babies are most likely to:

— leave school at 16 with the best qualifications?
— be better qualified in maths and science?
— continue in full-time education after the age of 16?
— go on to higher education and get a degree?
— drive a company car?
— be part of a group of only 3 per cent if they become engineers?
— earn one third less than the other two?
— put in more hours doing housework as well as doing a full-time job outside their home?
— find themselves as single parents bringing up young children?
— belong to a group of people that does two thirds of the world's work, yet owns only one hundredth of its property?

And one more thing . . .
Which two babies are girls and which two are boys?

Did you guess that the differences between these babies' expectations were mainly because of their sex? Beatrice and Chetna are likely to earn less, because they will have less chance than George and Li of gaining the kind of qualifications that lead to higher paid jobs. This is in spite of the fact that statistics suggest they will do better at school up to the age of 16.

This unit explores why, and how, this happens. To do this it asks you to think about *sex stereotyping* – the way people develop fixed views about what men and women should be like.

2. In a small group, look back at the list of questions on the previous page. The answers to the first five questions are all 'the boys' and to the remaining five, 'the girls'.

Do you think that the differences highlighted here are *innate* (caused by the biological differences between the sexes) or *social* (caused by the differences in their upbringing and experiences)? Or are they, perhaps, a mixture of both?

For each of the points, decide where your answer would fall on the following scale.

Women's work?

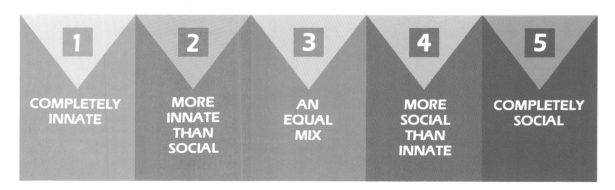

1	2	3	4	5
COMPLETELY INNATE	MORE INNATE THAN SOCIAL	AN EQUAL MIX	MORE SOCIAL THAN INNATE	COMPLETELY SOCIAL

The lesson of history

The comments on this page are taken from a variety of sources but the writers have one thing in common. Can you guess what it is?

> IF WE ARE GOING TO USE MEN AND WOMEN FOR THE SAME PURPOSES, WE MUST TEACH THEM THE SAME THINGS... THERE IS NO FUNCTION IN SOCIETY WHICH IS PECULIAR TO WOMAN AS WOMAN OR AS MAN TO MAN; NATURAL ABILITIES ARE SIMILARLY DISTRIBUTED IN EACH SEX AND IT IS NATURAL FOR WOMEN TO SHARE ALL OCCUPATIONS WITH MEN, THOUGH IN ALL WOMEN WILL BE THE WEAKER PARTNERS.

A Greek philosopher in about 380 BC

> The whole education of women ought to be relative to men. To please them, to be useful to them, to make themselves loved and honoured by them. To educate them when young, to care for them when grown, and to make life sweet and agreeable to them. These are the duties of women at all times, and what should be taught them from infancy.

A French writer famed for his liberal ideas in about 1770

> 'Q. Should the girl who wishes to fulfil her maternal duties avoid the influence of education? And should the educated woman remain celibate?
> A. On the whole, the answer is yes to both questions. Girls who are natural and would like to be well married would do well to avoid education, remembering that the personal advantage to the highly educated woman impairs her usefulness as a mother.
> Q. Is not the unmarried woman a wretched and unsolaced creature?
> A. This and more. She is a dull, unsocial repulsive being, floating down the stream of time like an unguided log in the river.'

An English writer in about 1850

> 'We try to educate our girls into becoming imitation men, and, as a result, we are wasting and frustrating the qualities of womanhood at great expense to the community . . . in addition to their needs as individuals, our girls should be educated in terms of their main social function – which is to make for themselves, their children and their husbands a secure and suitable home, and to be mothers.'

A Government Committee Report in 1963

3 First, discuss these comments with a partner of your own sex. Do you agree with them? If so, why? If not, why not? Try to back up your feelings with reasons drawn from your personal experience, or your reading. Then, if possible, form a group with a pair of the opposite sex and rerun the discussion. Compare your views. Jot down any differences in the reactions of the two groups, and your own thoughts and feelings about them. Be ready to report back to the class.

Women in the past

As you probably realised, all the opinions on page 85 were offered by men. Not many women found a way of making their side of the argument heard until the twentieth century. Women were not encouraged to pursue higher education – Cambridge University finally agreed to give degrees to women students only in 1947 – and they were certainly not expected to enter into public life. Some, though, managed to put their views forward through literature.

Jane Eyre was written by Charlotte Brontë in 1846. The story is well known: a poor orphan girl goes to work as a governess for the rich Mr Rochester at his home, Thornfield Hall. They fall in love, but on their wedding day, Jane discovers Mr Rochester's guilty secret: he is already married, and his insane wife is kept locked up in the attic.

Jane leaves him, returning to marry him only after many twists in the story. *Jane Eyre* is a classic love story but it is also a book which gives us insights into the attitudes held by many people at that time about the 'proper place' of women in society and how they should be educated to fit it.

In Victorian Britain, a woman's place was in the home. Women could not vote or hold public office. Many manual and most professional jobs were closed to them. Rich or poor, it was difficult for a single woman to support herself. Most women, like Charlotte Brontë herself (above) had to depend on the goodwill of a man – a husband or a brother – to provide them with a home.

Women in Victorian times were expected to be submissive and passive. They were not expected to experience strong feelings or passions. They were certainly not expected to take any interest in the world of ideas and politics; they were hardly encouraged to write novels. Even *Jane Eyre* was first published with the author's name shown as Currer Bell – a man's name.

Middle-class women were educated in 'accomplishments' like embroidery and singing to fit them to be ornamental wives. Working-class girls were expected to learn how to do housework and bring up children, unless they were needed to do routine work on farms or in factories, but that was not seen as needing much education in any case.

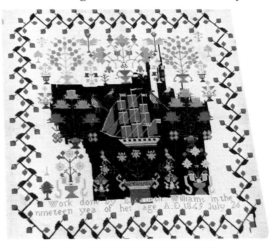

1857

On the following pages are three extracts from *Jane Eyre*. As you read them, think about the picture that emerges of middle-class and working-class women and how they were expected, or *not* expected, to behave.

JANE EYRE

...tte Brontë

1952

Jane is settling into Thornfield Hall. She is pleased to have a place to call home at last, after spending most of her childhood in a charity school. She gets some satisfaction from teaching her pupil, Adèle, and she also finds some company in Mrs Fairfax, the housekeeper. But still, there are times when she feels hemmed in by her life:

Anybody may blame me who likes, when I add further, that, now and then, when I took a walk by myself in the grounds; when I went down to the gates and looked through them along the road; or when, while Adèle played with her nurse, and Mrs Fairfax made jellies in the store-room, I climbed the three staircases, raised the trap-door of the attic, and having reached the leads, looked out afar over sequestered field and hill, and along dim sky-line – that then I longed for a power of vision which might overpass that limit; which might reach the busy world, towns, regions full of life I had heard of but never seen; that then I desired more of practical experience than I possessed; more of intercourse with my kind, of acquaintance with variety of character, than was here within my reach. I valued what was good in Mrs Fairfax, and what was good in Adèle; but I believed in the existence of other and more vivid kinds of goodness, and what I believed in I wished to behold.

Who blames me? Many, no doubt; and I shall be called discontented. I could not help it: the restlessness was in my nature; it agitated me to pain sometimes. Then my sole relief was to walk along the corridor of the third storey, backwards and forwards, safe in the silence and solitude of the spot, and allow my mind's eye to dwell on whatever bright visions rose before it – and, certainly, they were many and glowing; to let my heart be heaved by the exultant movement, which, while it swelled it in trouble, expanded it with life; and, best of all, to open my inward ear to a tale that was never ended – a tale my imagination created, and narrated continuously; quickened with all of incident, life, fire, feeling, that I desired and had not in my actual existence.

It is in vain to say human beings ought to be satisfied with tranquillity: they must have action; and they will make it if they cannot find it. Millions are condemned to a stiller doom than mine, and millions are in silent revolt against their lot. Nobody knows how many rebellions besides political rebellions ferment in the masses of life which people earth. Women are supposed to be very calm generally: but women feel just as men feel; they need exercise for their faculties, and a field for their efforts as much as their brothers do; they suffer from too rigid a constraint, too absolute a stagnation, precisely as men would suffer; and it is narrow-minded in their more privileged fellow-creatures to say that they ought to confine themselves to making puddings and knitting stockings, to playing on the piano and embroidering bags. It is thoughtless to condemn them, or laugh at them, if they seek to do more or learn more than custom has pronounced necessary for their sex.

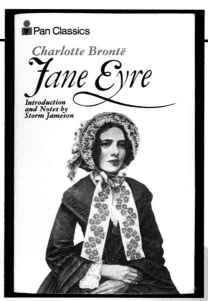

Pan Classics

Charlotte Brontë

Jane Eyre

Introduction
and Notes by
Storm Jameson

1967

After Jane discovers the truth about Mr Rochester and his marriage, she leaves. She has nowhere to go. The little money she has in the world she spends on a coach fare to put as much distance between herself and Mr Rochester as she can. She walks to the nearest village to look for work:

About two o'clock p.m., I entered the village. At the bottom of its one street, there was a little shop with some cakes of bread in the window. I coveted a cake of bread. With that refreshment I could perhaps regain a degree of energy; without it, it would be difficult to proceed. The wish to have some strength and some vigour returned to me as soon as I was amongst my fellow-beings. I felt it would be degrading to faint with hunger on the causeway of a hamlet. Had I nothing about me I could offer in exchange for one of these rolls? I considered. I had a small silk handkerchief tied round my throat; I had my gloves. I could hardly tell how men and women in extremities of destitution proceeded. I did not know whether either of these articles would be accepted: probably they would not; but I must try.

I entered the shop: a woman was there. Seeing a respectably-dressed person, a lady as she supposed, she came forward with civility. How could she serve me? I was seized with shame: my tongue would not utter the request I had prepared. I dared not offer her the half-worn gloves, the creased handkerchief: besides, I felt it would be absurd. I only begged permission to sit down a moment, as I was tired. Disappointed in the expectation of a customer, she coolly acceded to my request. She pointed to a seat; I sank into it. I felt sorely urged to weep; but conscious how unseasonable such a manifestation would be, I restrained it. Soon I asked her, 'if there were any dressmaker or plain-work-woman in the village?'

'Yes; two or three. Quite as many as there was employment for.'

I reflected. I was driven to the point now. I was brought face to face with Necessity. I stood in the position of one without a resource: without a friend; without a coin. I must do something. What? I must apply somewhere. Where?

'Did she know of any place in the neighbourhood where a servant was wanted?'

'Nay; she couldn't say.'

'What was the chief trade in this place? What did most of the people do?'

'Some were farm labourers; a good deal worked at Mr Oliver's needle-factory, and at the foundry.'

'Did Mr Oliver employ women?'

'Nay; it was men's work.'

'And what do the women do?'

'I knawn't,' was the answer. 'Some does one thing, and some another. Poor folk mun get on as they can.'

She seemed to be tired of my questions: and, indeed, what claim had I to importune her? A neighbour or two came in; my chair was evidently wanted. I took leave.

I continued the labours of the village-school as actively and faithfully as I could. It was truly hard work at first. Some time elapsed before, with all my efforts, I could comprehend my scholars and their nature. Wholly untaught, with faculties quite torpid, they seemed to me hopelessly dull; and, at first sight, all dull alike: but I soon found I was mistaken. There was a difference amongst them as amongst the educated; and when I got to know them, and they me, this difference rapidly developed itself. Their amazement at me, my language, my rules, and ways, once subsided, I found some of these heavy-looking, gaping rustics wake up into sharp-witted girls enough. Many showed themselves obliging, and amiable too: and I discovered amongst them not a few examples of natural politeness, and innate self-respect, as well as of excellent capacity, that won my good-will and my admiration. These soon took a pleasure in doing their work well; in keeping their persons neat; in learning their tasks regularly; in acquiring quiet and orderly manners. The rapidity of their progress, in some instances, was even surprising; and an honest and happy pride I took in it: besides, I began personally to like some of the best girls; and they liked me. I had amongst my scholars several farmers' daughters: young women grown, almost. These could already read, write, and sew; and to them I taught the elements of grammar, geography, history, and the finer kinds of needlework. I found estimable characters amongst them – characters desirous of information, and disposed for improvement – with whom I passed many a pleasant evening hour in their own homes. Their parents then (the farmer and his wife) loaded me with attentions. There was an enjoyment in accepting their simple kindness, and in repaying it by a consideration – a scrupulous regard to their feelings – to which they were not, perhaps, at all times accustomed, and which both charmed and benefited them; because, while it elevated them in their own eyes, it made them emulous to merit the deferential treatment they received.

I felt I became a favourite in the neighbourhood. Whenever I went out, I heard on all sides cordial salutations, and was welcomed with friendly smiles. To live amidst general regard, though it be but the regard of working-people, is like 'sitting in sunshine, calm and sweet': serene inward feelings bud and bloom under the ray. At this period of my life, my heart far oftener swelled with thankfulness than sank into dejection: and yet, reader, to tell you all, in the midst of this calm, this useful existence – after a day passed in honourable exertion amongst my scholars, an evening spent in drawing or reading contentedly alone – I used to rush into strange dreams at night: dreams many-coloured, agitated, full of the ideal, the stirring, the stormy – dreams where, amidst unusual scenes, charged with adventure, with agitating risk and romantic chance, I still again and again met Mr Rochester, always at some exciting crisis; and then the sense of being in his arms, hearing his voice, meeting his eye, touching his hand and cheek, loving him, being loved by him – the hope of passing a lifetime at his side, would be renewed, with all its first force and fire. Then I awoke. Then I recalled where I was, and how situated. Then I rose up on my curtainless bed, trembling and quivering; and then the still, dark night witnessed the convulsion of despair, and heard the burst of passion. By nine o'clock the next morning I was punctually opening the school; tranquil, settled, prepared for the steady duties of the day.

4 As a group, compare the extracts with the views expressed in the quotations on page 85 and the background information above. List all the examples you can find where conventional Victorian beliefs about how women should think, feel or behave are challenged by Charlotte Brontë's writing.

More recent times

Jane Eyre's story was set over 150 years ago. You might expect that some of the attitudes and opinions about the place of women in society which the story expresses would have changed since then.

At least, the coming of the twentieth century saw new opportunities for clever girls which were not open to Jane Eyre and her contemporaries. Girls who were able to pass a scholarship examination had the chance of a grammar school education very much like their brothers. However, conflict still arose in many families.

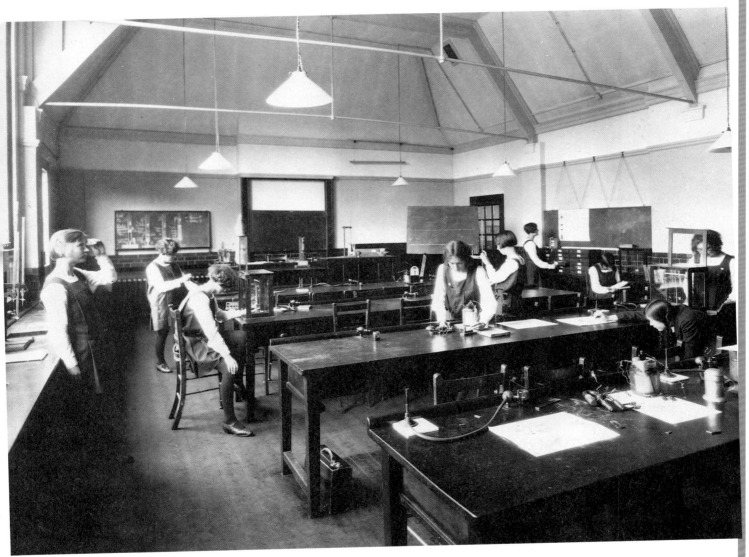

The next three extracts are from *No End to Yesterday*. This is the biography of the author's mother, Marjory, who grew up in the 1920s. Neglected and abandoned by her mother, Marjory was brought up by her father's strict parents. The household is a large one and Marjory has many aunts and uncles: Ron, Molly, Ada, Ellie and Ellie's daughter, Susie (a cousin of Marjory's own age) are all regular visitors.

Now, read the extracts.

From 1900 onwards, some grammar school places were made available to girls.

Marjory loves animals; the family dog, Buller, and the cat, Jimmy, are her best friends. At the age of ten, and coming up to taking her scholarship exam, she has been thinking about what she will do for a living. Here she tells the family of her plans:

'You and animals,' Uncle Ron said. 'I don't know. Why don't you train to be a coalwoman? Or a kennel-maid?'

'Animals are nicer than some people,' she said, louder than intended. Auntie Molly and Auntie Ada looked up, making Chuh! noises.

'– Or,' went on Ron, 'you could go and muck out stables or pig-sties?'

'Not at table, thank you,' Auntie Ada gasped a little.

'Or you could just be a good lady going round saving skinny horses, rescuing mice from traps, mending broken wasp wings, turning over upside-down beetles –'

'I want to be a vet.'

In the silence Marjory felt her throat rise in fear. It had been said, wallop, without her planning. She looked at Grandad.

'A *what*?' Gran's knife was in mid-air.

'A *vet*?' Molly laughed quite loudly.

'For goodness' sake,' Ada said.

'A vet, ugh,' said Susie.

Grandad was surprised, then grinned: 'Well, always said she's good with animals, didn't I?'

'Certainly fond enough of 'em,' said Ron, 'can't deny that.'

Gran's smile at her husband and son was tolerant. 'I hope we all are in this family, but it takes more than that, surely? Exams, hard work, like a doctor. But I don't know that it's a job for ladies, is it?'

'Mr Stopps said I could do it.'

'You asked Mr Stopps?' Gran almost gaped.

'When I took Buller. He said he didn't see why I shouldn't, if I worked hard.'

'Ha – *if*,' Auntie Molly said.

Marjory drummed the table leg instead of kicking her. 'Well I would, *wouldn't* I?' she cried.

'Marjory!' warned Gran.

'Can just see Marj as a vet,' Uncle Ron was elbowing her, doing his music-hall comedian act. 'Remember the time I caught you teaching Jimmy manners?' It was a favourite funny story. 'There she was, in the kitchen, how old was she – about six? What a scream, giving the cat his tea, letting him take a bit of food and then grabbing hold of his jaw, like this – ' Uncle Ron demonstrated on her – 'holding his mouth shut. I said to her, here, Marj, I thought you liked animals, what're you doing to poor Jimmy? You know what she said? I'm trying to teach him some manners, Uncle Ron. Eat with your mouth shut, Jimmy, stop yaffling. Uncle Ron, he will keep *yaffling*, it's not very polite.' Uncle Ron leaned back in his chair and laughed; they all echoed him.

'I was only little then,' she said.

'Oh hark at her,' Auntie Molly said, 'all grown up.'

Auntie Ellie said: 'I think it's a very *brave* idea, Marjory, I really do.'

'You'd have to do operations and things,' said Susie, 'cutting them open. How could you? Ugh, it makes me feel sick.'

'I wouldn't mind, they'd get better.'

'I suppose,' Grandad said, 'there must be lady vets nowadays.'

'I wouldn't know,' Gran sighed. 'The things the child thinks of.'

'I thought of it ages ago,' Marjory said.

'We'll just have to see how you get on at school then, won't we?' Grandad was reasonable. 'The scholarship and everything. You'd have to do mathematics I imagine, and I think Latin would be needed, so I've heard.'

'We'll have to see what your father thinks, anyway,' Gran said. 'It's Henry who will have to decide in the end about the child's education, after all.'

But they hadn't actually said no.

In the 1920s women began to show their legs for the first time in known history. They wore corsets to flatten their busts and kept their hair short.

Bathing belle, 1921, revealing a lot of leg!

Marjory and her friend Keziah take the scholarship exam:

Rows and rows of desks in a hall five times as big as Christ Church school. It was quiet, the children filed obediently, not looking much at each other. The whole room was pale and tense, a tall man with glasses waited with a pile of white papers. Sit down, children, when you have found your name. Arrange your pens and blotting paper. You will find plenty of ink in the ink-well. Papers, upside-down on the desks. Turn them over when the man says Now. Scratching pens, sighs, for an hour. Fifteen minutes' break, no talking, drink your milk. Another paper in two parts. Then it was the end. At lunchtime they could compare.

'Wasn't bad, was it?' Keziah bounced.

'It was easy. The English and General Knowledge anyway.' Marjory pulled sandwiches and an apple from a large greaseproof-paper bag. 'What did you think of the arithmetic?'

'All right really.'

Marjory looked into a sandwich. 'I couldn't do it all.'

'Some of it *was* hard, I suppose.'

'I made two mistakes, I know I did. *Stupid* ones. I knew as soon as I gave the paper, ugh.'

'Oh, that always happens,' Keziah was airy. 'You always think of something too late.'

'Did you then?'

'Not yet, but I bet I will.'

'Arithmetic came first, that was why,' Marjory said. 'I hadn't sort of settled down, wasn't in the mood.'

'Crikey, I wouldn't be in the mood for arithmetic any time of day,' Keziah laughed.

'I bet *you* passed,' Marjory said.

'Well if *I* did, *you* did,' Keziah told her. 'You always beat me in class, nearly always anyway. Don't be soppy.'

'Well?' Gran and Grandad asked. 'How did you get on?'

'Pass, did you?' Uncle Ron looked over his evening paper. 'Flying colours?'

'It was all right really.'

'All right *thank* you,' said Gran.

'Thank you.'

'Easy, was it?' Ron asked.

'Some was. The arithmetic was hard though.'

'Arithmetic!' Auntie Molly was doing her eyebrows at the mirror by the door. 'You'll need arithmetic if you're going to be a *vet*, my girl.'

'I know *that*.' With luck Auntie Molly would jab those tweezers in her eye.

'Oops, temper,' simpered Ada. 'I'm sure nobody'd want to take little Fido to a bad-tempered vet.'

'I expect you're a bit tired, aren't you, dear?' Auntie Ellie said. 'You do look a little pale.'

'Sallow,' Gran agreed.

'I'm fine, really, thank you.'

'So what about this arithmetic?' Uncle Ron said. 'It's not so important. Only have to count up to four – most animals have got four legs, haven't they?'

'It was the very first paper, that was the trouble. If it had come second, or last –'

'Really, Marjory,' said Gran, 'I hope you're not going to be one to make excuses. *Some*thing had to come first, be sensible. And if you've failed, you've failed, and that's all there is to it. I'm sure it's not the end of the world. Susie didn't pass the scholarship and I've no doubt she'll do quite well for herself, something nice and respectable and ladylike. Why didn't you finish your sandwiches?'

Mr Beach was waiting at the classroom door as the line of pupils filed from the playground. 'All right. Stop here.' He waved them into a queue against the corridor wall. 'I want you to wait quietly, and come into the classroom one at a time, when I call.' He hitched his shapeless trousers and at mystified whispers yelled: 'Quietly I said!' He went into the room, calling: 'Right. First one.'

He had called 'Next!' three times when Keziah said: '*I* know. It's the scholarship results. He's telling us one by one instead of in front of everybody.'

'Oh, Kez, how awful. I'd forgotten. I feel sick.'

'Course you don't. It's nerves, dope. *You* needn't worry.' She added some unwelcome logic: 'Anyway, you can't do anything about it now, can you?'

'You go first,' Marjory said at the door.

She watched through the narrow opening. Mr Beach murmuring briefly to Keziah. Keziah blushed, grinned, and walked to her desk. 'Next!'

Mr Beach smiled as she came to his side. 'Marjory Bell. Well, Marjory, I'm rather surprised. It was the arithmetic I'm afraid. Missed it by only five marks.'

Little hairs stood up cold on her neck and arms. She looked at him.

'In cases like this,' he was saying, 'where it's such a near decision, you have another chance to sit. You could do so at the end of the autumn term, near Christmas. You did extremely well in the other subjects, you'd pass them again easily. Indeed, I can't think how you missed the arithmetic, not like you, hm? Never mind, bad luck. Go and sit down.'

Keziah said: 'I don't believe it, Marj, are you pulling my leg?'

A buff envelope had come in the midday post.

'Mustn't cry over spilt milk,' Gran said.

'I'm not crying.'

'If you fail you fail, and that's that.'

'And you wanted to be a *vet*?' Molly had to laugh.

Auntie Ada followed her. 'My, my, imagine that. Really Marjory, you'll have to lower your sights just the teeniest bit.'

Uncle Ron said: 'What, only five marks? What a swiz. You'd think they'd give it to you.'

'I can take it again, Mr Beach said. When it's only a few marks they let you.'

'Goodness, Marjory,' Gran landed floating white linen on the big table. 'I don't think you want to go through all that again, do you?'

'I don't mind –'

'Facts must be faced. If you didn't make it, you didn't.'

'Mr Beach said –'

'I'm sure Mr Beach was very kind, as one would expect.'

'Can't I do it again? They let you, near Christmas. Can I ask Daddy?' A thought worse than any exam.

Grandad said: 'I don't see why not, really, if the child wants to have another try.'

'Oh, very well. We'll speak to Henry at the weekend.' Gran placed silver and table-mats. 'Come, Marjory, make yourself useful, bring the cruet and glasses.' And after a pause: 'I'm sure young ladies never needed examinations in my day.'

    *   *   *

'Your Gran has explained everything to me.'

Her father stood by the drawing-room fire, sharpening a pencil to a needle. He looked at Marjory; his glasses needed cleaning. It was the only thing about him not always immaculate. 'It's a pity about the scholarship exam. I hope you're not too disappointed.'

Gran, sitting in the sewing-chair, said nothing.

'I can take it again, Mr Beach said so, as I only missed the arithmetic by five –'

'So I understand. But I agree with your grandmother, my dear. Why put yourself through all that again, and especially when you've been so unwell. It's not so very important, hm?'

'I want to go to the High School, Daddy.' She didn't know if he knew, but rushed on. 'I want to do things like maths and Latin and everything. I want to be a vet.'

'Hm, yes, I heard about that.' He peered at the pencil. 'Well, don't we all have these grandiose ideas when we're very young, and we don't know what's involved? But your Gran has a very sensible plan for you, and I agree with it completely.'

She did not turn her head to look at Gran.

Flappers, named after the style of the dance of the time, on their way to vote

Her father said, 'It would mean you staying on at Christ Church until you're fourteen – that's the leaving age isn't it? – but you wouldn't mind that I'm sure. You like it there, don't you?'

'Yes it's nice, but –'

'Well then.'

'But I'd *rather* do the exam again and try and go to High School, I'd *rather* –'

'Marjory. Surely we've covered that.'

'Well if I can't be a vet, can I be a nurse? I want to do something sort of medical, and –'

'A nurse!' Gran jerked in her chair. 'Good heavens, Henry. A nurse! Whatever will she think of next? We all know about *nurses*, no decent girl becomes a *nurse*.' Her mouth was a small thin scratch on her face.

'They were nice, the nurses in hospital –'

'Nice! My dear child,' Gran made a half-smile towards Henry, 'you wouldn't understand what I mean.'

'But they *were* nice, and they worked hard and –'

'Don't argue with your grandmother, Marjory.' Her father, satisfied with the precise point of his pencil lead, put it away in his top pocket. 'You must accept that she knows best and has your welfare at heart. Being a patient in hospital –' he returned his mother's smile – 'hardly puts you in a position to judge.'

'But –'

'But nothing. We'll hear no more of it, that's final.' Now he took off his glasses and looked closely at the lenses. From his pocket came a clean white hanky. 'I'm surprised, I must say, that you haven't asked about your Gran's excellent idea.'

She said nothing, keeping her face stony, watching the ironed whiteness rubbing round and round the lenses.

Henry sighed at her rudeness. 'There is a very good college in Southwark, and your grandmother has taken a great deal of trouble to find out all about it.' He paused, but the only response was Gran's breathing. 'It is a college for girls, it teaches everything there is to know about domestic science, cookery and housecraft and all that sort of thing. If you do well, you finish up after two years with a fine diploma. It is a very good college with a first-class reputation, and altogether seems to me to be very suitable.'

'*Very*,' Gran said to him.

'There is an entrance examination,' her father went on through newly glinting spectacles, 'which you would take at thirteen and a half – in two years' time, that is, not long at all. No reason at all why you shouldn't pass, plenty of time to brush up on that arithmetic, hm? Wouldn't you say?'

She wouldn't say anything.

'*I* should say,' he continued, 'you are a very lucky girl, having a family that thinks about your future with such care and consideration.'

Gran nodded at the compliment. 'It is a highly thought-of college,' she looked only at Henry, 'and Marjory will be extremely well equipped for her life. The best kind of woman's work.'

'I hope,' Henry still looked at his daughter, 'you are grateful, Marjory.'

There were answers, but none would be acceptable.

'*Well*, Marjory? Surely it would be nice to have a proper diploma in domestic science? Don't you agree that would be quite an achievement? You would be qualified, an expert, when you are a grown person with a home of your own. You could probably even teach the subject if you wished. Come now, don't tell me you don't want to do it.'

She kept her face stiff: 'I don't care what I do.'

5 As a group, make a list of the traditional attitudes expressed in these extracts. Who expresses them? Do gender issues seem to influence what the characters say or how they react? Are there other factors as well?

What does Marjory want? Make a list of the things she says (or does not dare say) which cause her conflict with the family. What is your opinion of the way her wishes are treated? Could a situation like this still happen nowadays?

PRESENT DAYS

The chart on the following pages shows some of the things which could have affected the beliefs, attitudes and behaviour of boys and girls much more recently . . .

Toys

Images

What people say

Such a pretty little thing. And she hardly ever cries . . . not like her brother.

There, there, let mummy kiss it better.

Keep an eye on that Tina. She can be a real madam and push the others around if she chooses to.

Tracey is polite and cooperative and has helped with the library this term. Her classwork is neat and nicely presented.

EMPLOYMENT BY OCCUPATION:

Occupational group	Females (Thousands)	%	Males (Thousands)	%
Professional and related supporting management and administration	383	4	1,110	8
Professional and related in educational, welfare and health	1,490	14	733	5
Literary, artistic, sports	135	1	204	1
Professional and related in science and engineering, technology and similar fields	111	1	936	7
Managerial	691	6	1,920	13
Clerical and related	3,250	30	1,011	7
Selling	1,044	10	746	5
Security and protective service	45	0	357	3
Catering, cleaning, hairdressing and other personal service	2,311	22	577	4
Farming, fishing and related	97	1	365	3

Physics
Other sciences
Geography
Economics
Chemistry
Mathematics
History
English
Music, drama, visual arts
Religious studies
French
Other social studies
Biology, botany, zoology
Vocational subjects

The percentage distribution of girls and boys in GCSE, O level and CSE entries

What people say

> What a big bonny baby. And listen to the lungs on him.

> Big boys don't cry . . . now let's see you do it this time . . .

> Dean's holding his own in the rough and tumble, I see.

> Jim will be a great addition to your junior management sales group. His one GCSE in RE shows he really is capable of good results. His competitive spirit will, I'm sure . . .

Images

Toys

Girls	Boys	Total entries
28	72	220,040
29	71	254,700
42	58	259,730
43	57	45,440
44	56	186,640
49	51	519,640
51	49	217,300
51	49	557,020
54	46	214,230
59	41	89,630
60	40	229,680
60	40	81,400
64	36	246,950
73	27	246,210

(1987–88)
Source: HMSO

EMPLOYMENT BY OCCUPATION:

Occupational group	1988			
	Females (Thousands)	%	Males (Thousands)	%
Processing, making, repairing and related (excl. metal and electrical)	477	5	1,158	8
Processing, making, repairing and related (metal and electrical)	112	1	2,260	16
Painting, repetitive assembling, product inspection, packing and related	390	4	558	4
Construction and mining	4	0	870	6
Transport operating, materials moving and storing and related	86	0	1,341	9
Miscellaneous	21	0	192	1
Inadequately described/not stated/don't know	5	0	39	–
Data not available	30	0	54	–
All persons in employment	10,681	–	14,433	–

(*Source:* Labour Force Survey 1988)

6 Work in pairs of the same sex. First, study the chart on pages 96-7 and analyse the picture it gives of people's expectations of the opposite sex. You will need to consider:

— appearance
— interests
— behaviour
— personality and character
— attitudes towards the opposite sex
— hopes and ambitions
— how the picture changes as a child grows up.

Decide between you what should go in each of the blank boxes.
Draw or write your version.

Now, compare your ideas as a group or as a class. Discuss which of these statements best describes the chart for you:

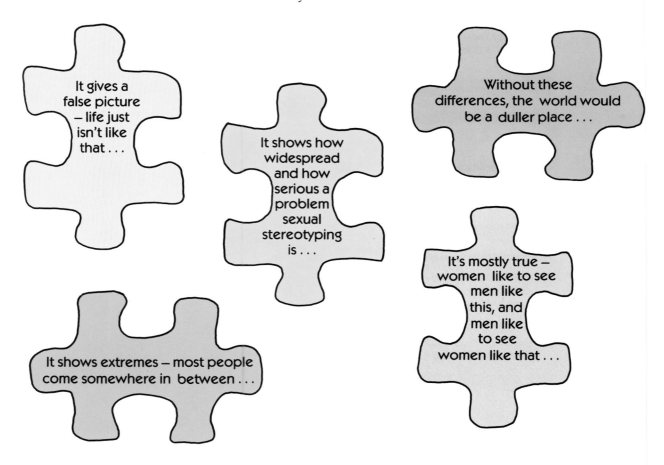

It gives a false picture – life just isn't like that . . .

It shows how widespread and how serious a problem sexual stereotyping is . . .

Without these differences, the world would be a duller place . . .

It's mostly true – women like to see men like this, and men like to see women like that . . .

It shows extremes – most people come somewhere in between . . .

As you discuss, notice your own contribution to the talk which takes place. It is an observed fact that, in most discussions of this kind, the men taking part:

— speak for longer
— speak louder
— interrupt more frequently
— interrupt women more than they do other men
— tend to ignore women's contributions and respond to those made by other men.

Now, write . . .

Below is an extract from *Bill's New Frock*, a story for younger children which examines the issue of sex stereotyping in an amusing but revealing way.

Not only does Bill find that he has become a girl overnight, he also has the problem of being sent to school in a very pretty pink dress with shell buttons! Here, he tries to borrow the football from the boys to take up a bet to kick a ball through an open cloakroom window:

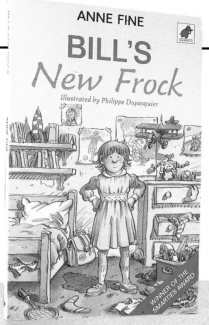

Right then, thought Bill. No reason to hang about. It was a simple enough shot. All he needed was a football.

He walked towards the footballers in order to borrow theirs for a moment. Just as he did so, the game happened to swing his way and several boys charged past – knocking Bill flat on his back on the tarmac.

'Get out of the way!'

'*We're* playing here!'

Bill picked himself up. He was astonished. Usually if anyone walked into the football game, the players just thought they'd decided to join in. 'Come in on *our* side!' they'd yell. 'Be our goalie! Take over!'

This time it was as if they weren't so much playing football around him as *through* him.

'Get off the pitch!'

'Stop getting in our way! Go *round*!'

It was the frock again! He knew it!

'I want the ball,' yelled Bill to all the other players. 'I just want to borrow it for a minute – for a bet!'

Games always stopped for bets. It was a rule. But they all acted as if they hadn't even heard him.

'Out of our *way*!'

'You're spoiling the *game*!'

The ball happened to bounce Bill's way again, so he leaped up and caught it in his hands.

'I *need* it,' he explained. 'Just for a moment.'

The footballers gathered in a circle round him. They didn't look at all pleased at this interruption of the game. In fact, they looked rather menacing, all standing there with narrowed eyes, scowling. If this was the sort of reception the girls had come to expect, no wonder they didn't stray far from the railings. No wonder they didn't ask to play.

'Give the ball back,' Rohan was really glowering now.

'Yes,' Martin agreed. 'Why can't you stay in your own bit of the playground?'

Mystified, Bill asked Martin:

'What bit?'

'The girls' bit, of course.'

Bill looked around. Girls were still perched along the nursery wall. Girls were still huddled in the porch. Girls still stood in tight little groups in each corner. No girl was more than a few feet into the playground itself. Even the pair who had been trying to mark out the hopscotch game had given up and gone away.

'Where's that, then?' asked Bill. 'Where's the girls' bit? Where *are* the girls supposed to play?'

'*I* don't know,' Martin answered irritably. '*Anywhere*. Just somewhere we're not already playing football.'

'But you're playing football all over *every single inch* of the playground!'

Martin glanced up at the clock on the church tower next door to the school. There were only two minutes left before the bell rang, and his team was down by one tiny goal.

He spread his hands in desperation.

'*Please* give the ball back,' he pleaded. 'What's it worth?'

For the life of him Bill Simpson couldn't understand why, if Martin wanted the ball back so badly, he couldn't just step forward and try to prise it away from his chest. Then he realised that Martin simply didn't dare. The two of them might end up in a bit of a shoving match, and then a real fight – and *no one* fights a girl in a pretty pink frock with fiddly shell buttons.

7 Use this idea as the starting point for a piece of writing of your own. So far, this unit has highlighted the expectations and limitations of female roles. But you could argue that men and boys are excluded from other kinds of behaviour and activities.

Write a short scene from a story that features a boy or girl who wakes up to find they have changed sex. Make sure your story questions the stereotypes, rather than reinforces them. You can write in the first or the third person and you can write about either sex.

The age of your central character is important. Refer back to the chart to help jog your memory if you choose a character who is younger than you are now.

Tips for Success

◆ As you read the extracts describing the situation in the past, try to put yourself in the writer's place and visualise the frustration they felt and the doors that were closed to them.

◆ As you write try to think about the little actions – trivial in themselves – which groups of boys or girls use to exclude the opposite sex.

◆ As you discuss in other situations think about what is said on page 98 about the different roles that the sexes tend to play in argument and conversation.

TIME MANAGEMENT

This unit explores the way you think about time, the way you use it, and the way it affects you.

Many poets and writers have written about time and many scientists and philosophers have studied it. More recently, experts have tried to analyse how we can make more use of the time that we have. You will be asked to apply some of their ideas to your own lifestyle.

Never enough . . .

The passing of time is something we all take for granted but it is a part of our lives which is very hard to understand.

While we live in the present we talk about the past and the future as if they exist separately from our own present-day thoughts. But, do they? And why is it that we are not surprised that time seems to move quickly when we are at a party or enjoying a film but much more slowly during the last lesson of a long day? Why do people say that everyone wastes time and yet no one has enough of it?

Reading time

Science fiction writers often make time an important ingredient of their stories. They write mostly about the future and their stories describe a possible future from the viewpoint of the present.

The story overleaf by Robert Sheckley is called *The Robot Who Looked Like Me*. It looks at time from a new perspective, by setting a story in the future which raises questions about the ways we make use of time today.

Read the story in a small group, or as a whole class.

you will be . . . .

- **Responding to literature**
- **Relating personal experience**
- **Sharing ideas**
- **Arguing a point of view**
- **Writing a narrative**

The robot who looked like me

Snaithe's Robotorama is an ordinary looking shop on Boulevard KB22 near the Uhuru Cutoff in Greater New Newark. It is sandwiched between an oxygenator factory and a protein store. The store front display is what you would expect: three full-size humanoid robots with frozen smiles, dressed occupationally – Model PB2, The French Chef; Model LR3, The British Nanny; Model JX5, The Italian Gardener. All of Them Ready to Serve You and Bring a Touch of Old-World Graciousness Into Your Home.

I entered and went through the dusty showroom into the workshop, which looked like an uneasy combination of slaughterhouse and giant's workshop. Heads, arms, legs, torsos were stacked on shelves or propped in corners. The parts looked uncannily human except for the dangling wires.

Snaithe came out of the storeroom to greet me. He was a little grey worm of a man with a lantern jaw and large red dangling hands. He was some kind of a foreigner – they're always the ones who make the best bootleg robots.

He said, 'It's ready, Mr Watson'. (My name is not Watson, Snaithe's name is not Snaithe. All names have been changed here to protect the guilty.)

Snaithe led me to a corner of the workshop and stopped in front of a robot whose head was draped in a towel. He whisked off the towel.

It is not enough to say that the robot looked like me; physically, this robot was me, exactly and unmistakably, feature for feature, right down to the textures of skin and hair. I studied that face, seeing as if for the first time the hint of brutality in the firmly cut features, the glitter of impatience in the deep-set eyes. Yes, that was me, I didn't bother with the voice and behaviour tests at this time. I paid Snaithe and told him to deliver it to my apartment. So far, everything was going according to plan.

I live in Manhattan's Upper Fifth Vertical. It is an expensive position, but I don't mind paying extra for a sky view. My home is also my office. I am an interplanetary broker specialising in certain classes of rare mineral speculations.

Like any other man who wishes to maintain his position in this high-speed competitive world, I keep to a tight schedule. Work

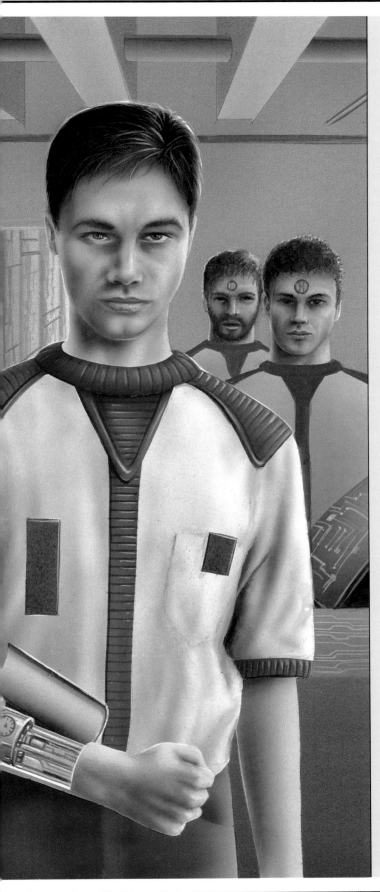

consumes most of my life, but everything else is allotted its proper time and place. For example, I give three hours a week to sexuality, using the Doris Jens Executive Sex Plan and paying well for it. I give two hours a week to friendship and two more to leisure. I plug into the Sleep-Inducer for my nightly quota of 6.8 hours and also use that time to absorb the relevant literature in my field via hypnopaedics. And so on.

Everything I do is scheduled. I worked out a comprehensive scheme years ago with the assistance of the Total Lifeplan people, punched it into my personal computer, and have kept to it ever since.

The plan is capable of modification, of course. Special provisions have been made for illness, war and natural disasters. The plan also supplies two separate sub-programmes for incorporation into the mainplan. Sub-programme one posits a wife and revises my schedule to allow four hours a week interaction time with her. Sub-programme two assumes a wife and one child and calls for an additional two hours a week. Through careful re-programming, these sub-programmes will entail a loss of no more than 2.3 per cent and 2.9 per cent of my productivity respectively.

I had decided to get married at age 32.5 and to obtain my wife from Guarantee Trust Matrimonial Agency, an organisation with impeccable credentials. But then something quite unexpected occurred.

I was using one of my leisure hours to attend the wedding of one of my friends. His fiancée's maid of honour was named Elaine. She was a slender, vivacious girl with sun-streaked blonde hair and a delicious little figure. I found her charming, went home and thought no more about her. Or, I thought I would think no more about her. But in the following days and nights her image remained obsessively before my eyes. My appetite fell off and I began sleeping badly. My computer checked out the relevant data and told me that I might conceivably be having a nervous breakdown – but the stronger inference was that I was in love.

I was not entirely displeased. Being in love with one's future wife can be a positive factor in establishing a good relationship. I had Elaine checked out by Discretion Inc. and found her to be eminently suitable. I hired Mr Happiness, the well-known go-between, to propose for me and make the usual arrangements.

Mr Happiness – a tiny white-haired gentleman with a twinkling smile – came back with bad news. 'The young lady seems to be a traditionalist,' he said. 'She expects to be courted.'

'What does that entail, specifically?' I asked.

'It means that you must videophone her and set up an appointment, take her out to dinner, then to a place of public entertainment, and so forth.'

'My schedule doesn't allow time for that sort of thing,' I said. 'Still, if it's absolutely necessary, I suppose I could wedge it in next Thursday between 9.00 and 12.00 p.m.'

'That would make an excellent beginning,' Mr Happiness said.

'Beginning? How many evenings am I supposed to spend like that?'

Mr Happiness figured that a proper courtship would require a minimum of three evenings a week and would continue for two months.

'Ridiculous!' I said. 'The young lady seems to have a great deal of idle time on her hands.'

'Not at all,' Mr Happiness assured me. 'Elaine has a busy, completely scheduled life, just like an educated person in this day and age. Her time is completely taken up by her job, family, charities, artistic pursuits, politics, education, and so forth.'

'Then why does she insist upon this time-consuming courtship?'

'It seems to be a matter of principle. That is to say she wants it.'

'Is she given to irrationalities?'

Mr Happiness sighed. 'Well . . . she is a woman, you know.'

I thought about it during my next leisure hour. There seemed to be no more than two alternatives. I could give up Elaine or I could do as she desired, losing an estimated 17 per cent of my income during the courtship period and spending my evenings in a manner I considered silly, boring and unproductive.

Both alternatives were unacceptable. I was at an impasse.

I swore. I hit the desk with my fist, upsetting an antique ashtray. Gordon, one of my robot secretaries, heard the commotion and hurried into the room. 'Is there anything the matter, sir?' he asked.

Gordon is one of Sperry's Deluxe Limited Personalised Series Androids, number 12 out of a production run of 25. He is tall and thin and walks with a slight stoop and looks a little like an old film star called Leslie Howard. You

would not know he was artificial except for the government-required stamps on his forehead and hands.

Looking at him, the solution to my problem came to me in a single flash of inspiration.

'Gordon,' I said slowly, 'would you happen to know who handcrafts the best one-shot individualised robots?'

'Snaithe of Greater New Newark,' he replied without hesitation.

I had a talk with Snaithe and found him normally larcenous. He agreed to build a robot without government markings, identical to me, and capable of duplicating my behaviour patterns. I paid heavily for this, but I was content: I had plenty of money, but practically no time to spend. That was how it all began.

The robot, sent via pneumo-express, was at my apartment when I arrived. I animated him and set to work at once. My computer transmitted the relevant data direct to the robot's memory tapes. Then I punched in a courtship plan and ran the necessary tests. The results were even better than I had expected. Elated, I called Elaine and made a date with her for that evening.

During the rest of the day I worked on the spring market offers, which had begun to pile up. At 8.00 p.m. I dispatched Charles II, as I had come to call the robot. Then I took a brief nap and went back to work.

Charles II returned promptly at midnight, as programmed. I did not have to question him: the events of the evening were recorded on the miniature concealed video-camera that Snaithe had built into his left eye. Using a mixture of playback and fast forward, I watched and listened to the beginning of my courtship with mixed emotions.

It went beyond impersonation; the robot was me, right down to the way I clear my throat before I speak and rub my forefinger against my thumb when I am thinking. I noticed for the first time that my laugh was unpleasantly close to a giggle; I decided to phase that and certain other annoying mannerisms out of me and Charles II.

Still, taken all together, I thought that the experiment had come off extremely well. I was pleased. My work and my courtship were both proceeding with high efficiency. I had achieved an ancient dream; I was a single ego served by two bodies. Who could ask for more?

What marvellous evenings we all had! My

experiences were vicarious, of course, but genuinely moving all the same. I can still remember my first quarrel with Elaine, how beautiful and stubborn she was, and how deliciously we made up afterwards.

That 'making up' raised certain problems, as a matter of fact. I had programmed Charles II to proceed to a certain discreet point of physical intimacy and no further. But now I learned that one person cannot plan out every move of a courtship involving two autonomous beings, especially if one of those beings is a woman. For the sake of verisimilitude I had to permit the robot more intimacies than I had previously thought advisable!

After the first shock, I did not find this unpalatable. Quite the contrary – I might as well admit that I became deeply interested in the films of myself and Elaine. I suppose some stuffy psychiatrist would call this a case of voyeurism, or worse. But that would be to ignore the deeper philosophical implications. After all, what man has not dreamed of being able to view himself in action? It is a common fantasy to imagine one's own hidden cameras recording one's every move. Given the chance, who could resist the extraordinary privilege of being simultaneously actor and audience?

My drama with Elaine developed in a direction that surprised me. A quality of desperation began to show itself, a love-madness of which I would never have believed myself capable. Our evenings became imbued with a quality of delicious sadness, a sense of imminent loss. Sometimes we didn't speak at all, just held hands and looked at each other. And once Elaine wept for no discernible reason, and I stroked her hair, and she said to me, 'What can we do?' and I looked at her and did not reply.

I am perfectly aware that these things happened to the robot, of course. But the robot was an aspect or attribute of me – my shadow, twin, double and Doppelganger. He was a projection of my personality into a particular situation; therefore whatever happened to him became my experience. Metaphysically there can be no doubt of this.

It was all very interesting. But at last I had to bring the courtship to an end. It was time for Elaine and me to plan our marriage. Accordingly, exactly two months after its inception, I told the robot to propose a wedding date and to terminate the courtship as of that night.

'You have done extremely well,' I told him. 'When this is over, you will receive a new personality, plastic surgery, and a respected place in my organisation.'

'Thank you, sir,' he said. His face was unreadable, as is my own. I heard no hint of anything in his voice except perfect obedience. He left carrying my latest gift to Elaine.

Midnight came and Charles II didn't return. An hour later I felt disturbed. By 3.00 a.m. I was in a state of agitation, experiencing erotic and masochistic fantasies, seeing him with her in every conceivable combination of mechano-physical lewdness. The minutes dragged by. Charles II still did not return, and my fantasies became sadistic. I imagined the slow and terrible ways in which I would take my revenge on both of them – the robot for his presumption and Elaine for her stupidity in being deceived by a mechanical substitute for a real man.

The long night crept slowly by. At last I fell into fitful sleep.

I awoke early. Charles II still had not returned. I cancelled my appointments for the entire morning and rushed over to Elaine's apartment.

'Charles!' she said. 'What an unexpected pleasure!'

I entered her apartment with an air of nonchalance. I was determined to remain calm until I had learned exactly what had happened last night. Beyond that, I didn't know what I might do.

'Unexpected?' I said. 'Didn't I mention last night that I might come by for breakfast?'

'You may have,' Elaine said. 'To tell the truth, I was much too emotional to remember everything that you said.'

'But you do remember what happened?'

She blushed prettily. 'Of course, Charles, I still have marks on my arm.'

'Do you, indeed!'

'And my mouth is bruised. Why do you grind your teeth that way?'

'I haven't had my coffee yet,' I told her. She led me into the breakfast nook and poured coffee. I drained mine in two gulps and asked, 'Do I really seem to you like the man I was last night?'

'Of course,' she said. 'I've come to know your moods. Charles, what's wrong? Did something upset you last night?'

'Yes!' I cried wildly. 'I was just remembering how you danced naked on the terrace.' I stared at her, waiting for her to deny it.

'It was only for a moment,' Elaine said. 'And I wasn't really naked, you know. I had on my body stocking. Anyhow, you asked me to do it.'

'Yes,' I said. 'Yes, yes.' I was confused. I decided to continue probing. 'But then when you drank champagne from my desert boot . . .'

'I only took a sip,' she said. 'Was I too daring?'

'You were splendid,' I said, feeling chilled all over. 'I suppose it's unfair of me to remind you of these things now . . .'

'Nonsense, I like to talk about it.'

'What about that absurd moment when we exchanged clothing?'

'That was wicked of us,' she said, laughing.

I stood up. 'Elaine,' I said, 'just exactly what in hell were you doing last night?'

'What a question,' she said. 'I was with you. But, Charles – those things you just spoke about . . .'

'I made them up.'

'Then who were you with last night?'

'I was home, alone.' Elaine thought about that for a few moments. Then she said. 'I'm afraid I have a confession to make.'

I folded my arms and waited.

'I too was home alone last night.'

I raised one eyebrow. 'And the other nights?'

She took a deep breath. 'Charles, I can no longer deceive you. I really had wanted an old-fashioned courtship. But when the time came, I couldn't seem to fit it into my schedule. You see, it was finals time in my Aztec pottery class, and I had just been elected chairwoman of the Aleutian Assistance League, and my new boutique needed special attention . . .'

'So what did you do?'

'Well – I simply couldn't say to you, "Look, let's drop the courtship and just get married." After all, I hardly knew you.'

'What did you do?'

She sighed. 'I knew several girls who had gotten themselves into this kind of a spot. They went to this really clever robot-maker named Snaithe . . . Why are you laughing?'

I said, 'I too have a confession to make. I have used Mr Snaithe, too.'

'Charles! You actually sent a robot here to court me? How could you! Suppose I had really been me?'

'I don't think either of us is in a position to express much indignation. Did your robot come home last night?'

'No, I thought that Elaine II and you . . .'

I shook my head. 'I have never met Elaine II, and you have never met Charles II. What happened, apparently, is that our robots met, courted and now have run away together.'

'But robots can't do that!'

'Ours did. I suppose they managed to re-program each other.'

'Or maybe they just fell in love,' Elaine said wistfully.

I said, 'I will find out what happened. But now, Elaine, let us think of ourselves. I propose that at our earliest possible convenience we get married.'

'Yes, Charles,' she murmured. We kissed. And then, gently, lovingly, we began to coordinate our schedules.

I was able to trace the runaway robots to Kennedy Spaceport. They

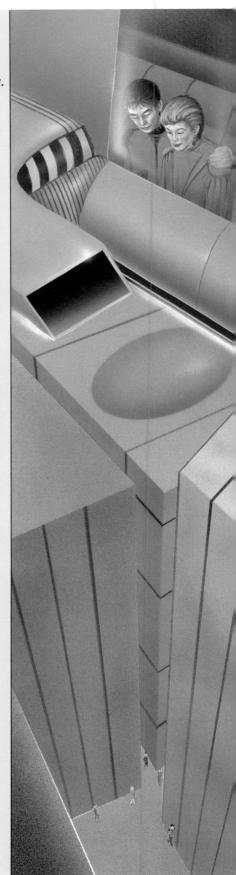

had taken the shuttle to Space Platform 5, and changed there for the Centauri Express. I didn't bother trying to investigate any further. They could be on any one of a dozen worlds.

Elaine and I were deeply affected by the experience. We realised that we had become over-specialised, too intent upon productivity, too neglectful of the simple ancient pleasures. We acted upon this insight, taking an additional hour out of every day – seven hours a week – in which simply to be with each other. Our friends consider us romantic fools, but we don't care. We know that Charles II and Elaine II, our alter egos, would approve.

There is only this to add. One night Elaine woke up in a state of hysteria. She had had a nightmare. In it she had dreamed that Charles II and Elaine II were the real people who had escaped the inhumanity of earth to some simpler and more rewarding world. And we were the robots they had left in their places, programmed to believe that we were human.

I told Elaine how ridiculous that was. It took me a long time to convince her, but at last I did. We are happy now and we lead good, productive, loving lives. Now I must stop writing this and get back to work.

Time to talk

1. Discuss the story as a group and agree on exactly what happens in it. You may need to pay special attention to the end. Decide what you think the writer is saying about time and people's use of it. Report back to the class, as a group, each taking a section of the story to summarise and comment on.

2. With a partner, draw a chart like the one below. In the first column note down some of the things – names, ideas or events – that are different about this future world. In the second column see if you can suggest what Sheckley has seen in the present to make him think that things will turn out like this. Include the names of places and companies mentioned in the story and some details about homes, work and lifestyles.

Present and future

Robert Sheckley's story is set in the future and he has created a future that a reader can believe in. He has invented a busy world where companies seem to be responsible for almost everything and computers have advanced to the stage where they can simulate human beings. But the background of New York and the lovers' emotions are almost as they might be today. Once you know that Newark is now a suburb close to New York and that Alpha Centauri is the nearest star system to the Earth then you can see why he writes about Greater New Newark and why there might be a Centauri Express. This technique of taking something today and projecting or developing it into the future is one of the skills of the science fiction writer. It underlines the idea that the past, the present and the future are different aspects of the same time.

SHECKLEY'S FUTURE	OUR PRESENT

Future and present

Setting a story in the future is not enough to make it into science fiction – a good science fiction story examines some of the human dilemmas that life in the present may hold.

When Robert Sheckley refers to the 'simple, ancient pleasures' he could be warning us against allowing our responses and lifestyles to become so controlled that they become almost robotic – to the extent that eventually we cannot tell people and robots apart.

For example, do people lead increasingly programmed lives – committed to work – with less and less time for friendship, conversation, and so on? Do we manage our time as well as we should? If you could do it, would it be a good thing to be completely organised with every day planned?

To talk about how *you* manage time you first need to look at what you do with it now. What do you spend your time on, in a typical day?

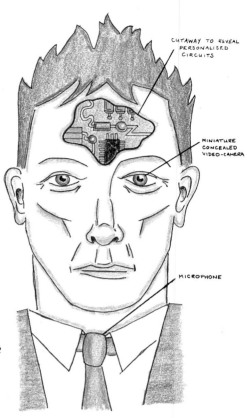

CUTAWAY TO REVEAL
PERSONALISED
CIRCUITS

MINIATURE
CONCEALED
VIDEO-CAMERA

MICROPHONE

3 Make a chart like the one below and use it to map your activities over the course of an average week. Keep this 'time diary' for three days – two weekdays and one day of the weekend. Make it detailed and informative about how you spend your time without going into unnecessary detail. Include sleeping, eating, work, sport, TV/video, going out, and so on. Try to cover all 24 hours in the day.

DAY :	MONDAY	WEDNESDAY	SATURDAY
0000 midnight :			
0600			
0900			
1200			
1500			
1800			
2100			

4 Compare your time diary with those made by the rest of your group. What does the chart tell each of you about your particular lifestyle? Are there any differences between the lifestyles of girls and boys, and between people who have part-time jobs and those who do not? In what ways can home circumstances affect someone's use of time?

Make another chart and choose one of the following ideas to help you complete it. Afterwards, share your ideas with your group.

■ Imagine that a parent saw your outline of how you spend your time. If they wanted to turn you into the perfect daughter or son, how would they change it?

■ Place yourself ten years into the future. Imagine that you are married with two children. Fill in the chart once more allowing for the ways it will have changed.

■ Imagine yourself one hundred years in the future in a world like Robert Sheckley's. Fill in your chart for a typical few days.

Writing time

5 Having completed your own charts and talked about them with your group, work independently on a piece of writing which gives your opinion. Decide whether you agree or disagree with the view that we lead increasingly programmed lives. What evidence can you draw together to back up your ideas? As you plan and draft your writing, think about:

— The way people plan, or fail to plan, their careers – schools, training, higher education, apprenticeships and work.
— How people use their leisure time – satellite television, package holidays, DIY, evening classes.
— How much time and effort people give to resolving problems and difficulties – from plumbing to personal relationships.
— 'The simple, ancient pleasures' that people may have already lost the ability to enjoy – conversation with friends, walking in the country, time to reflect and dream.

Remember that in this writing you are giving your point of view. As you put forward your opinions, be careful to support them with examples. Organise the writing carefully so that your reader can see how your ideas are developing and how each one follows on from the one before.

6 Now, use the science fiction writer's technique of focusing on an aspect of life in the present which concerns you, or which you think should concern everybody. Write a story and develop your theme to show what could happen in the future. Use some of Robert Sheckley's techniques to make your writing convincing and make sure that, although your story is set in the future, it raises relevant and important questions for those of us living in the present.

Tips for Success

◆ As you read, spot the subtle ways that Robert Sheckley relates his future to the present.
◆ As you write your viewpoint, try to present your ideas in a subtle way to show that what you are writing about might happen – not that it definitely will.
◆ In preparing the final draft of your viewpoint and the story, make sure that your handwriting is neat and legible and use your dictionary to check your spelling.

WAR STORIES

War is one of the most demanding and difficult subjects to read and write about, or to discuss objectively. For most people, the subject of war is both repellent and yet, oddly, compelling. Perhaps this is because war is a situation in which people are tested to their very limits.

War has always been written about, in different ways, from different standpoints and to different ends. In this unit, you will explore the way experiences of war and attitudes towards it are revealed through various forms of writing.

Men at war – the frontline

For most people who have lived through a war, it is the single most affecting experience of their lives. Their accounts which relive wartime memories, frequently reveal mixed and strong emotions. Opposite, an American soldier describes a single moment of great danger as his platoon is ferried by helicopter into a battlefield during the long series of wars in Vietnam which ended in 1976.

Read through the passage with a partner.

From the mid-sixties to the end of the Vietnam war, anti-war protests spread across America.

WE had been airborne less than ten minutes when the H-34 Helicopters started down towards the landing zone, a field bounded on the north by tangled woods and a stream whose still, brown waters, flecked with white, reminded me of dirty milk. To the south, a low ridge separated the Landing Zone (LZ) from a swamp, beyond which rose the dusky slopes of Hill 270. Circling down, the helicopters began to draw ground fire; the rounds made a noise like corn popping as they whipped past the aircraft. The fire was not heavy, but it produced in us the sensation of helplessly waiting for a bullet to pierce the fuselage and plough through a foot or groin. Trapped, we were little more than pieces of human cargo, with no means of defending ourselves and nowhere to take cover. The door gunner, sitting on a folded flak jacket, was tensed behind his machine gun; but he could not return fire without the risk of hitting another aircraft. Hearing that pop-pop-pop outside, I could only think of what a pilot had once told me: 'If a chopper gets hit in the right place, it has the flying characteristics of a falling safe.' Nevertheless, the experience — our first of a hot LZ — was not entirely unpleasant. There was a strange exhilaration in our helplessness. Carried willynilly down toward the landing zone, with the wind slapping against our faces and the trees rushing in a green blur beneath us, we felt a visceral thrill. It was like the feeling of being on a roller coaster or in a canoe careering down a wild rapid; the feeling, half fear and half excitement, that comes when you are in the grip of uncontrollable forces.

Suddenly we were on the ground. I leaped out of the door and was grateful when my boots touched the soft, damp earth. I was back where an infantryman belonged, on his feet and in the mud. Bent at the waist, we dashed toward the woods at the northern edge of the clearing. Opposite, Lemmon's men were assembling in a swathe of elephant grass at the base of the low ridge. The grass rippled in the wind churned up by the helicopters' rotor blades. The Viet Cong [VC] were still taking potshots at the landing zone; we heard the sounds smacking overhead and the distinctive crack of Russian SKS carbines. The two sounds occurred almost simultaneously, so it was impossible to tell where the snipers were. But now that we were back in the foot soldier's natural element, the firing did not seem half so frightening. It was just the usual, sporadic, harassing fire, and we had learned by this time that it was not serious sniping, rather a VC tactic intended to fray our nerves. We ignored it. ▶

The last wave came in, dropped Tester's platoon, and flew off. There was a brief crackling as the VC turned their rifles on the aircraft, but none of the H-34s was hit. Watching them climb until they were just specks in the sky, some us felt a momentary but deep longing to go with them back to the small comforts and relative safety of what was called, for lack of a better term, the rear. It was the same feeling we had experienced on the first operation, a sense of being marooned on a hostile shore from which there was no certainty of return. Drawn up in mass formation back at base camp, C Company had looked formidable — two hundred heavily armed marines. But there in the LZ, surrounded by those high, jungled hills, it seemed such a small force.

Forming a column, my platoon started toward its first objective, a knoll on the far side of the milky-brown stream. It was an objective only in the geographical sense of the word; it had no military significance. In the vacuum of that jungle, we could have gone in as many directions as there are points on a compass, and any one direction was as likely to lead us to the VC, or away from them, as any other. The guerrillas were everywhere, which is another way of saying they were nowhere. The knoll merely gave us a point of reference. It was a place to go, and getting there provided us with the illusion we were accomplishing something.

A Vietnamese woman grieves for her husband.

The first reading should give you a basic understanding of the situation. With your partner, briefly agree on the main points which the writer makes. What impressions do you think he most wants to convey to his readers about this episode?

1 Now, working in small groups, use talk and improvisation to study the writing more closely.

■ Using the extract as a starting point, imagine that members of your group are the writer and one or two of the other foot soldiers who took part in this landing. Improvise your conversation, later that day, after you have reached the knoll.

■ Then, imagine that you are the same people who meet up ten years later and recall the events of that day. How might your views and feelings about the event have changed?

■ Now, imagine that you are war correspondents (news reporters) who have been invited to fly on this mission. The radio stations you work for are very popular and have always supported the war. Many of their listeners will have members of their families involved. Each compose a two-minute report for the radio station you work for. In your group, record some of the reports.

■ Although hundreds of people are clearly involved – including the Viet Cong fighters on the ground – the extract focuses only on the writer's feelings. Imagine now that you are some of the young teenagers who were working in the rice fields by the river when the raid took place. Ten years later a radio reporter asks you for your recollections of that day. Improvise the interviews and record some of them.

How are the four viewpoints different? Show your best improvisations to the class, or listen to the recordings, and talk about what they reveal about the extract.

2 The extract uses a powerful **emotional map** to achieve its effect. An emotional map highlights the inner thoughts and feelings of the people involved in a situation, independently of the events which take place. Three emotional stages might be identified in this particular map:

— an increasing fear and apprehension, a mounting tension and a sense of not being in control
— some regaining of control and an accompanying release of tension
— then, teamwork, training and organisation take over and emotions are put into second place.

With a partner, discuss how this same kind of map is used in many television films and series. Start by thinking of a typical episode from a police series and another from a series about a hospital. Then, use an idea of your own to write a story which has a similar emotional map.

Key emotional stages in the story of Platoon

A war, for anyone involved in it, is a unique, scarring experience which involves the emotional extremes of fear, anger and hate as well as many other horrifying or terrible experiences. People who relive their wartime experiences in writing reveal these powerful feelings and often provoke a strong sense of sympathy from their readers.

There have been many films made about the Vietnam War – *The Deer Hunter, Apocalypse Now, Good Morning Vietnam, Platoon, Casualties of War* and *Born on the Fourth of July* are just some of them. They show different views of the war and what it meant to different groups of people. Some of them make war exciting and glamorous, some suggest that war is dirty and unpleasant but necessary, while others suggest that war is rarely justified and is often morally wrong.

If you have the chance, watch one or more of these films. Notice how they use emotional maps and how they develop and extend them at both the beginning – the feeling of being a rookie recruit and not knowing the rules, for example – and at the end – a feeling of sadness and nostalgia as the characters look back.

Women at war – the homefront

In the last section, you read about action on the frontline of war. But war is not only about direct combat – although that is generally the aspect which is most written about. War involves the lives of all groups of people and in many different ways. The pictures, extracts and information on the following pages show a view of the part played by women in the Second World War which lasted from 1939 to 1945.

Training to use a lathe as part of her war work (1941)

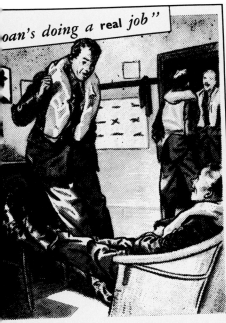

"*oan's doing a real job*"

That's what I like about her. She's not playing at war work. Once she heard my story of what women could do for our chaps she was off like a flash to join the W.A.A.F. Gets her stripe soon . . . and deserves it."

The R.A.F. wants more women like Joan . . . and that means more women like *You*. You'll wear a proud uniform. You'll get a close-up of the war. *And you'll share responsibility with airmen who are making history.*

These jobs need recruits most of all . . .

NURSING ORDERLY
BALLOON OPERATOR
ADMINISTRATIVE AIRWOMAN
RADIO OPERATOR
METEOROLOGIST
CLERK

The age limits for all trades are 17½ to 43 with few exceptions. Go to the R.A.F. Section of the nearest Combined Recruiting Centre (address from any Employment Exchange) or fill in the coupon for leaflet giving full particulars.

JOIN THE WAAF

To Air Ministry Information Bureau, Kingsway, London, W.C.2. *Please send me full details of service with the W.A.A.F.*

I am interested in.. *trade*

Mrs./Miss..

Address

W.F. 203/JAN.

Eggless Puddings

You needn't stint your family of nourishing puddings even when eggs are scarce, because you can make them without eggs.

Spiced Raisin Puddings

½ lb. flour	½ teaspoon mixed spice
½ teaspoon baking soda	½ cup golden syrup
¼ cup treacle	2 tablespoons melted butter or margarine
½ cup weak coffee	
½ cup chopped raisins	Little fat for greasing moulds
¼ teaspoon salt	

Grease 6 fair-sized pudding moulds. Sift the flour with the salt, soda and spice. Heat the fat slowly with the syrup and treacle until the latter are tepid, then add the coffee. If you've any sour milk you can substitute it for the coffee. Stir into dry ingredients. Add raisins. Three-quarter fill the moulds. Cover with greased greaseproof paper. Steam for ¾ hour. Serve with custard or sweet white sauce, flavoured with vanilla essence to tast

If li
mixtur
instead
1½ hou
If
add ½
meat
candie
of sul
dates

Don't get Slack!

"It is every woman's job to wear her gayest clothes—and a smile!" says the actress RUBY MILLER—reminding us that cheerfulness is war work.

WOMEN in wartime should not relax their efforts to look attractive. I went through the last war, so .... much our appearance meant to men on active service. It was a tonic. In the first dark days the thought of dress and beauty treatment may .... think: "Oh,

MRS F. HUGHES, *of Benchill, Manchester, worked in Ferranti's as a capstan machine operator, until giving it up shortly before the birth of her first child:*

'I'm not coming back in the morning'

They said, if you can work that machine, you can work anything. It was like three motorbikes joined together, with all sorts of different levers. You were given two weeks to learn it. I thought, I'll never get the hang of this in two years – I'm not coming back in the morning! But, on going home, I took one look at my Dad's face when I told them and I was back at work the next morning all right. Funnily enough, I actually learned to work it in two days.

We had to work very hard there, but on the whole we were a happy bunch. We sang most of the time. The roof of the building was made of glass and painted black because of the air-raids. Lord Haw Haw announced on the radio that they were coming to bomb Ferranti, which wasn't very nice to hear. In the beginning we used to go to the underground shelters outside when there was a raid on, but after a few weeks we decided just to stay put inside and work on. I remember saying to my friend, 'Won't we be lucky if we're still alive when the war is over.'

Mrs Hughes survived the war, as did her husband, and they had two sons. Widowed in 1979, she still lives in the Manchester area.

GRIM MEMORIES OF SWANSEA BLITZ

SCENES LIKE THESE greeted the people of Swansea when dawn broke on the morning after the fire blitz on the town nearly a year ago. The picture above is of High-street and Castle-street, with gaunt ruins—now pulled down—and debris on the road, contributing to a scene of desolation. The work of demolition had already begun when the picture was taken on the Saturday morning. The picture below of Castle Bailey-street, shows the last of Messrs. Evans' store, with firemen still playing on the ruins, while piles of debris litter the building block.

Auchinle...

Co...

MEN WHO ESCAPED FROM HONG-KONG

POST OFFICE TELEGRAM
NO CHARGE FOR DELIVERY

Kohler

POST OFFICE
TELEGRAM

Charges to pay
s.   d.
RECEIVED

Prefix.   Time handed in.   Office of Origin and Service Instructions.   Words.
53
10.22 SWANSEA 9

From
KOHLER 4 VALMONT RD BRAMCOTE NOTTINGHAM =

ALL SAFE = BETTY +

For KOHLER +   ...tful words telephone "TELEGRAMS ENQUIRY" or call, with...
at office of delivery. Other enquiries should be accompanied by this form, and, if possible, the envelope

35, Glanbrydan Ave,
Swansea.
'16-3-41.

Dear Joan, First of all I
must apologise for forgetting
David's birthday. It wasn't till
last night that I found in
my address book that his
birthday was on the 8th. Nigie
and I both sent cards for
I am sure he must have been
disappointed. Still you must
forgive us for things haven't
been normal lately. We again
have had a dreadful week
of raids which have lasted
every night from eight till
2-30 and 3 o'clock in the
morning. On Wed. night some
people were killed in the H'fod
and in Landore. The railway

still unable to
town. Well Joan
never recognise
for it is in ruins
have just gone 9 o'clock)
burnt to the ground
Chapel have also
Trinity church, Pell St
St Mary's Church were
the ground. Dynevor
be had and the Grammar
burnt also the Nursery
Nelson St. All the
be burnt. Part of the
llege was hit. If you
the fires that night
never forget the
whole place was
daylight. Fires
up townhill and
St Thomas, well I should say
everywhere for as I mentioned
in my last letter the

After all these years
I can still close my eyes and see
her sitting there,
in her big armchair,
grotesque under an open sky,
framed by the jagged lines of her broken house.

Sitting there,
a plump homely person,
steel needles still in her work-rough hands;
grey with dust, stiff with shock,
but breathing,
no blood or distorted limbs;
breathing, but stiff with shock,
knitting unravelling on her apron'd knee.

They have taken the stretchers off my car
and I am running
under the pattering flack
over a mangled garden;
treading on something soft
and fighting the rising nausea –
only a far-flung cushion, bleeding feathers.

They lift her gently
out of her great armchair,
tenderly,
under the open sky,
a shock-frozen woman trailing khaki wool.

Lois Clark

Ordinary people on both sides huddled in shelters to escape the bombing.

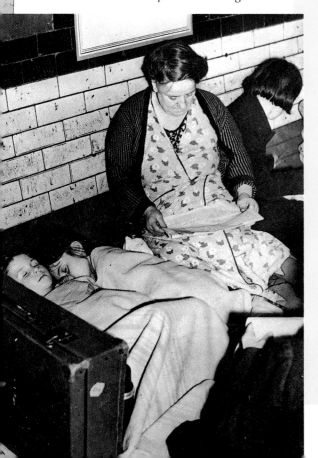

HANNA LAMBRECHT, of Langen, near Frankfurt-am-Main, spent her war years in the north of Germany. Her account is a concise and telling depiction of the brutal effect of war on one family:

'Words would not come, only tears'

At the outbreak of the war we were a complete family: father, mother, two brothers who were soldiers, and myself. We lived in Bremerhaven, which suffered throughout the war as it was on the direct flight-path of bombers approaching Germany. So it was sirens day and night for the whole of the war, and I spent most of my youth in cellars and bunkers.

In 1942, when I was just 19, I met my future husband, a chief petty officer in the German navy. Three days after we met he was off on a tour of duty again. After six weeks of intensive letter writing, we got engaged. Times were so uncertain, no one knew whether they were going to live or die. We married in March 1943. My husband got three weeks' marriage leave from the Norwegian front.

Dark clouds were gathering over us. My elder brother was badly wounded in the Crimea and lost both his legs. My first child was born in a hospital cellar in the middle of an air-raid. It was a boy, and for a while I was the happiest mother alive, cherishing and protecting him. But night after night I had to take him out of his warm bed and go with him to the ice-cold bunker. It was too much for his delicate health. When he was only 14 weeks old he went down with acute meningitis and died within three days, on 17 November 1943. On 16 November my husband had come home on leave. It was his first since we got married. He just had time to see his son alive and then we buried him together. I was inconsolable.

Not long after that, on 13 February 1944, whilst my husband was stationed in Wilhelmshaven and I was living with him a telegram came: 'House bombed. Mother injured. Come at once.' My husband got three days' compassionate leave and we left. That evening we reached the spot where our house had once stood. All we found was ashes and rubble, the smoke still rising from them. Sticking up in the middle was the charred frame of our little boy's pram. All around was darkness and the chill of the night. We held each other close and wept helplessly and uncontrollably. What should we do? Where were they all, Mum and Dad, Granny and Grandad? Were they alive or dead?

My brother – the one who had lost both legs – had a little flat nearby, so we went there and found them all. My mother had severe burns. Words would not come, only tears. We couldn't stay there, it was already full. Neighbours took us in and for three nights lent us their sofa. Then my husband had to go back to the war and I was alone again. My parents' suffering was so great that there was no sympathy left for me.

The day after the bombing I heard that an enemy aircraft had been shot down and that pieces of the aircraft were scattered all over the area where our house had been. I saw the wreckage and in it a human torso, probably the pilot, burnt beyond recognition. They said it was a British plane. I felt nothing. My own tragedy had numbed all my feelings. Later, when working in the garden, I found a human arm lying there between the dungheap and the cabbages. It was a man's arm, quite hairy, with the hand still attached. Probably what was left of one of the crew. That shocked me deeply. I reported the find to the authorities.

On 18 September came the massive raid that just about destroyed Wesermünde. As the bombs rained down I was in the bunker. It was two days before the ruined town emerged from the fire and smoke. Thousands of human beings and animals suffered a terrible death. The clearing-up operations were hindered for days by the stench of rotting and burnt flesh. Emergency kitchens were set up for the bomb-victims. I felt somehow predestined for this work and reported to the emergency services. Together with other women I peeled mountains of potatoes, boiled soup in huge washtubs and looked after women and babies. That was the hardest thing for me. I couldn't get my own dead baby out of my mind.

3 In a small group, identify from these extracts some of the ways in which the lives of women were changed by the Second World War. Think about:

— the additional responsibilities and pressures which the War placed on women in their traditional roles as wives, home-makers and mothers
— the new, and different, roles which women were expected to adopt and play as part of the war effort
— the personal tragedies women suffered or witnessed.

4 Use one or more of the pictures or extracts as the starting point for improvisations of your own. For example, you could work on a situation where:

— a group of friends meet together in the street after a severe night of bombing
— two people are talking about the stresses and strains involved in their new work
— a number of newspaper or radio interviews take place after a bombing raid
— after the War, a small group of people look back on their lives then.

Link your group's improvisations together and show them to the class.

5 In your group, talk about how you might have reacted to the pressures of wartime on the homefront. How do you think they compare to those faced by soldiers? You might consider:

— the comparative danger of battle and air-raids
— the balance between responsibility for one's own survival and responsibility for others
— the levels of work and hardship involved
— the balance between having to leave home to fight and having to stay at home to cope.

A family welcome for Private Bill Martin as he returns home from action in 1945

Families at war

In the first section of this unit you read about men at war fighting in a different country. In the second section you read about how women worked on the homefront to achieve victory in the 1939–45 war which engulfed much of the world. But future wars are unlikely to be waged by men or women as separate groups fighting in different places. Because of the power and range of modern weapons, it is impossible to safeguard any group of people from the consequences of war. Children of all ages, mothers, pensioners and the sick are all potential targets in the wars of the future.

The pity of war

Early in the morning of 6 August 1945, an American airplane dropped a single bomb over the thriving Japanese city of Hiroshima. The detonation of this atomic bomb signalled the end of the 1939–45 war and made sure that warfare between major powers would never be the same again.

Something like 70,000 people died instantly, another 70,000 within six months and by 1950 the death toll was 200,000. After 1950 many more people died as a result of the radiation.

The extracts below and on the next two pages give only the slightest idea of what that day was like. They show that there are limits on the power of words to convey such human tragedy and destruction. Read them through on your own.

Below is an account by Junko Morimoto of what happened to her on that day. She was a high school student and she wrote this many years later as a children's story so that young readers might know about the horror of the bombing.

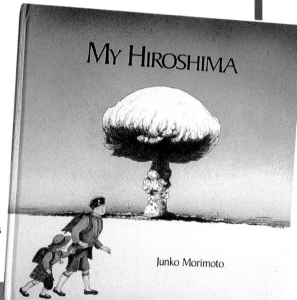

8.15AM 6 AUGUST 1945

The people of Hiroshima had just begun their day's work. Suddenly, the sirens sounded, warning that a plane was approaching, but the sirens soon stopped and everyone went about their work.

This day I had a pain in my stomach and was not going to school. My sister and I were in our room talking.

I thought I heard the sound of a plane, but it seemed a long way off and very high up.

I was hit by a thunderous flash and an explosion of sound.

My eyes burnt – everything went black. I held my sister.

Everything faded away – I thought I was dying.

I woke up. I was alive. But my home was completely destroyed.

When I crawled outside, I found that the whole of Hiroshima was destroyed. Everything was blown away, torn apart. Everything was burning.

This account of the Reverend Tanimoto's journey into Hiroshima immediately after the bombing is related by John Hersey, an American writer and war correspondent. In his short book, *Hiroshima*, the ordinariness of the account and the way it unfolds makes compelling reading. There is no attempt to dramatise what is seen and the most awful injuries are described in a matter-of-fact way.

Mr Tanimoto, fearful for his family and church, at first ran towards them by the shortest route, along Koi Highway. He was the only person making his way into the city; he met hundreds and hundreds who were fleeing, and every one of them seemed to be hurt in some way. The eyebrows of some were burned off and skin hung from their faces and hands. Others, because of pain, held their arms up as if carrying something in both hands. Some were vomiting as they walked. Many were naked or in shreds of clothing. On some undressed bodies, the burns had made patterns – of undershirt straps and suspenders and, on the skin of some women (since white repelled the heat from the bomb and dark clothes absorbed it and conducted it to the skin), the shapes of flowers they had had on their kimonos. Many, although injured themselves, supported relatives who were worse off. Almost all had their heads bowed, looked straight ahead, were silent, and showed no expression whatever.

After crossing Koi Bridge and Kannon Bridge, having run the whole way, Mr Tanimoto saw, as he approached the centre, that all the houses had been crushed and many were afire. Here the trees were bare and their trunks where charred. He tried at several points to penetrate the ruins, but the flames always stopped him. Under many houses, people screamed for help, but no one helped; in general, survivors that day assisted only their relatives or immediate neighbours, for they could not comprehend or tolerate a wider circle of misery. The wounded limped past the screams, and Mr Tanimoto ran past them. As a Christian he was filled with compassion for those who were trapped and as a Japanese he was overwhelmed by the shame of being unhurt, and he prayed as he ran, 'God help them and take them out of the fire.'

Long after 1945, James Kirkup visited the rebuilt Hiroshima. This is his view of the city and its people then.

No More Hiroshimas

At the station exit, my bundle in hand,
Early the winter afternoon's wet snow
Falls thinly round me, out of a crudded sun.
I had forgotten to remember where I was.
Looking about, I see it might be anywhere —
A station, a town like any other in Japan,
Ramshackle, muddy, noisy, drab; a cheerfully
Shallow permanence: peeling concrete, litter, 'Atomic
Lotion, for hair fall-out,' a flimsy department-store;
Racks and towers of neon, flashy over tiled and tilted waves
Of little roofs, shacks cascading lemons and persimmons,
Oranges and dark-red apples, shanties awash with rainbows
Of squid and octopus, shellfish, slabs of tuna, oysters, ice,
Ablaze with fans of soiled nude-picture books
Thumbed abstractedly by schoolboys, with second-hand looks.

The river remains unchanged, sad, refusing rehabilitation.
In this long, wide, empty official boulevard
The new trees are still small, the office blocks
Basely functional, the bridge a slick abstraction.
But the river remains unchanged, sad, refusing rehabilitation.

In the city centre, far from the station's lively squalor,
A kind of life goes on, in cinemas and hi-fi coffee bars,
In the shuffling racket of pin-table palaces and parlours,
The souvenir-shops piled with junk, kimonoed kewpie-dolls,
Models of the bombed Industry Promotion Hall, memorial ruin
Tricked out with glitter-frost and artificial pearls.

Set in an awful emptiness, the modern tourist hotel is trimmed
With jaded Christmas frippery, flatulent balloons; in the hall,
A giant dingy iced cake in the shape of a Cinderella coach.
The contemporary stairs are treacherous, the corridors
Deserted, my room an overheated morgue, the bar in darkness.
Punctually, the electric chimes ring out across the tidy waste
Their doleful public hymn — the tune unrecognisable, evangelist.

Here atomic peace is geared to meet the tourist trade.
Let it remain like this, for all the world to see,
Without nobility or loveliness, and dogged with shame
That is beyond all home of indignation. Anger, too, is dead.

And why should memorials of what was far
From pleasant have the grace that helps us to forget?

In the dying afternoon, I wander dying round the Park of Peace.
It is right, this squat, dead place, with its left-over air
Of an abandoned International Trade and Tourist Fair.
The stunted trees are wrapped in straw against the cold.
The gardeners are old, old women in blue bloomers, white
   aprons,
Survivors weeding the dead brown lawns around the Children's
Monument.

A hideous pile, the Atomic Bomb Explosion Centre, freezing
   cold,
'Includes the Peace Tower, a museum containing
Atomic-melted slates and bricks, photos showing
What the Atomic Desert looked like, and other
Relics of the catastrophe.'

The other relics:
The ones that made me weep;
The bits of burnt clothing,
The stopped watches, the torn shirts,
The twisted buttons,
The stained and tattered vests and drawers,
The ripped kimonos and charred boots,
The white blouse polka-dotted with atomic rain, indelible,
The cotton summer pants the blasted boys crawled home in,
   to bleed
And slowly die.

Remember only these.
They are the memorials we need.

---

6 As a group, end this unit by talking about all you have read and
your own views of war. You might consider these questions:

___ Is war inevitable because of the way people and nations are certain
to compete and argue among themselves?

___ What are the circumstances which justify war between nations?

___ If war is justified, what principles would you be prepared to fight
for?

___ In what ways do the nations of the world seem to encourage the
likelihood of war? How do they discourage it?

Tips for Success

◆ Whenever you read, think about bias. Ask yourself, what does this writing or picture want me to think?

◆ Do not be afraid to let bias show in your own writing. Often, it is the way a writer's opinion shows through which makes their work interesting.

◆ As you discuss the extracts, imagine what their writers might be like. In talking about the idea of war, do not forget their real stories.

HOLD THE FRONT PAGE

In this unit you will be investigating and comparing the front pages of different newspapers and the way they tell you about the stories which are in the day's news.

What's in the news?

Newspapers, television and radio are continually giving us the kind of information called **news**. But what exactly is news?

1 In groups, discuss these questions:

■ Where do people get news from? Who in the group watches television news regularly; reads newspapers; listens to radio? Who gets their news through hearing friends or family discussing it?

■ Look at this list of possible news items. Which of them do you agree *are* news?

- USA and Libya negotiate hostages deal
- ferry sinks off Finland — all survive
- 95 per cent of Intercity trains arrive on time
- Revolution in Chile
- Number One pop star to marry
- Liverpool win
- man shot dead in Northern Ireland
- flared trousers make a comeback
- Birmingham teenager killed by hit-and-run driver
- Prince and Princess of Wales open computer factory in Coventry
- Miss World resigns to marry schoolteacher
- Government to issue identity cards to under 18s
- Second World War general spied for Russia
- Stoke City beat Manchester United at Old Trafford
- Duchess of York spotted at nightclub with friends
- baby panda born at London Zoo
- Britain's oil reserves will be exhausted by 2050

■ Ask yourselves:

— Is something only news the first time it happens?
— Does something have to have actually happened to be news?
— Which countries, people, animals and football clubs are most *newsworthy*? Is everything they do news?
— Does news have to be serious to be important?

The people who produce 'news' have to make decisions all the time about which stories are news. Stories in every news programme or newspaper have been selected, and are presented, in order to interest and appeal to a particular audience.

you will be . . . .

Relating personal experience

Reporting on group discussion

Commenting on language use

Recognising and presenting non-literary material

Busy editorial office at The Times

2 Look back at the list of potential news items. Which of them do you think you would be most likely to find in the following places? Say why you think as you do.

— on the front page of *The Sun*
— on the back page of *Today*
— on the front page of *The Times*
— on 'News at Ten' as the last item
— on a local radio news round-up.

When you have agreed in your group, choose one person to report back to the rest of the class. Then, talk about any differences in ideas between the groups and where there was clear agreement.

Making the news

The **newsdesk** is the place where newspapers and broadcasters gather their news. In fact, it is more like a large office which gathers and sorts information about what is taking place all over the world. Stories come to the newsdesk from all kinds of people and organisations. A national newspaper, for example, would receive 'news' from all these *sources*:

Its own team of reporters sent out to cover particular stories, to find out details and to interview any people involved.

Its specialist reporters who cover particular areas like sport, politics, foreign affairs and business.

National and international *news agencies* which give out information on events around the world.

Freelance reporters who do not work for a particular paper but 'sell' the stories they cover to any newspaper which is interested.

Local newspaper reporters who are known as *strin-gers* and who report to the national paper when something happens which might be newsworthy in their area.

Press conferences and *press releases* where governments companies an pressure group invite reporters come and find about somethi which they wa to be include in the news.

The **news editor** who is in charge of the newsdesk makes decisions about which stories are worth investigating and what information should be printed or broadcast as news. Newsdesks also watch, or monitor, rival news organisations to see what other newspapers and news programmes are saying is news. Occasionally, a reporter uncovers an original story and then they can print it as a **scoop**.

The decisions that news editors take about what stories to follow up may help to make some of those stories into news. In this way, what we read in newspapers or watch on television news is never an exact record of what happened on any one day. Instead, it is a selection from those events and a description of them in a particular way. What you read as a newspaper front-page story is the result of a whole range of decisions taken as to what is newsworthy or important.

3 Take a large piece of paper. Write THIS WEEK'S NEWS in the centre of it. Then give yourselves three minutes to jot down as many news stories as you can remember from the past two or three days. Do not think about what is important but jot down your ideas as fast as you can.

After three minutes, stop writing. Read what each of you has noted about the news. Talk about what you have written and find out about any stories which you do not know about. As you talk, ask yourselves these questions:

- Which stories did you all note? Have they been major front-page stories and reported on all the news programmes?

- Which stories are only familiar to some of you? Is this because they have only appeared in some newspapers or on one news programme? Or, are they stories you would not have been interested in and so might have missed?

Front-page story

Although many people now rely on television for their news, more newspapers are sold in Britain per head of population than anywhere else in the world. Nevertheless, newspapers still have to compete for readers. The more readers a newspaper has, the more advertising it can attract and advertising earns the newspaper money.

Newspapers usually try to create a group of regular readers – and, indeed, people are often very loyal to one newspaper. They know what to expect from it in terms of the way it looks, the sort of stories it covers and its writing style. For any newspaper, an important factor both in keeping the interest of its regular readers and in attracting new ones, is the impact of the front page.

You are going to look closely at how three different newspapers presented their front page on the same day. But first you will need to know some of the terms used to describe a newspaper's layout.

Tabloid newspapers are those which have a relatively small page size, like *The Sun, Daily Mirror* and *Daily Star*. On a tabloid front page there are only two or three stories. In contrast, **broadsheet** newspapers, which have a larger page size, always carry several front-page reports as well as their major story. *The Times, The Guardian* and *The Independent* are broadsheet papers. On this page is a typical broadsheet newspaper, with some of its layout features named.

Labels around the image: masthead, ears, date, line, copy, cartoon, masters, contents, picture, caption, byline, jumpline

THE INDEPENDENT

No 1,026 — FRIDAY 26 JANUARY 1990 — Published in London 35p

SUMMARY

MacGregor redraws the curriculum

The Government has been forced to redraw the national curriculum, the central plank of its education changes, creating a two-tier system for pupils in examination classes. John MacGregor, Secretary of State for Education, admitted that schools would not be able to fit GCSE courses in the 10 compulsory subjects into the general timetable..........Page 3

Stalker papers

John Stalker handed in to the Home Office the document that he says shows senior civil servants were involved in his sacking from the Ulster shoot-to-kill inquiry..........Page 4

Romanian demo

Hundreds of protesters gathered in central Bucharest, despite the National Salvation Front's restrictions on street demonstrations..........Page 8

Walesa boycott

Lech Walesa boycotted a speech to the Polish parliament by President Vaclav Havel of Czechoslovakia..........Page 8

Soviet jobless

Soviet statisticians have admitted 13 million people, out of a total workforce of 164 million, are unemployed..........Page 8

Shias 'massacred'

Iraqi exiles accused President Saddam Hussein's government of killing or wounding up to 10,000 people in a two-week military campaign against Shia Muslim villages in southern Iraq..........Page 10

China protests

China condemned strongly the House of Representatives vote to allow Chinese students to stay in the US..........Page 10

INSIDE

FILM

THE ELECTRIC CINEMA
OPEN THURSDAY 25
CALL 792 2020

Reopening the Electric.....25

ARTS
Oblomov updated..........12

CANNES MUSIC
Publishers 'do lunch'..........13

THE PEACE DIVIDEND
Spending expected defence savings 19

COMMONWEALTH GAMES.....30,32

Toll likely to rise after hurricane-force winds leave trail of damage and transport chaos

32 killed in storm devastation

By Phil Reeves and James Cusick

AT LEAST 32 people died as hurricane force winds swept across southern Britain yesterday, leaving a trail of disruption and damage estimated at many hundreds of millions of pounds.

Buildings were blown down, trees ripped off their roots, and roofs torn off as the second severe storm to affect Britain in three years crossed the country from west to east.

Large areas were without electricity, telephone services were disrupted and London ground to a virtual standstill as all public transport was thrown into chaos.

An emergency meeting of senior ministers, chaired by David Waddington, the Home Secretary, was held last night to review the effects of the storm. The Government announced emergency funds would be given to local authorities in the worst-affected areas, although the amount was not specified.

Road, rail, sea and air travel was severely disrupted for much of the day, by winds gusting at more than 100 mph. Dozens of vehicles were blown over – one policeman said they were "thrown about like toys".

The actor, Gorden Kaye, star of BBC television's 'Allo 'Allo series, was among the dozens who were seriously injured. A plank of wood from an advertising hoarding crashed through the windscreen of his car as he was driving through London.

Mr Kaye was taken to Charing Cross Hospital, West London, where an emergency brain operation was carried out. Last night he was in intensive care and doctors described his condition as critical.

Britain's weathermen were quick to deny any suggestions that they failed to give adequate warning – one of the criticisms levelled after the 1987 storm. The Met Office said the severe conditions had been widely forecast since Sunday, and warnings had been broadcast on the media.

The South-east, West Country, Wales and the Midlands were the worst affected areas, although there were heavy snow and blizzards in Scotland and northern England. Thousands of homes suffered power cuts.

Last night the death toll was set at 32, although it was expected to rise as the extent of the destruction became clearer. Among the victims were two young school girls. One, aged 11, was killed when the roof blew off Grange Junior School in Swindon, Wiltshire. Another was killed when a conservatory collapsed at St Brandon's School, Clevedon, near Bristol.

In Hampshire, a policeman, Chief Insp John Smith, 51, who had five children, died when a tree fell on his car as he was travelling to work.

Others were killed in similar incidents in Hertfordshire, south Devon, Cornwall and Kent. Falling masonry claimed victims in Southampton and south-east London. Uprooted trees crashing down on vehicles were responsible for most of the casualties. But fallen chimneys, collapsing scaffolding and walls, and falling roots increased the death toll.

The Thames from Lambeth Bridge yesterday, lashed by hurricane-force winds of up to 100mph as the centre of London

'Awesome' wind ripped off school roof

By Phil Reeves

AN OFF-DUTY policeman described how he saw the entire roof of a school being blown off by a hurricane-force blast of wind which killed one child and seriously injured another.

PC Adrian Wys was walking past the Grange Junior School in Swindon, Wiltshire, at 1.36pm yesterday when he heard a "terrific noise". The felt and wooden roof was ripped off and hurled 50 yards by an "awesome" wind.

An 11-year-old girl was killed and five other pupils — three boys and two girls — were hurt by falling masonry after a wall on the building's first floor collapsed. One boy, aged 11, was last night in intensive care at Princess Margaret's Hospital, Swindon.

PC Wys, 23, said: "I heard a ripping noise, and I saw the roof of the school seemed to be moving." When he reached

the 240-pupil school the children were already being escorted out to a nearby community centre.

"We went to one of the worst-affected areas on the first floor and found there were four large classrooms where the roof had been totally removed. It was just open air. In the first room we saw the worst of the casualties. We found the dead girl. There was no pulse. There was nothing we could do for her.

"We searched through the classrooms for other kiddies but there weren't any. Luckily the roof was removed. If it had collapsed, the casualties could have been higher."

Police were last night withholding the names of the dead girl and severely injured boy until identification procedures were completed.

Four of the children received minor injuries, police said. PC Wys added that other pupils, sheltering from the storm, were in "one hell a state — every time the wind gusted they screamed".

Two buildings workers watched as a large tree crashed on to a van near Hemel Hempstead, Hertfordshire, killing both people inside.

One of the workers, Chris Brooks, 36, said there was "a mighty crack . . . there were two men driving past in their pick-up truck. They never had an earthly chance. The tree just smashed down on them. It was awful.

"We rushed over to see what we could do. The engine was still running but they had no chance. The truck was flattened...

Mandela stands by ANC line on nationalisation

From John Carlin in Johannesburg

NELSON MANDELA, in a surprisingly provocative political move, has issued a statement describing as "inconceivable" any notion of dropping the African National Congress's nationalisation policy, which extends to key sectors of the South African economy now in private hands.

A senior spokesman for the United Democratic Front, which is allied to the ANC, released the statement yesterday "on the request of Comrade Nelson Mandela himself". The single-paragraph statement read:

"The nationalisation of the mines, banks and monopoly industries is the policy of the ANC and a change or modification of our views in this regard is inconceivable. Black economic empowerment is a goal we fully support and encourage, but in our situation state control of certain sectors of the economy is unavoidable."

The timing of the statement,

Writing at its best in new Sunday paper

SOME OF Britain's best writers make their appearance this Sunday in The Independent's new sister paper, The Independent on Sunday. The first issue has pieces by Alan Bennett, Martin Amis and Germaine Greer, as well as André Brink writing from South Africa and Yevgeny Yevtushenko from the Soviet Union. There are weekly columns from Neal Ascherson and Alexander Chancellor, and a distinguished list of critics includes Irving Wardle, Mark Lawson and Anita Brookner.

---

4 This newspaper is from a day in January 1990 when a major story drove all the other news from the front pages. Opposite, are the front pages of two tabloid newspapers from the same day. Working with a partner, check that you can identify all the elements which make up the front pages before you go on to look at them in detail overleaf.

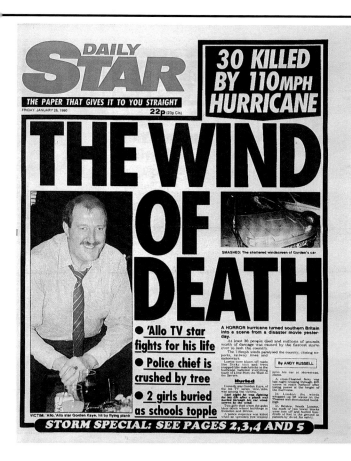

DAILY **STAR**

THE PAPER THAT GIVES IT TO YOU STRAIGHT

FRIDAY, JANUARY 26, 1990   22p (23p Cls.)

30 KILLED BY 110MPH HURRICANE

THE WIND OF DEATH

SMASHED: The shattered windscreen of Gorden's car

- 'Allo TV star fights for his life
- Police chief is crushed by tree
- 2 girls buried as schools topple

VICTIM: 'Allo 'Allo star Gorden Kaye, hit by flying plank

STORM SPECIAL: SEE PAGES 2,3,4 AND 5

By ANDY RUSSELL

A HORROR hurricane turned southern Britain into a scene from a disaster movie yesterday.

At least 30 people died and millions of pounds worth of damage was caused by the fiercest storm ever to lash the country.

The 110mph winds paralysed the country, closing airports, railway lines and motorways.

Lorries were blown off roads like Dinky toys and trees snapped like matchsticks as the hurricane battered everything south of a line from the Wash to the Severn.

Hurled

Comedy star Gorden Kaye, of the hit TV series 'Allo 'Allo, was among the victims.

Last night he was fighting for his life after a plank was hurled through his car windscreen by the wind.

Two girls died when the gales blew down school buildings in Swindon and Bristol.

A police inspector was killed when an uprooted tree toppled onto his car at Morestead, Hants.

A cross-Channel ferry was last night limping through 40ft waves to reach harbour after losing power at the height of the hurricane.

In London the winds whipped up 5ft waves on the Thames and demolished buildings. In Brixton, South London, the roofs of two tower blocks were torn off and hurled hundreds of feet to the ground as passers-by dived for safety.

TV TRAGEDY: PAGE 13   FRIDAY, JANUARY 26 1990 ★★★★   DAILY SALE 596,651   (Week Ending Jan 13)   22p (Republic of Ireland 35p)

'ALLO STAR FIGHTS FOR HIS LIFE

Today
FOR A BRIGHTER TOMORROW

SPECIAL STORM ISSUE
DRAMATIC STORY AND PICTURES
PAGES 2, 3, 4, 5, 13 and CENTRE PAGES

DAY OF DEVASTATION: A red Ford, one of hundreds of vehicles wrecked by the hurricane, lies crushed beneath a fallen tree off Redcliffe Gardens, London

Hurricane kills 35 after warning no-one heard

DEADLY SILENCE

GORDEN: Critical

Turn to Page 3

---

by JAMES MURRAY and TONY GALLAGHER

THEY left their homes armed with umbrellas, expecting nothing more than the breezy, showery British weather of a winter's day.

But they found themselves exposed to killer 120 mph winds from which there was no protection – and at least 35 lost their lives.

The weathermen claimed last night that they had warned of the storm – but it was a warning so bland that no one heard it.

The forecasters' deadly silence left millions of workers trapped in their factories and offices.

Even indoors there was no hiding place. Two schoolchildren were crushed in their classrooms by falling masonry.

Actor Gorden Kaye, star of TV's 'Allo 'Allo, was fighting for his life last night after a plank smashed through his car windscreen.

The news in close-up

THE HEADLINES

Headlines are intended to grab the reader's attention at a distance. They have their own rules, they miss out unnecessary words, they use emotive language, they abbreviate words or use short informal alternatives. Tabloid newspapers with their large headline size and smaller pages are especially limited by space as to the number of words they can use.

Look at each headline on the previous two pages and agree on:

— What point in the story is highlighted?
— Which headline is the most sensational?
— How might any of the headlines be rewritten for use in one of the other newspapers?

THE LAYOUT

The way a page is set out is designed to catch a person's attention as he or she quickly passes a news-stand or glances at a newsagent's display. The arrangement of the story on the page, the amount and size of the copy and the way the story is broken by photographs has an important effect. Look at the layouts on pages 128–129 and agree on your answers to these questions:

— What differences in layout do you immediately notice?
— What is the overall effect of each of the pages?
— How successful do you think each of them is in attracting your attention?

THE COPY

Every newspaper story follows a similar pattern. It opens with a paragraph which contains the most interesting points in the story, and develops them in the rest of the report. Paragraphs are short – very often consisting of only one sentence – and carry one main idea only. All good news reports are supposed to contain answers to the five Ws – Who? What? When? Where? Why? – although not necessarily in that order.

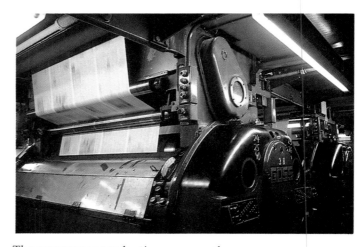

The newspaper production process: the reporter on the street; the sub-editor preparing the copy; the printing press.

5 Read through each report of the storm and note where the answers to these questions are given. Compare how each of these reports concentrates on different aspects of the storm by drawing a chart like the one here and noting the differences in the separate columns.

	Daily Star	Today	The Independent
WHAT: list the details which are given about the storm and its impact.			
WHEN: how much are you told about the time of day that it struck or the time when things happened?			
WHERE: name the places which are mentioned in the article.			
WHO: list the details given about how the storm affected people.			
WHY: what is said to explain the storm or the things which took place during it?			

In doing this, you will need to think about:

— the importance attached to the casualties of the storm
— the space allocated to Gorden Kaye's accident
— the viewpoint that the disaster might have been avoided
— the amount of detail given about what happened
— the language used to describe the storm
— the complexity of the writing.

THE PHOTOGRAPHS

These can 'say' as much as the headline and so add enormously to the impact of the front page. A good photograph tells a story and works with the headline and copy to build up an overall impression. Look at how photographs are used on these pages and decide:

— which photograph best sums up the story of the storm
— which is the most successful linking of photograph and text
— whether the photographs tell you anything about the readers of the newspapers.

News round-up

6 In your group, analyse a selection of newspaper front pages from this week's newspapers. Try to collect copies of *The Sun, Daily Mail* and *The Guardian* for the same day.

Study all the headlines and lead stories. Remember that, in one day, there are literally thousands of stories a newspaper could pursue and print. Only a tiny number of these find their way into the papers at all and even fewer end up on the front page.

As a group, talk about the pages you have in front of you and compare them. You will need to discuss:

— why you think these particular lead stories were chosen
— the language they are written in and the detail they provide
— their headlines
— the layout of each page as a whole. Look at the other stories on the front pages, as well as any headlines and captions which are used
— whether the same stories are covered in different newspapers. If so, how does the treatment of the story differ in each newspaper?

7 Now, individually, write a comparison of the front pages. Make sure that you back up your comments by referring to the pages you have looked at. You will need to say something about the points which have arisen in your group discussion and you could use the points above to help you organise your writing.

Students writing their own front page story

Your own front page

8 Now, choose one of the mastheads from the newspapers you have studied. Place it at the top of a large sheet of paper and then write and edit your own newspaper front page.

Listed on the right are the stories which you considered at the beginning of this unit. Decide which ones you will use on the front page of your newspaper.

When you have decided on the lead story, mock up the front page showing where you would put the headline or headlines, any photographs and the report or reports. Indicate where other elements such as tasters and jump lines should go as well.

Finally, write the main story as you think it would appear in that newspaper. Use a suitable headline and a sketch of any photographs you would include. If you can, use a word processor to print out the story as it should appear on the page.
Alternatively, draw up your layout, write out your main story and mount them together for a wall display or to keep in your file.

- USA and Libya negotiate hostages deal
- ferry sinks off Finland – all survive
- 95 per cent of Intercity trains arrive on time
- Revolution in Chile
- Number One pop star to marry
- Liverpool win
- man shot dead in Northern Ireland
- flared trousers make a comeback
- Birmingham teenager killed by hit-and-run driver
- Prince and Princess of Wales open computer factory in Coventry
- Miss World resigns to marry schoolteacher
- Government to issue identity cards to under 18s
- Second World War general spied for Russia
- Stoke City beat Manchester United at Old Trafford
- Duchess of York spotted at nightclub with friends
- baby panda born at London Zoo
- Britain's oil reserves will be exhausted by 2050

Tips for Success

◆ Keep looking out for the differences between newspapers as you read them.
◆ Get used to using the proper names and labels for the elements of a newspaper page.
◆ As you study them, always remember that a newspaper is a commercial business selling a product – itself – to its readers. Think about the readers as you write your own front pages.

ALL IN A DAY'S WORK

This unit is about oral communication at work. You will be asked to look at a day in the life of a small company and to use role-play, improvisation and discussion to explore some of the issues that arise.

Introducing Marathon Bikes

MARATHON BIKES
Annual Report

2

INTRODUCTION

Marathon Bikes is a relatively young company, situated on the outskirts of Manchester. The company assembles a small but sophisticated range of all-terrain bikes for a variety of clients. These range from large chainstores to small retail outlets and even individual clients requiring customised cycles. There is also a developing export market.

STAFF

The company now employs 19 people in total in the following capacities:

- Managing Director
- Company Secretary
- Production Manager
- Sales Manager
- Designer
- 2 Production supervisors
- Administration supervisor
- 4 Sales representatives
- 6 Workshop fitters
- Clerical worker
- Switchboard operator/receptionist

3

NEW PREMISES

The company has recently purchased and relocated to converted warehouse premises in a mixed area of residential housing and commercial properties. The move has increased the company's overheads but the extended workshop facilities were much needed and, as the area is rapidly improving, the company's assets are likely to improve also. The new accommodation is organised as shown:

Workshop store	Production office	General office
Workshop		Reception
		Company Secretary
Cloak rooms	Sales Manager	Managing Director

POLICY STATEMENT

Marathon Bikes aims to stay ahead of its competitors by offering reasonably priced quality products, meeting deadlines and providing a friendly, helpful service. Marathon Bikes intends to build on its existing network of clients and to continue to take advantage of its skilled workforce.

CURRENT POSITION

After a boom period when all-terrain bikes were very popular, it has become more difficult to sell the company's products. There are now similar bikes available from other companies. There is a growing need for Marathon Bikes to begin to open up new markets and develop new products.

The staff

TOBIAS MORRIS: Managing Director and company founder. Thirty-five years old and very fit. Has always been a cycling fanatic and worked with a major cycling manufacturer after leaving polytechnic. Ten years later moved to Manchester and, with the help of a new business grant, set up Marathon Bikes.

JING YEE CHEUNG: Company Secretary and accountant, she is responsible for the company's finances and legal affairs. Recently, the company has been spending more than it earns, but Christmas and summer are both good times for sales so future is hopeful.

MIKE FIELDING: Sales Manager. Manages team of sales representatives, visits buyers from the big stores and organises yearly sales campaign for Marathon Bikes, including special promotions.

Four members of the sales team, based in different parts of the country, work from home. They visit a number of shops every day, introducing Marathon Bikes.

LAURENCE DOE: Production Manager. Handles workshop and store. Responsibility to make sure that work is scheduled effectively and that materials are available to assemble the cycles. Worked with Tobias before and was recruited by him. Moved to Manchester to join the company eight years ago.

SARAH KNELL: Designer. Appointed three months ago. Has excellent qualifications in design. Worked for a large design consultancy before joining Marathon Bikes. Young and forward-looking, she was recruited by Tobias after Bill Wheatley retired.

JONATHON SPEDDING: Production Supervisor. Has been with the company for five years, during which time has completed his engineering apprenticeship.

JULIET BRAY: Production Supervisor. Has been with the company 18 months. Crossed China on her bicycle and is a keen supporter of cycling events. She and Jonathon work alongside fitters in the workshop, taking particular responsibility for training and quality control.

Six workshop fitters – three men and three women – assemble the different models of cycle produced by Marathon Bikes. They have varying degrees of expertise on joining the company but receive training. They are paid a basic wage and a bonus based on productivity.

ESTHER RIDGE: Office supervisor. Office deals with all clerical work – issuing invoices, arranging deliveries, doing company correspondence, keeping track of orders and operating switchboard and reception. Office is responsible to finance, sales and production, as well as to Tobias Morris. Two young women office workers assist with office work.

The gossip

[1] Any group of people who work together have to relate to one another if the company is to succeed. This is not necessarily the same as liking one another and tensions between individuals in the workplace are very common. With a partner, look at these snippets of conversation overheard during one day at Marathon Bikes. Decide who you think is speaking, who they could be talking to and who they might be talking about.

'He doesn't seem to understand that if all his orders come in at the end of the month, and the invoices have to be paid the next month, that's bound to upset the cash flow.'

'It makes life hard down here too – and he always wants them by yesterday.'

'My qualifications are just ignored. We simply bolt them together now. I don't use my training. I think he's got it in for me – that's why I've never been promoted.'

'It's hard physical work but I don't mind it. I get on all right with the rest of them except for him. He thinks he's above the rest of us.'

'Progress is vital. We can't stand still. We need this sort of person to keep us on our toes. Times might be hard just now but that mustn't stop product development.'

'I've been making bikes for years and I know them inside out. I don't need anyone coming up with some fancy ideas which have never been tried out before.'

'It's all very well on paper. She doesn't have to fit them together.'

'At least she's better than old Haystacks. He didn't do anything new if he could avoid it.'

A day in the life

Now you are going to work as a group to explore some of the situations that develop at Marathon Bikes in the course of the day. It is unlikely that these things would all happen on the same day, but they are the kinds of situations managers and workers have to face from time to time.

Before you begin each scene, think about it and talk it through. Decide what you think the different characters are thinking and feeling at the point where the role-play begins.

Imagine a typical Thursday at Marathon Bikes three weeks before the company closes for a fortnight's break. Work starts at 8.30am.

Managers and employees

9.00AM *The phone rings in the workshop. Laurence answers. It is Dave, one of the workshop fitters, ringing in to say he cannot come to work. Dave is a single parent and his little boy is ill. He feels bad about it but has no choice but to stay at home. Laurence is not a parent himself. He knows that an important order needs to go out today and that all hands are needed. Dave is the most experienced fitter they have.*

2. In pairs, role-play the phone conversation between the two men. First, discuss the position for each of them. What will they be thinking about and how will they be feeling? Remember, Laurence is Dave's boss.

9.30AM *After the phone call, Laurence realises that someone with enough experience is going to have to work late to get the order off. That means one of the two supervisors or himself. Jonathon Spedding has already asked for the afternoon off. Laurence suspects he is going for an interview. Juliet is keen to leave on time because she has a new date. Laurence himself is due to fly to Aberdeen to look at some new machinery.*

3. In groups of three, hold the conversation between Laurence and the two supervisors. Discuss first what you think Laurence is trying to achieve and how he might best do that. And what would be the best course of action for Jonathon or Juliet to take?

Office talk – dealing with colleagues, on or off the telephone, is an essential workplace skill.

136

Management meeting

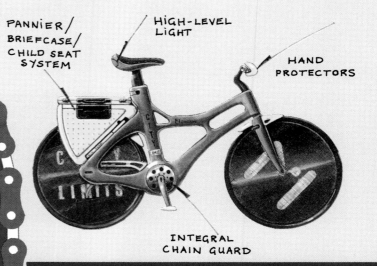

PANNIER/ BRIEFCASE/ CHILD SEAT SYSTEM

HIGH-LEVEL LIGHT

HAND PROTECTORS

INTEGRAL CHAIN GUARD

10.00 AM *Tobias, Jing, Mike, Laurence, Sarah, Jonathon, Juliet and Esther meet together for a special management meeting in Tobias's office. The main item on the agenda is 'future developments'. Tobias and Sarah have been keeping under wraps a new prototype design which is about to be unveiled.*

The design which Sarah has come up with is for a bike called Citycycle. *It is chunky like an all-terrain bike, but it is designed for town use. It has large panniers on the back for shopping or work, and can be modified to fit a seat for a child. The frame is made of a new carbon fibre material which should make the bike very light and strong. It is intended to appeal to both women and men.*

The alternative to developing this product is to relaunch the old model with a new European-style saddle, and to put extra money and effort into marketing it overseas. However, the successful launch of an entirely new product might be the best way to ensure the long-term future of Marathon Bikes.

Management talk – members of the board present their points of view.

4 Improvise the discussion at the meeting and try to reach a decision about whether, or when, to begin work on the new project. Before you begin, spend a few moments jotting down the views of your character taking into account the factors on the right. Think about who you will need to persuade to your way of thinking and how you might best go about achieving this.

TOBIAS – keen to go for a new part of the home market, and has supported Sarah in early stages of the design. Knows that if the *Citycycle* is to happen, it will need support and expertise of everyone in the company, particularly senior sales and production staff.

JING – concerned about cost of new investment at the moment. Would probably mean no salary rises, and raising loans against high-risk project.

MIKE was not consulted about new design early enough to have a say in what it should be like and who it should be for. For him, prospect of opening up the overseas market with the 'European' is not without certain appeal.

LAURENCE has not worked with carbon fibre for years and remembers it was always difficult to fit carbon fibre components to other parts of the cycle. If the idea is developed, it will mean total reorganisation of workshop procedures.

SARAH sees enormous potential for introducing her new concept at a time when traffic congestion in towns and increasing environmental awareness are causing more people to take up cycling. Besides, this is simply the best thing she has ever done.

For JONATHON, the new project could mean an exciting new area of work and increased promotion prospects. He has some criticisms of the design and so far, surprisingly, his views have not been invited.

JULIET – keen to move into a less specialised market that specifically includes women. Welcomes prospect of more responsibility, and obviously, more pay.

ESTHER's main concern is for continued stability of the company and a cheerful sociable atmosphere.

Shop floor

1.15PM *The shop steward, one of the fitters, has called an emergency meeting for all those on the shopfloor, including the clerical staff. It has come to light through an advert in the local paper that, after the holiday, the company is planning to bring in temporary workers to help prepare the Christmas orders. Their pay is to be almost twice the rate of the permanent workshop staff.*

You are going to role-play the shopfloor meeting. It is a fairly formal meeting, at the end of which a decision must be made about the next step to take and a statement prepared for the management.

5 But first, you have a few minutes before the meeting begins to talk with one of the other production fitters about this situation:

▪ Bringing in new people could disrupt your own rate of work and hence your bonus. How serious is this for you?

▪ You have worked in the company long enough to know you do not get what you do not ask for. What *do* you want to ask for?

▪ What about the principles involved? Bringing in other workers is bad enough without the way it is being done. What changes would you want to see?

▪ If management refuses to do anything, what action could you or would you take to get them to change their mind, without putting your own future at risk?

6 Begin the meeting by agreeing who should be the chairperson. You have been given a strict time limit before you have to return to work, so concentrate on covering all the business in hand.

Points to cover in a formal meeting

- The situation should be described for the benefit of everyone present by the chair or someone appointed by the chair.
- The chair should invite as many views as possible and allow a brief discussion of them.
- The chair should invite two or three of those present to each put forward a motion, i.e. to propose a particular view and course of action.
- Each motion should be discussed briefly and then voted on by a show of hands.
- After the vote, a written statement should be prepared which sums up the majority view for the management. Note, this is not a once-and-for-all statement. You may plan to change your stance at a later time.

Union talk – members of the union NUPE discuss their official position.

An angry customer

7 Work in a group of five or six, and pick up the phone without any prior discussion. Esther can deal with the caller herself, or can transfer the caller to any of the staff who make up the group. Each have had a part to play in producing the cycles. Jonathon Spedding, the production supervisor responsible for checking that batch, has left for the afternoon, and Tobias is still at lunch. Each staff member can also choose how to deal with the caller:

JANICE McFEE, the production fitter who assembled that batch
LAURENCE DOE, the production manager responsible for the general running of the workshop
MIKE FIELDING, the sales and publicity manager who has put a lot of effort into persuading local shops to take the cycles
JING YEE CHEUNG, who would handle any financial or legal claims on the company
ESTHER herself arranged the delivery at Jonathon's request.

Informal talks – shop stewards swap news and views.

8 The situation clearly needs sensitive handling. After the phone call, Tobias returns and calls for Jing, Laurence, Mike, Juliet (in Jonathon's absence) and Janice to talk over what has happened. In your group, review the situation and agree what action should be taken and by whom.

Some points to consider:

– **Safety** Are any other bikes affected?

– **Customer satisfaction** The firm's reputation is at stake. How was the phone call handled?

– **Publicity** The news could find its way into the press. How could this be dealt with?

– **Production procedures** What can prevent it happening again?

Health and safety

3.15PM *During the afternoon tea break, Tobias chats to a group of his senior staff and lets it be known that he is set on making the firm a non-smoking workplace. It would be good for the company's 'health and fitness' image. Tobias himself is a fervent anti-smoker.*

9 In a group of three or four, hold this conversation. It is an informal chat, but Tobias is still the boss. Laurence Doe is a smoker and so are several of the non-managerial staff. A total ban would be popular with some people, but extremely unpopular with the smokers. There is no space for a smoker's room and most of the premises are open plan. Tobias seems to be indicating that if people cannot stop smoking they will just have to leave.

At the end of the discussion, Tobias asks this group to tell the rest of the workforce about the new rule and to let him know by the end of the day how quickly it can be put into action.

10 Individuals should talk to small groups of workers, which include both smokers and non-smokers. Their task now is to try to introduce this new measure in a way that is least likely to cause division and ill-feeling, and to persuade everyone to accept the new rule. The workers will need to decide where they stand on this and try to influence their manager to take account of their views.

Telephone talk – presenting a positive image to the customer is always important.

5.15PM *The managers get ready to report back to Tobias. The issue has sparked a good deal of discussion and most of the others gather round to listen in.*

In the meantime, however, Tobias has been talking to Jing and for whatever reason appears to have changed his mind, although he is not saying so directly. Far from insisting that people will have to stop smoking or leave, he now appears willing to be persuaded of any other measures that will improve the situation for everyone.

11 Hold this discussion. As a group of managers, try to find ways of feeding back to Tobias some of the views of the workforce. You will need to do this in a way that does not make Tobias lose face.

At the end of the day

12 As a group, discuss what the management or workers at Marathon Bikes might have done to avoid any of the situations which developed during the day. You might think about ways in which:

— communications within the company could be improved
— the workforce could be involved in company decision-making
— the structure of the company could be changed.

13 Now suppose that you work for a firm of management consultants which has been asked to look at the working practices at Marathon Bikes and to advise on how the company might become more efficient. On the basis of what you now know and the evidence of the day, write a report. Say what the company's good points appear to be as well as where the weaknesses lie.

◆ Good role-play depends on your willingness to be involved in a situation. Think about the interests of the characters you play and about what they would wish to see happen.

◆ As you improvise the scenes, try to stay in role. This means that you should try to think and react as a character even when you are not actually speaking.

◆ As you write your report, remember that it must be constructive and helpful to the company even though you may wish to make major criticisms of individuals or the way that things have been done.

Some options to consider:

● amending the personnel structure and identifying ways in which key people need to relate to each other
● setting out a promotion structure which gives employees a chance to progress and move into new work areas
● suggesting ways in which communications might be improved.

Include in the report your independent advice, and your reasons for supporting or rejecting the proposed development of the *Citycycle*. Now, write your report.

BURNING ISSUES

In this unit you will be thinking about, discussing and writing about a major issue in the world today.

This unit asks the questions, 'Where will we obtain new sources of energy as we use up those we have?' and 'How can our world continue to use energy at the rate it does?'

TAKE ISSUE:

RUNNING OUT OF POWER

The way people lead their lives in Britain, North America and the European Community depends on enormous supplies of power for heating, lighting and transport. Every year there are more cars and lorries on the road; more people own televisions, refrigerators and dishwashers; factories use more energy to produce more goods. Yet everyone knows that there are not endless sources of coal or oil in the ground and that our power supplies will neither last forever nor meet the increasing demands placed upon them.

Where to get power and energy from in the future is a real question and a real issue that will not go away. You need to think about it, discuss the alternatives and decide what you think should be done.

you will be . . . .

 Solving problems

 Relating personal experience

 Recognising non-literary material

 Locating and selecting information

 Commenting on language use

 Interviewing another person

Arguing a point of view

STAGE 1

THE PROBLEM

At the present time, we use vast quantities of oil for power. In fact, oil is the largest of all our energy sources. But present world oil supplies are rapidly running out. They are only likely to last about another 50 years.

There are problems relating to other sources of energy too:

 There is a lot of coal, but mining damages the environment. When it is burned for power, coal is the worst contributor to the acid rain which has destroyed vast areas of forest in northern Europe.

 Our present supplies of natural gas are also running out. There is plenty of natural gas in other parts of the world, but these may be difficult and expensive to obtain.

 Plans to build more nuclear power stations have been cut back mainly due to the costs involved in disposing of extremely dangerous nuclear waste. Opinion research data indicates a recent drop in public support for nuclear power.

 'Renewable' sources of energy like the sun, wind, waves and the movement of the tides are cheap to run and less polluting. They do, however, require expensive research and development, and need huge and elaborate pieces of equipment and installations to capture quite small amounts of energy.

There is clearly a crisis about the future of energy supplies. It is the focus of much debate and research by individuals and governments. You are now going to join in that debate. First, establish between you what you already know.

1. In a small group, jot down some of the main points you already know about energy sources. You should know something about energy use from your work in Science, Geography and Technology. One of you might have visited Sellafield, or you may remember something about places such as Sizewell or Chernobyl from watching, reading or listening to the news. You might have seen pictures of the fields of windmills in Denmark and California, or heard something about how it is possible to adapt coal-fired power stations so that they emit less sulphur. Make a note of the energy sources you know *least* about.

STAGE 2

CONFLICTING VIEWS

As you find out more about energy sources, you will come across many conflicting views and arguments. For instance, companies and organisations who are connected with the current power-producing industries are likely to support their development along broadly similar lines. **Pressure groups**, on the other hand, are often organisations which are pushing for changes. All of these groups produce information for politicians, journalists, the public and schools presenting their point of view. It is therefore important to study carefully the 'factual information' that is put forward and to think about whose argument it supports.

One of Britain's biggest tunnelling machines at work in a coalmine (top) and a machine cutting coal at the coalface. The water sprays suppress coaldust (bottom).

2 With a partner, read through the pieces of information below. They are about what are called fossil fuels; that is, fuels based on coal and oil. These were created over millions of years by layer after layer of tiny sea creatures being squeezed by the pressure from layers of rock above them into carbons and hydrocarbons which can be burnt to give energy.

First, read these statements about coal from some of the companies and campaign organisations which support the use of coal:

A There is enough coal available for two to three hundred years.
B Coal has wide uses as an energy fuel — from homes, to trains, to factories.
C Miners are highly paid professional workers from close-knit mining communities. These towns and villages depend on mining for their prosperity.
D Coal does not leave dangerous wastes when it is burnt.

However, some people argue against the use of coal. They point out that:

E Remaining reserves of coal are in the most inaccessible places or are difficult to mine for other reasons.
F Mining remains a very dangerous and unpleasant occupation.
G Coal mining scars the land.
H It has been discovered that the burning of coal in power stations causes acid rain and other pollutants, and contributes to global warming.

3 All eight points are worth considering in a discussion about energy use and the environment. In your group, look back at the two lists and decide:

— which arguments contradict one another
— which arguments interpret (make sense of) the same evidence in different ways.

Next, copy the eight statements on to slips of paper, marking A–D with one colour and E–H with another. Talk about how you would rank the eight statements on a ladder according to which you think are the most important. When you have decided, look at whether there are more of one colour than the other at the top of your ladder.

Most important

Least important

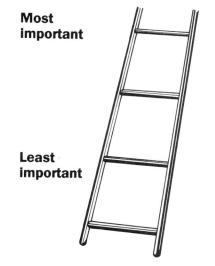

[4] Now study these arguments about the future use of oil and natural gas. Decide whether each argument is on the side of the companies and campaign organisations which support the use of oil and natural gas, or on the side of those organisations which oppose their use.

Make two lists headed FOR and AGAINST and summarise the arguments in your own words.

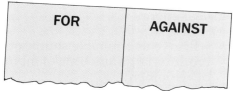

FOR	AGAINST

A   Transporting oil over vast distances by tanker has already caused damage to the environment when spillages have occurred.

B   The world has plenty of natural gas supplies. There are many more sources already available in the world and new sources are being discovered all the time.

C   Oil-producing countries are realising the real value of their oil reserves. Prices are bound to rise.

D   By the time Britain needs to import a lot more oil and natural gas, pipelines will have been built or cheap methods of transporting them found so that supplies can be continued.

E   A substitute for natural gas can be produced from coal.

F   Transporting gas and oil by pipeline or tanker can be very expensive.

G   Unlike other fossil fuels, natural gas contains almost no dangerous sulphur dioxide. Nor does it leave ash or dirt.

H   The transport system runs on oil – without it the economy of a country like Great Britain would collapse.

I   New supplies of natural gas may be in countries which do not have close links with Britain or which are very far away. If there are disputes between countries anywhere along the gas route, supplies could be threatened.

J   Many oil and gas products are hazardous because the products themselves and their vapours are extremely inflammable.

K   Substitute 'natural gas' is very expensive to manufacture.

L   Oil is getting more difficult and expensive to refine.

M   Oil can be used for many purposes beyond burning it for energy – for example, the plastics industry depends on oil.

N   Oil reserves are not generally located in Europe so there are no industrial eyesores to blight the landscape.

A gas-drilling platform off the Lancashire coast and (inset) a cormorant – victim of an oil spill

STAGE 3

THE NUCLEAR ENERGY DEBATE

5 In the longer extracts below and on the next few pages, some very different views about the value and safety of nuclear power are given. Read them with a partner. Then study the seven points below and match each of them with one of the extracts. Putting two copies of *New Dimensions* together (open at this double-page and the next) will allow you to see all the extracts at once.

Nuclear energy . . .

— will give us a reliable source of power well into the next century
— requires large amounts of money still to be spent on research and development
— is as safe, for those who produce it, as any other source of power
— can allow accidents to happen where dangerous radiation escapes into the surrounding areas
— does not damage the ozone layer, produce acid rain or contribute to the greenhouse effect
— is no more dangerous to people than the natural radiation in rocks and the atmosphere
— creates waste that is dangerously radioactive for thousands of years.

A
Safety and radiation

Government figures show that the nuclear industry is one of the safest industries to work in. It has always paid great attention to health and safety and operates under Acts, regulations, and codes of practice, based on internationally accepted safety standards. Independent safety inspections are made by the Health and Safety Executive and by Government Departments.

Nuclear reactors cannot blow up like atom bombs. This is physically impossible. To prevent lesser accidents elaborate safety systems are built into nuclear power plants. In particular, there are multiple barriers to the escape of radiation. For example, the fuel is inside cans which contain the fission products. The containment of the reactor also provides shielding from radiation.

Radiation is a natural phenomenon. People are constantly exposed to radiation from outer space and from materials in the earth's crust. All the activities of the British nuclear power industry account for less than one-fifth of one per cent of the average radiation received from all sources. This is less than the radiation from a single chest X-Ray and many times lower than the additional radiation resulting from moving house from chalk downs to granite hills.

All employees at nuclear power stations must monitor themselves after working in an active area.

B

Energy supplies from both **coal and nuclear power** could be increased considerably and both would be able to meet increased demand for centuries to come. With fast reactors nuclear power could last for thousands of years. Oil and natural gas will contribute significantly for well over 30 years at current rates of use but have no prospects for long-term expansion.

The price of all fossil fuels must increase as reserves are depleted and more difficult sources have to be brought into production. Nuclear electricity costs need not increase significantly above those now experienced because fuel costs are a smaller part of the total cost of its production, particularly in the fast reactor.

Nuclear power is available, proven and has the greatest potential in resource terms. It is also among the cheapest options. Its use will be environmentally and economically beneficial.

C

People worry about the safety of nuclear power and the effects on the environment of having to deal with nuclear wastes. The nuclear industry is confident that both safety and wastes can be managed so that the risks to the public and the workforce are kept at levels at least as low as those from other industries.

Pine trees in Czechoslovakia devastated by acid rain

E

Fossil-fuel power stations produce CO_2 which contributes to the Greenhouse Effect. **Fact**

Nuclear power stations do not. **Fact**

In France and Belgium, for example, they generate more than two-thirds of their electricity from nuclear power.

This has helped to reduce their output of carbon dioxide faster than the rest of Europe.

In Britain, we would also reduce our output of carbon dioxide by increasing our investment in nuclear power.

D

To put into perspective discharges from Sellafield into the Irish Sea, a person eating large quantities of Cumbrian seafood would only receive an additional one per cent of the radiation dose he would be exposed to if he lived in certain parts of Cornwall.

F

Nuclear power has been used to generate electricity in Britain for the last 30 years. It originally developed out of the military programme in the 1950s and is still closely linked with weapons manufacture. Nuclear power currently accounts for just over six per cent of the total energy used by consumers. In providing this energy, it poses a variety of risks to society, ranging from the problems of radioactive waste disposal to increasing nuclear weapons proliferation.

A nuclear reactor operates at extremely high temperatures and continues to generate heat long after power production has stopped. This means that it must be kept cool at all times. A loss of coolant accident could lead to the eventual melting of the uranium fuel and the release of large quantities of radiation into the atmosphere. This would contaminate large areas of land and many of the local population, resulting in high cancer and leukaemia death rates. A number of serious accidents have already occurred. In 1957, fuel in one of the Windscale nuclear reactors caught fire and radioactivity contaminated large areas of the surrounding farmland. Millions of gallons of milk were thrown away as a result. The accident may have caused up to 100 deaths, but according to official studies the most likely number will be lower and may be zero.

G

Nuclear reactors currently rely upon finite sources of uranium, a metal which is not found in economic quantities in Britain. In order to prolong the lifespan of nuclear power therefore, the Fast Breeder Reactor has been developed. This uses plutonium as a fuel. Plutonium produced by the Fast Breeder can also be used to make nuclear weapons, and is one of the most dangerous substances known to mankind.

There is a growing understanding that nuclear power cannot solve all of Britain's energy problems. Because it only produces electricity, it cannot easily substitute for other fuels used in the transport or chemical industries. The large amounts of research and development capital currently spent on nuclear power, could be used instead to reduce our energy consumption by increasing energy efficiency, and to develop renewable sources of energy such as solar and wind power.

Hinkley Point Nuclear Power Station

H

The actual volumes of radioactive waste produced by the nuclear industry are relatively small when compared to other industrial wastes. Their radioactive nature, however, means that they are dangerous for enormous periods of time. For example, high level wastes and intermediate level wastes will need to be isolated from the biosphere for hundreds of thousands of years. The bulk of the waste produced in this country comes from Sellafield, approximately 80% of the intermediate level waste and 70% of the low level waste. In addition the routine discharges from Sellafield are the main contributor to population exposure in the UK and Europe from civil nuclear installations. There is increasing concern that plutonium which has been discharged is coming back to contaminate the human environment with measurements of house dust in the Sellafield area showing up to 1000 times higher plutonium levels than elsewhere. Controversy over a childhood leukaemia cluster in the Seascale area next to Sellafield led to the publication of the Gardner Report in February 1990. The report indicated that there was a link between the work that men carried out at Sellafield and their children developing leukaemia.

6 Now, look at the extracts again. As you re-read each one think about these questions:

— What point of view does the argument want its readers to adopt?
— How much of the argument is factual information and how much is opinion?

As you compare them, think about:

— places where the same information is used to support two different arguments
— arguments which contradict one another
— which arguments you find most convincing.

Together, write a brief comment on each extract using the points listed above to help you. Say, whether you found the extract persuasive or not and what made you think as you do.

The Fuel Handling Plant at Sellafield where spent fuel is stored (left) and activists trying to prevent the dumping of nuclear waste in the sea.

THE ALTERNATIVES

Renewable energy

One form of energy which is receiving considerable interest now concerns what are called 'renewable' energy sources. There is nothing new about renewable energy. Windmills were in use in Europe in the twelfth century. Another example of a renewable resource which has been common for centuries is water power – once used for mills to produce bread and cotton – and now used to produce electricity called hydro-electric power or hydro-electricity.

Hydro-electricity is generated from flowing rivers, using dams and reservoirs. It currently generates 7 per cent of the world's electricity.

A great deal of research has been carried out in recent years into ways of harnessing renewable energy – by using the winds, waves and tides to generate electricity, or by using the sun's rays directly to provide heat or electricity, or through types of vegetation (biofuels) which could be grown to provide new fuels.

Read this extract from a book called *Energy without End*:

Old style windmill

THE UK is rich in *renewable* energy resources, and yet has hardly begun to tap them. The only resource that is currently used commercially on any significant scale is water power, an indirect form of solar energy. But the country's wind and wave resources are amongst the best in the world; and there are vast quantities of organic wastes which could be turned into useful fuel – these, too, are indirect forms of solar energy. There is also major potential for harnessing the tides and tapping heat from the ground.

Within 40 or 50 years the country could meet *one-fifth* or more of its energy needs from these indigenous resources – and perhaps half or three-quarters by AD2050.

Implementing such a programme will be a major challenge, but far less daunting than the consequences of continuing with the haphazard and reckless energy policies that are now being pursued by the Government.

Renewables are now on the political agenda in many industrial and developing countries – and for good reason.

They are *indigenous* and offer a secure source of energy supply.

They can eventually *supply a major part of the energy* used in most countries.

Their *diversity* and range of sizes offer great *flexibility* in planning and reduce dependence on coal and oil.

Their use can *reduce chemical, radioactive and thermal pollution.*

They offer the prospect of major new *export markets.*

They are *popular* – people like the idea of using the sun and the wind to provide their energy.

As with all sources of energy, there are problems in harnessing renewable energy. The resources:

are often *intermittent* and *variable* – storage or back-up is therefore necessary if firm supply is required;

involve *less concentrated forms of energy* – which makes it necessary to cover large areas and this can be expensive.

Some of the current generation of technologies involve *financial risks* because they are novel or immature, *high unit costs,* because of pilot scale production, and more *supervision,* because they are more temperamental than conventional energy sources – at least at this early stage.

There may also be *conflicts of interest* arising from environmental factors – for example, whether to put wind turbines along a beautiful stretch of coastline, or build a tidal barrage which might upset an established wildlife sanctuary.

Within 50 years, the UK could be using 30 per cent less energy than it does today, and providing 20 per cent or more of this from 'home grown' renewable sources of energy. It could phase out nuclear power altogether and cut its use of fossil fuels by 40 per cent – and it could achieve all this at a much lower cost to society and the environment.

Modern windmill on a farm in Holland

Others, however, disagree with such views about the use of renewable energy sources. Read these comments:

Renewable forms of energy have an important contribution to make. However, it is likely that they will only meet a small proportion of energy needs. Further research and development needs to be carried out to determine their reliability, economic and environmental suitability.

(British Nuclear Fuels)

A tidal barrage across the Severn . . . could generate as much power as two power stations, but it might kill as many as 200,000 birds and destroy forever the habitat of many more.

Wave-power would be no better. Using present technology, the output of two power stations could only be achieved by covering the sea with wave-generators from Edinburgh to the Wash.

(Evening Standard)

Energy efficiency

Another very important alternative concerns the issue of saving energy and so reducing the demand for more energy.

Did you know that at the present time only 40 per cent of the energy released from fossil fuels and uranium actually provides a useful service like keeping people warm or supplying light? One-third of what is known as primary energy is lost when it is made into electricity. More wastages happen through draughty buildings, petrol-hungry vehicles and inefficient appliances.

Everyone would agree that with many energy sources becoming scarcer, this situation has to change. Here are some ways of saving energy:

- Make buildings energy-efficient through wall, roof and floor insulation, double-glazing and draught-proofing.

- Use rail rather than road transport; a two-track railway can carry the same traffic as a six-lane motorway and so uses less fuel.

- Introduce 'combined heat and power' systems. In most present-day power stations over 60 per cent of the heat produced goes to waste. The 'combined heat and power' system puts this waste heat to work, using it to heat water which can be supplied to local homes, offices or factories. Such systems are expensive to build but they can lead to big savings.

- Introduce alternative, energy-saving fuels or power to run cars.

7. Talk about these arguments and ideas about energy sources with your group. Which do you agree with? Which do you disagree with? At the end of your discussion, choose one alternative energy source to research further.

Manufacturers testing solar panels (above) and a self-build house with wind generator and solar panels

STAGE
5

FINDING OUT MORE

Find out more about one energy resource – perhaps one of the resources which you know very little about when you started this unit. Use books in the library, newspapers and magazines, videos and television programmes. (In recent years, energy sources have often been the focus of newspaper and magazine articles and television programmes.)

Some useful organisations:

Friends of the Earth
Greenpeace
Centre for Alternative
** Technology**
Nuclear Electric
National Power
PowerGen
British Coal
British Nuclear Fuels
British Gas
Association for the Conservation
** of Energy**
Scottish Nuclear
World Information Service on
** Energy**

8 Pick one organisation and write to them asking for further details about energy resources or the answer to particular questions. Write a formal letter to the Customer Relations Department asking for more information. Remember that all of the campaign groups have limited funds and time to deal with enquiries. Try to organise things with others who are researching the same energy source, so that one letter is sent on behalf of all of you.

Here are some examples of material produced by various organisations.

STAGE 6

ENERGY FORUM

9 You are now going to put your views to the test in an 'energy forum' where your group and others can challenge your knowledge, your point of view and your ability to put it forward convincingly. For this, you are going to role-play a particular point of view and answer questions from an audience. (The point of view you are going to argue may be very different from your own!)

A **Government Minister** who supports a combination of options: keeping a nuclear power programme, developing more renewable energy sources and promoting energy efficiency.

The **managing director** of a proposed nuclear power station who believes in nuclear power and whose job depends on it.

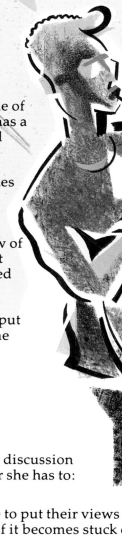

First, choose your viewpoint by adapting the role of one of the people described here. Each of them has a clear view about particular energy resources and policies.

Divide the class into four, so that each of you takes the point of view of *one* of the four people.

Now, write some notes on all the points you can think of to support the argument or point of view of the person you are role-playing. (Remember that you are acting the role of another person and need to see the issues as that person would see them.)

And, prepare some questions you would like to put to your opponents on the panel. Also, think of the questions they are likely to put to you.

Hold your 'energy forum' with another group or with the whole class. Each group can make up a panel and another group or groups provide the chairperson and audience.

The *chairperson* is responsible for organising the discussion and for making sure that it runs smoothly. He or she has to:

— introduce the speakers
— make sure that all the speakers have a chance to put their views
— move the discussion forward to a new issue if it becomes stuck on one point
— calm the discussion down if it is turning into a personal argument
— allow some time for the audience to give their views on what has been said
— conclude the discussion and thank the speakers for taking part.

The **Green Party political candidate** who is standing for election in the same area as the proposed nuclear power station. She, of course, is in favour of renewable sources of energy and energy saving.

A **trade union official** representing miners in a major mining area. He feels that coal should be mined to a greater extent, and that technologies should be introduced to make sure that it does no harm to the environment.

After the introductions by the chairperson, the forum can begin with each member of the panel making a short statement about their position and what they stand for.

The chairperson should ask the first round of questions – one to each speaker – but each member of the forum should be allowed to comment on it if they wish. Then, there can be questions from the audience – addressed to the whole panel or to individual speakers.

At the end of the session, find time to talk with your group about the success of your role-play. A session like this may reveal how some arguments are more convincing than others, how the way a speaker puts an argument forward can make it more or less convincing and how the same facts can be used to support different points of view.

STAGE 7

YOUR OWN ARGUMENT

So far, you have researched your information and talked about one aspect of energy in detail. But what is your own line of argument? This is your opportunity to argue in support of your own solutions and to set out in detail what you think is best for you and for the place where you live.

Writing an argument like this is not difficult so long as you remember to state your opinions clearly and to support them with information and evidence.

As you write, your ideas will develop. Some will become clearer, some may change altogether as you find out more and think more deeply about the issue.

10 To trace how your ideas are developing, and to give you space to redraft and revise what you want to say, start a fresh double-page, and write your own points on the left-hand side only. Use the right-hand page for thoughts, comments, revisions, further information, and so on.

■ First, write notes on the main points you want to make. This session is a good time to *brainstorm* the question and jot down anything that occurs to you. If you note down separate points leave plenty of space between each one.

■ At this point you may well need to collect further information or to reorganise the information you already have. Remember that other people in the group or class may be experts in some of the aspects you are interested in.

■ Write an outline, so that you are clear about the direction your argument is going in. Having a structure helps you write, but you are always free to change it if it does not work. This pattern may help:

— Give your piece a sub-title or headline. Think carefully about exactly what attitudes and opinions you are trying to convey.

— Write the opening paragraph or your opening sentences, which will say clearly what your viewpoint is.

— Check back, and add to, the various ideas you are going to put across and the information you will use to back them up. Decide how you will order your points.

— Summarise what you will say at the end of your piece. Write the final sentence.

Have you been *swimming* again, Baby?

VROOOM

VROOOM!

VROOM!

VROOM

CYCLISTS UNITE! – YOU HAVE NOTHING TO LOSE BUT YOUR CHAINS

VROOM

A.K

(clockwise from top) Used nuclear material in strong container survived 100 mph train crash; cartoon; geothermal hot dry rock programme – the water bubbles up from deep underground and energy is tapped from it; postcard; tidal power station, Rance Estuary, France; checking radiation levels outside Dungeness Nuclear Power Station; solar power station, Odeillo, France – the mirrors reflect sunlight onto a furnace.

Write a first draft. How do you feel about it? Underline the words, phrases and passages you like. Where do you need more information or to sound more convincing? Add some new passages or rephrase others. Do they make the points more strongly? Write down thoughts, plans and how satisfied you feel with the writing so far on the right-hand page.

You need to make sure that your draft is a successful argument before you go on to write and present your final version.

Ask a friend to read your draft and, playing the part of a reader who disagrees with the viewpoint you have presented, to argue against what you have written. Expect him or her to spot a lack of evidence or unconvincing arguments. Note the points you may need to change because of this.

Only write another draft if you feel that major changes are required. Otherwise, rewrite what you need to on the right-hand page of the book.

Now, edit your work. Check for spelling, punctuation and paragraphing.

Write your final draft. As you write check that your arguments move from point to point smoothly and that your paragraphs are linked. Keep your handwriting neat and legible throughout. At the end write a **bibliography**. That is a list of the sources – books, organisations, leaflets or whatever – that you obtained your information from.

Tips for Success

◆ For the role-play to be a success you need to have the right information at your fingertips. Prepare carefully and try to think as your character.

◆ As you read an argument try to get an understanding of what the writer believes in a general way as well as seeing what the specific point is.

◆ Work carefully through the different stages, and check back and revise at the end, to achieve a satisfying and successful result when you write your own argument.

Write from the heart

This unit explores the way people speak and write about places and people associated with times when they were especially happy.

Writing seriously about something that means a lot to you may seem a bit of a risky business. But, in the end, it is probably the kind of writing that you will be most pleased with because it matters most to you. In this unit, you will have the chance to read some writing that is quietly expressive of deep-felt feelings – and to do some personal writing of your own.

you will be . . . .

- **Responding to literature**
- **Locating information**
- **Writing a narrative or poem**
- **Relating personal experience**

A special sort of person

Most people know someone who is, or has been, a very special person for them. The writing which follows is from *Crick Crack, Monkey* by Merle Hodge. The story is about her childhood in the Caribbean and describes one person in particular, who influenced her. Each summer, Tee and her brothers and sisters were sent to spend the final part of their summer holiday with their grandmother, Ma in a place called Pointe d'Espoir:

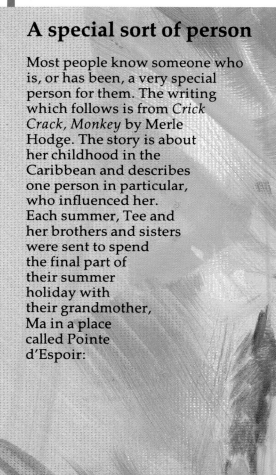

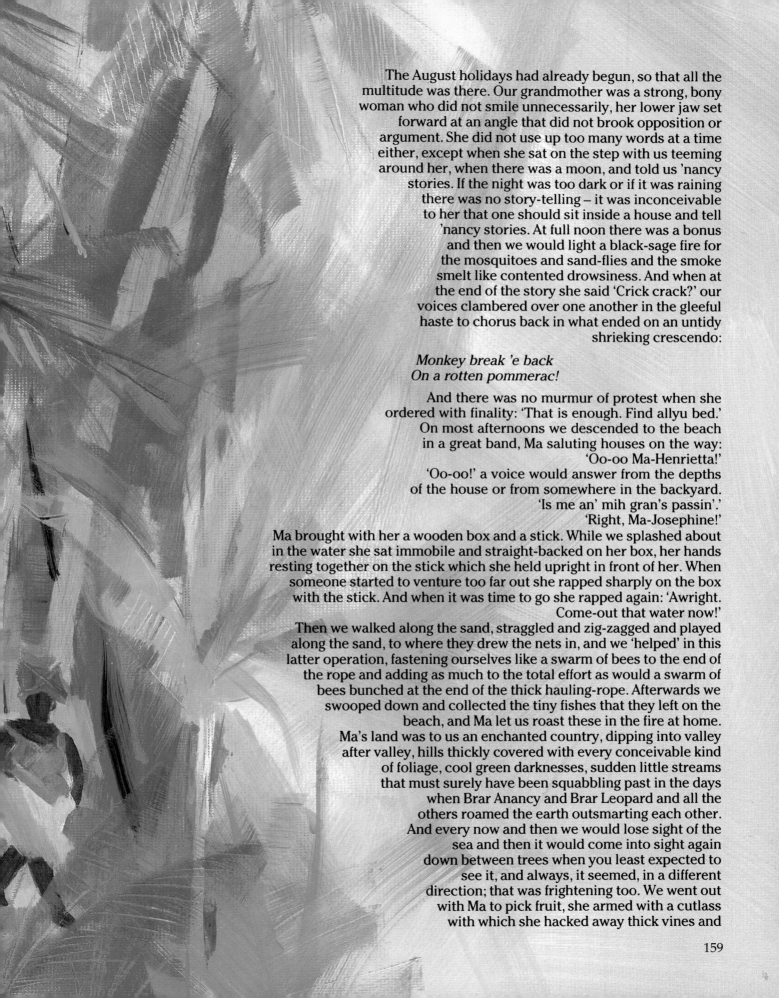

The August holidays had already begun, so that all the multitude was there. Our grandmother was a strong, bony woman who did not smile unnecessarily, her lower jaw set forward at an angle that did not brook opposition or argument. She did not use up too many words at a time either, except when she sat on the step with us teeming around her, when there was a moon, and told us 'nancy stories. If the night was too dark or if it was raining there was no story-telling – it was inconceivable to her that one should sit inside a house and tell 'nancy stories. At full noon there was a bonus and then we would light a black-sage fire for the mosquitoes and sand-flies and the smoke smelt like contented drowsiness. And when at the end of the story she said 'Crick crack?' our voices clambered over one another in the gleeful haste to chorus back in what ended on an untidy shrieking crescendo:

Monkey break 'e back
On a rotten pommerac!

And there was no murmur of protest when she ordered with finality: 'That is enough. Find allyu bed.' On most afternoons we descended to the beach in a great band, Ma saluting houses on the way: 'Oo-oo Ma-Henrietta!'
'Oo-oo!' a voice would answer from the depths of the house or from somewhere in the backyard. 'Is me an' mih gran's passin'.'
'Right, Ma-Josephine!'
Ma brought with her a wooden box and a stick. While we splashed about in the water she sat immobile and straight-backed on her box, her hands resting together on the stick which she held upright in front of her. When someone started to venture too far out she rapped sharply on the box with the stick. And when it was time to go she rapped again: 'Awright. Come-out that water now!'
Then we walked along the sand, straggled and zig-zagged and played along the sand, to where they drew the nets in, and we 'helped' in this latter operation, fastening ourselves like a swarm of bees to the end of the rope and adding as much to the total effort as would a swarm of bees bunched at the end of the thick hauling-rope. Afterwards we swooped down and collected the tiny fishes that they left on the beach, and Ma let us roast these in the fire at home.
Ma's land was to us an enchanted country, dipping into valley after valley, hills thickly covered with every conceivable kind of foliage, cool green darknesses, sudden little streams that must surely have been squabbling past in the days when Brar Anancy and Brar Leopard and all the others roamed the earth outsmarting each other. And every now and then we would lose sight of the sea and then it would come into sight again down between trees when you least expected to see it, and always, it seemed, in a different direction; that was frightening too. We went out with Ma to pick fruit, she armed with a cutlass with which she hacked away thick vines and

159

annihilated whole bushes in one swing. We returned with our baskets full of oranges, mangoes, chennettes, Ma bent under a bunch of plantains that was more than half her size.

Ma had a spot in the market on Sunday mornings, and she spent a great part of the week stewing cashews, pommes-cythères, cerises, making guava-cheese and guava jelly, sugar-cake, nut-cake, bennay-balls, toolum, shaddock-peel candy, chilibibi. . . . Oh these days we hung slyly about the kitchen, if only to feed on the smells; we were never afforded the opportunity of gorging ourselves – we partook of these delicacies when Ma saw fit, and not when we desired. She was full of maxims for our edification, of which the most baffling and maddening was:

> *Who ask*
> *don't get*
> *Who don't ask*
> *don't want*
> *Who don't want*
> *don't get*
> *Who won't get*
> *don't care*

For her one of the cardinal sins of childhood was gluttony: 'Stuff yu guts today an' eat the stones of the wilderness tomorrow.' (Ma's saying often began on a note of familiarity only to rise into an impressive incomprehensibility, or vice versa, as in 'Them that walketh in the paths of corruption will live to ketch dey arse.') She was equal to all the vagaries of childhood. Nothing took her by surprise – she never rampaged, her initial reaction was always a knowing 'Hm'. Not that one permitted oneself the maximum of vagaries in Ma's house – her eye was too sharp and her hand too quick. But there were the odd times that somebody thought she wasn't looking. Sometimes there would be a chase, exciting but brief, when the culprit was hauled back panting to face the music in front of us all. Sometimes he was merely set free again, since he was already frightened to death and would certainly never try that one again.

Just as there were enough of us to play Hoop and Rescue and every conceivable game, so there were enough of us for the occasional outbreak of miniature gang-warfare. We sat for hours under the house in two camps proffering hearty insults. The division usually fell between those who were kept by Ma and those of us who didn't really live there. Ma's children were the 'bush-monkeys' and 'country-bookies' and they in turn made it known to us how deep was their longing for the day when we would all depart so they could have their house and their yard and their land to themselves again. This stung deep for though we knew beyond doubt that it was equally our house and yard and land yet it was those fiends who lived in the house all year round and played in the yard and went on expeditions into the land with Ma when we were not there. If hostilities lasted till a mealtime, then we placed ourselves on opposite sides of the table and eyed each other with contempt. And if they lasted until night-time, then going to bed was an uncomfortable affair, for it took rather longer to fall asleep when every muscle of your body and every inch of your concentration was taut with the effort of not touching your neighbour. But we the vacation batch always had our revenge when it was time to go home and our big-people had come to fetch us and we were all dressed up for the trip home and being fussed over – Ma's children looked a little envious then.

Ma awoke every morning with a groan quickly routed by a brief loud cheups. She rose at a nameless hour and in my half-sleep I saw a mountain shaking off mist in one mighty shudder and the mist falling away in little drops of cloud. The cheups with which Ma greeted the day expressed her essential attitude before the whole of existence – what yu mus' beat-up yuself for? In the face of the distasteful and unavoidable, the unexpected and irreversible, all that Ma could not crush or confound with a barked word or surmount with her lioness strength, she reacted to with a cheups, more or less loud, more or less long. Thus she sucked her teeth loudly and without further comment when the iron pot full of rice spitefully tipped itself over into the fire; when the sun took to playing monkey-wedding with the rain the moment she had put the final clothes-peg to her miles of washing strung from the breadfruit tree to the zaboca tree, from the zaboca tree to the house-post and from the house-post to the chicken-run post, Ma sucked her teeth and turned her back.

And there were the days of real rain. We could see it coming, down across the water, a dark ceiling letting down slow grey streamers into the horizon (that was God pee-peeing into his posie) and then it would be pounding the earth like a thousand horses coming at us through the trees. It was frightening and exciting. A sudden greyness had descended upon everything and we had seconds in which to race about the yard like mad-ants helping Ma to place her assortment of barrels and buckets in places where they would catch the water. And all the time the rain pounding nearer, racing to catch us. When the first messenger spray hit us there was pandemonium – we stampeded into the house, some squealing with a contagious excitement. We ran round shutting the windows, pulling out buckets and basins to place under the leaks, still squealing and colliding with each other. As the windows were closed one by one a cosy darkness crept in, and we felt as if our numbers were growing. We all collected into one room. Sometimes we piled on to the big-bed and made a tent of the coverlets, tying them to the four posts of the bed. Under the tent the commotion was sustained rising to squealing pitch at every flash of lightning and crack of thunder, or every time the tent collapsed about us, or when a lath fell so that a part of the bed caved in under some of us; or when someone chose this situation of inescapable intimacy to emit an anonymous but very self-assertive poops. It was impossible to detect the owner, and chaos ensued while every man accused his immediate neighbour. In the end we had to count the culprit out by means of Ink-Pink-Mamma-Stink, and the man thus denounced was emitted bodily amidst a new burst of commotion.

Meanwhile Ma bustled about the house – we knew that she was just as excited as we were, barricaded into the darkened house with the rain drumming on the galvanize and surrounding us with heavy purring like a huge mother-cat. Ma seemed to be finding things to do so as not to yield to the temptation to come and crawl under the sheets and play tent with us. Then she came in with a big plate of sugar-cake and guava-cheese, and pretended to be scandalized at the way we were treating the bedclothes.

And when the rain had stopped we dressed up in Grampa's old jackets and went out with Ma to look at the river. This was like a ritual following upon the rain – she had to go and see the river. We walked behind her squelching joyously in the new puddles and mud. The air smelt brown and green, like when the earth was being made. From a long way off the river was calling to us through the trees, in one continuous groan, so that when we finally came to it, wet and splashed from the puddles and from the bushes we had brushed against, it was as though we had been straining along in it the whole time. Ma stopped abruptly and spread out both her arms to stop us, as though it were likely that we would keep on walking right into the fast ochre water. We counted how many trees it had risen past on the bank. If the river came down every week Ma's rapture would be quite as new.

'Eh!' she exclaimed, and then fell back into her trance. Then a little later on 'Eh!' shaking her head from side to side, 'Well yes, well yes!' We stood around her in an unlikely silence like spattered acolytes in our jumble-sale clothes, in the bright air hanging out crisp and taut to dry, and the river ploughing off with the dirt and everything drenched and bowing and satisfied and resting before the world started up again from the beginning. We roamed the yard and swarmed down to the water and played hoop around the breadfruit tree as if we would always be wiry-limbed children whose darting about the sun would capture like amber and fix into eternity. Although Ma exclaimed upon our arrival each year at how big we'd got, yet all the holidays at Pointe d'Espoir were one August month, especially in the middle part of the day when everything seemed to set in the still, hanging brightness – our games and squabbling; the hens with their heads down scratching about the yard; the agreeableness of sitting clamped between Ma's knees having one's hair plaited. The cream air in the middle part of the day was like Time staring at itself in a mirror, the two faces locked dreamily in an eternal gaze.

162

Remembered times, remembered faces

Several things seem to come together to make Tee's summers with Ma so happy: the special character of Ma, the beauty and wilderness of the place and the company of the other children.

1. With a partner, look back at the extract and at how the characters are described. First, talk about Ma. Ma is obviously a very remarkable woman and much of Tee's happiness at Pointe d'Espoir seems linked with her feelings towards Ma.

▬ Note down all the words which immediately come to mind to describe Ma and some of her best known sayings.

▬ Make a spidergram, like the one below, which lists all the things Tee describes Ma doing so well. Put these in your own words in the spidergram, or use short quotations from the story.

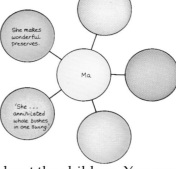

Next, think about the children. You may have noticed that the children who stayed and lived with Ma are not described as individuals – the reader is not even told how many there were!

▬ Re-read the extract and note down the ways Merle Hodge refers to the children.

▬ Discuss why you think she has chosen not to describe them in detail and as individuals. How is their description different from the way that Ma is described?

Now, write . . .

2. Suppose that Tee was asked by someone who had never met her grandmother what Ma was like. Write a short piece giving her reply.

3. Write the conversation Tee has years later with her cousin as they recall some of the games they used to play each summer at Ma's.

Special friends

Read this poem by Grace Nichols. She describes a similar warmth towards her neighbour as that expressed by Tee in the story extract.

Waiting for Thelma's laughter

You wanna take the world
in hand
and fix-it-up
the way you fix your living room

You wanna reach out and crush
life's big and small injustices
in the fire and honey
of your hands

You wanna scream
cause your head's too small
for your dreams
and the children
    running round
acting like lil clowns
    breaking the furniture down

while I sit through
it all watching you
knowing any time now
your laughter's gonna come

to drown and heal us all

4 Write some notes about an older person – perhaps a grandparent like Ma. Use these headings to help you:

Appearance	Things he/she does	Favourite sayings	Personality

Then, write an account – or a poem – describing a time you spent with that person. It does not have to be a long time. Try to convey a real sense of how the person is, perhaps in the way Merle Hodge does for Ma or Grace Nichols for Thelma, by including examples of the way they speak and the kinds of things they say. Try to show, also, your feelings towards that person.

A special place

Like Tee, most people can think of a place which holds a particular meaning – often associated with happy times or with times when they were younger.

Sometimes life can take people right away from those places to a quite different environment. Then, such thoughts are particularly heightened. The poems which follow are by writers from Jamaica and Barbados, who have travelled far away from their islands as adults. This may be a reason why they express such strong feelings about the places of their childhood.

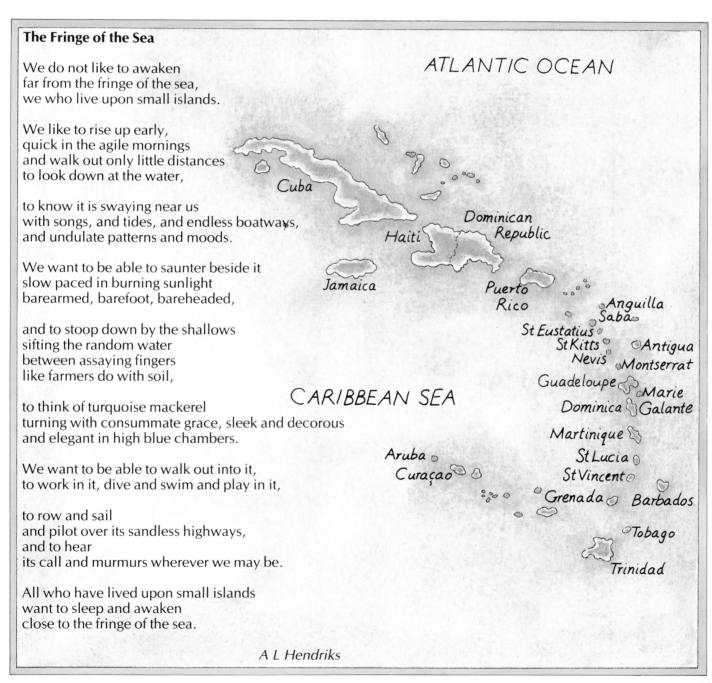

The Fringe of the Sea

We do not like to awaken
far from the fringe of the sea,
we who live upon small islands.

We like to rise up early,
quick in the agile mornings
and walk out only little distances
to look down at the water,

to know it is swaying near us
with songs, and tides, and endless boatways,
and undulate patterns and moods.

We want to be able to saunter beside it
slow paced in burning sunlight
barearmed, barefoot, bareheaded,

and to stoop down by the shallows
sifting the random water
between assaying fingers
like farmers do with soil,

to think of turquoise mackerel
turning with consummate grace, sleek and decorous
and elegant in high blue chambers.

We want to be able to walk out into it,
to work in it, dive and swim and play in it,

to row and sail
and pilot over its sandless highways,
and to hear
its call and murmurs wherever we may be.

All who have lived upon small islands
want to sleep and awaken
close to the fringe of the sea.

A L Hendriks

SOUTH

But today I recapture the islands'
bright beaches; blue mist from the ocean
rolling into the fishermen's houses.
By these shores I was born: sound of the sea
came in at my window, life heaved and breathed in me then
with the strength of that turbulent soil.

Since then I have travelled: moved far from the beaches:
sojourned in stoniest cities, walking the lands of the north
in sharp slanting sleet and the hail,
crossed countless saltless savannnas and come
to this house in the forest where the shadows oppress me
and the only water is rain and the tepid taste of the river.

We who are born of the ocean can never seek solace
in rivers; their flowing runs on like our longing,
reproves us our lack of endeavour and purpose,
proves that our striving will founder on that.
We resent them their wisdom, this freedom: passing us
toiling, waiting and watching their cunning declension down
to the sea.

But today I would join you, travelling river,
borne down the years of your patientest flowing,
past pains that would wreck us, sorrows arrest us,
hatred that washes us up on the flats;
and moving on through the plains that receive us,
processioned in tumult, come to the sea.

Bright waves splash up from the rocks to refresh us,
blue sea-shells shift in their wake
and *there* is the thatch of the fishermen's houses, the path
made of pebbles, and look!
Small urchins combing the beaches
look up from their traps to salute us:
they remember us just as we left them.
The fisherman, hawking the surf on this side
of the reef, stands up in his boat
and halloos us; a starfish lies in its pool,
And gulls, white sails slanted seaward,
fly into limitless morning before us.

From *Rights of Passage* by Edward Brathwaite

Tips for Success

◆ As you talk about Ma, try to picture in your mind that time and the faces and settings which Merle Hodge describes.
◆ When you read an account like Tee's, read it slowly and carefully. Try to see the place and the people through her young eyes and to *empathise* with her feelings and reactions.
◆ When you write, use the note-making and drafting stages to add details as they come back to you. Try to include some little points of detail in your writing – it is these which can make it especially convincing.

Some of you may have had the same experience as these writers – of moving to another place or country and thinking back to the sights, sounds and emotions which you associate with that earlier place. For others, your favourite place may be somewhere you are still very much in contact with.

5 Think of a place which makes you very happy. Without stopping to work your thoughts out in detail, write down all the words which come to mind to describe that place.

Then, again without first thinking at length, write down all the feelings you have when you picture that place.

Now, write about a time you spent there. Try to use language in a way that captures what is special about the place for your readers – and make them feel something of what the place means to you.

THE BOOK OF

THE FILM

This unit explores how a piece of writing can be adapted and changed to suit different purposes and different audiences.

After you have planned and drafted a piece of writing, you may think of the final, neat copy as a finished product. Once you have handed it to your teacher, you do not expect to work on it again. But, for a professional writer, the final version can often be the starting point for another writing task.

The book of the film

When a new film has been a great success you can be fairly sure that the 'book of the film' will soon be in your local bookshop. Of course, the reverse is also true – many films start life as a book or, increasingly, as a television series. Both books and films are also made into plays.

This process of **adaptation** where the same story is used in another *medium* or form has become especially important as increasing numbers of new titles compete for the attention of the public. The money spent on promoting and advertising a particular film, say, helps to create a situation where people are already interested in the book version of that story.

1 With a partner, list any books, films and television series which you know have been adapted from one form to another. What do you know about how each of them started off? Copy the chart below and use it to record all the examples you can think of.

Write the title in the correct box to show where the story was first told (as a book, a film, TV programme or whatever). Then, tick the other boxes to show the adaptations you know about.

you will be . . . .

- Responding to a range of texts
- Commenting on language use
- Responding to a writer
- Writing a narrative or playscript

ADRIAN MOLE - book - tv series - play

HENRY V - play - film - comic strip

THE YOUNG ONES - tv series - book - record/tape

RAINMAN - film - book

THE WITCHES - book - film

SHE-DEVIL - book - tv series - film

TEENAGE MUTANT TURTLES - tv cartoon - books - toys - films

STAR TREK - tv series - films - cartoon - books

Books	Films	Television	Plays	Other things
Tintin				Toys
			An Inspector Calls	
		Mutant Turtles		Toys, games

Changing the words . . .

Jan Needle is a popular writer for teenagers who has
adapted his own writing, and other people's, on
many occasions. Below he writes about how he
does this. Read what he writes and talk about it
with a partner.

' The best thing about the written word, in my opinion, is that you can change
it. I write by hand, with a ballpoint pen, and if something comes out wrong I
can scrub it through and start again. Likewise, if I write a novel and someone
wants me to turn it into a television script or vice versa, wonderful things can
be made to happen. Characters can disappear, change sex, or multiply,
settings can become sparser or more ornate, and time can be telescoped or
expanded. When people complain that a film is not 'like' the book it springs
from, they are missing a very important point. A film and a book are
completely different things: one cannot and should not be like the other. As
the French say — vive la différence!

Ah, you might think — easy for Jan Needle to say. And it's true that having
done about seven or eight adaptations from novel to television (or vice versa)
plus a couple of script/novel/stage permutations, I'm a lot more relaxed
about it than I was when I started. But confidence is the best tool you can
develop for adaptation, and confidence soon sets in once you've made this
basic realisation; when you adapt, some things will have to change
drastically, or be cut ruthlessly — and there is nothing you can do about it.

Other people's words

My first awareness of the need to change and cut was forced upon me as
soon as I set out on my first adaptation. I had been asked to turn Phil
Redmond's six-part television series for teenagers, *Going Out*, into a novel.
The series, which became a cult success despite being shown at midnight in
most areas because of its frankness about teenage lifestyles, depicted a
group of school-leavers in their first six weeks on the jobs/dole market.
I loved the series, and by coincidence it was filmed in Portsmouth, my home
town, so I knew the settings inside-out. The trouble was — I could not find a
way to start the novel.

The problem was that the first episode started with an extremely strong visual sequence of two boys barging down a crowded school staircase, full of physical exuberance, shoving, shouting, and generally messing about. It was obviously a special occasion, and all the other pupils were also excited and physical. At the bottom of the staircase, a teacher intervened and was nasty to the boys. Simple on film, and very effective. But in prose, on the page, it was a mess. Without the camera to 'pick out' our heroes, and without us knowing or caring about them this early into the book, the physical excitement and the interest in the characters seemed merely contrived. An actor's face and body and attitude give you instant rapport, or sympathy, with a character. On page, these 'heroes' were just two boys being loutish. We needed to know them, and we needed to know it was a special occasion and why.

This is how I started the book:

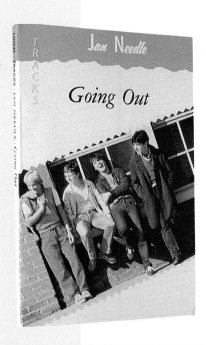

Going Out

Chapter 1

Sean Tinnersley didn't know exactly what he was expecting, but whatever it was, it didn't happen. For the last ten minutes of the last 'lesson' he couldn't keep his eyes off his watch. Mr Dyer (of Dyer here fame) kept rubbishing on, but no one, just nobody, was listening. The noise level was fantastic, and Sean had a pretty fair idea that it was the same all over their floor. Who wanted to hear about the great big outside world from Dyer, anyhow? In ten minutes' time they'd be out in it. For good. He glanced at his watch. Eight minutes. Seven and a half. It was the last lesson of the last day of the last term of the last year. Of the lot. They were on their way.

He nudged Roger, who was lounging next to him, about to flick a lump of dead chewing gum across the room at Sammy, their mate.

'Hey,' he said. 'This is it, Rog. In five minutes' time we're free. I will kiss the Sergeant Major, no more lousy school for me!'

'Don't give me that,' said Roger, with a grin. 'You'll be back, Tinnersley, you can't leave it alone. You'll get two dozen O levels and you'll be down that sixth form college like a shot. It's me and Sammy who'll be out, mate. On our own.'

Mr Dyer was winding up: 'So anyway, men,' he said, 'I really do wish you all the very –'

The school bell clicked, which meant it was about to go off like a thing demented. A cheer went up, which drowned out Dyer – and the bell – totally. It turned into a chant: 'Dyer here, Dyer here, Dyer'ere, Dyer'ere, Diarrhoea!'

Mr Dyer smiled broadly, and raised his hands for silence after a couple of minutes.

'Thanks, lads,' he said. 'I think that just about sums you up! Best of luck. The very best of luck!'

4

5

Shortly after that, they were on the stairs, causing mayhem, and meeting the teacher, who accused them of being hooligans. But we knew them by now, and knew they were all right. It was a different route than Redmond took in his script — but we had achieved the same effect.

Having been made aware on the very first page of my novel that not only could I make certain large decisions about my method of adaptation but that I would be forced to by the material, I sat back and had a think. Clearly, if I wanted to, I could use the scripts as a flying-off point. I could read them and digest them, then write a 'free-form' version of them as a novel. Alternatively, I could keep as close to the dialogue and action 'as seen on television' as possible. As I became more experienced in the process, I came to realise that either way is equally valid.

[2] Above, Jan Needle shows an important difference between telling a story in pictures and in print or 'writing' with a camera rather than a pen. Now, try adapting the opening of *Going Out* into yet another form, that of a comic strip or a photostory using a sequence of drawings or photographs. Include something to set the scene, the characters' words and, perhaps, their thoughts to accompany the visual images.

As you work, think about:

— how to put across the excitement of the last day at school
— what to show in each frame of your story
— where to use close-ups
— whose point of view you are showing the events from
— what words you definitely need to include or leave out
— how to use the 'rules' of comic strip writing to make these few 'frames' tell a simple story.

Now, read on about Jan Needle's way of adapting his own writing:

Changing your own words

When I adapt my own work, I am able to make basic changes for different reasons. *A Game of Soldiers* is a good example.

A Game of Soldiers started life as a three-part television serial about a year after the Falklands crisis of 1982. It tells the simple story of three children who find a young, badly wounded enemy soldier lying in a sheep-shelter. At first they decide it is their patriotic duty — to help the war effort — to murder him. Later, however, they get to know and like him, and decide he must be saved. Unfortunately, an army patrol is already on its way.

Writing a television play and a novel threw up all sorts of interesting points about the difference between the different media. Practically everything I included in the television script — including people — had to be worked out by calculator. When I came to write the novel, anything could be used. I'll give you a simple example — parents.

In the television serial, the cast had to be kept down to a very small minimum, for cost reasons. Only Thomas had visible parents and they were only seen at a distance, so that we did not hear them talk, which cost extra. But in the novel all three children — Sarah, Michael and Thomas had parents, not unnaturally. In the event, they played a useful part in the story. All three talk to them, and seek advice and comfort about the brutal events that take place.

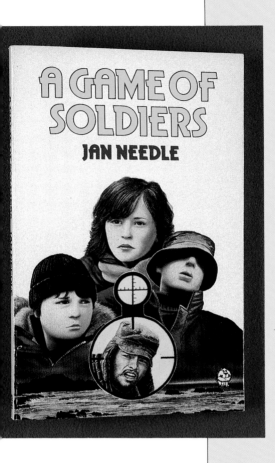

Sarah lay between her parents' warm bodies, comforted but still afraid. Her father was asleep again. Genuinely, she guessed, not just putting on an act to reassure her. He was breathing softly and evenly, his large chest expanding and contracting under his working shirt. Her mother was not asleep. But the conversation was over.

Both of them had petted her, and told her not to worry, and told her that everything would be all right, but she could not pin them *down*, that's what frustrated her. She wanted to *know*, she wanted to hear the details, to learn what they *felt* about the dangers. But that was not their way.

'Listen, you bum,' her Dad had said. 'Don't you worry your ugly little head about it. It's all in hand. I've given my men their instructions, and they're carrying them out. This noisy stuff is a diversion – I organised a fireworks display to keep the boys happy. You know what children soldiers are.'

He usually called her a bum, or something less polite, and he always called her ugly, and lazy, and a savage and so on. She loved his jokiness, and his niceness. But sometimes it did not help. She wanted an opinion. A straight, serious, honest opinion.

'There's no chance,' said her mother, when Dad had turned over for sleep. 'He'd be joking as they took him to the gallows, your Dad. That's why I married him.'

Sarah sighed.

'All right, *you* then,' she said. 'What do *you* think will happen?'

'Oh give up, Sarah,' replied her Mum. 'The best thing you can do is take his advice, isn't it? Don't *worry*.'

Hhm, thought Sarah. That was the trouble with getting on with your Mum and Dad. You couldn't even scream at them . . .

Listening to the guns, the bombs, the wind, the quiet rhythmic breathing . . . she went to sleep.

12

Conversations like this help to give an insight into Sarah and her attitudes. The medium of the novel allowed me to explore the characters' thinking, in a way that television didn't.

The Thief

The Thief by Jan Needle also started life as a television series but has since been adapted into both a novel and a stage play. Below, Jan Needle writes about some of the issues which arise in doing this.

The Thief is a story about a boy called Kevin Pelham who finds some criminals' loot hidden in a network of caves near his home. His responses are complicated by the fact that his father is a habitual burglar, now in jail, and he himself has the reputation at school of being a thief. It's a fairly complex moral story, which on television — because of the constraints of time and money — had to be very simply told, but in the novel, it was possible to expand some of the points further.

At the start of both the serial and the play, a five-pound note is stolen (unknown to Kevin, who is later blamed for it) from a teachers' cloakroom. On television we see, in a brief shot, that the thief is a girl. The point which comes across is simply a technical and dramatic one. It could not have been Kevin who took the money, because it was a girl, so we shouldn't get involved in an irrelevant guessing game. In the novel, though, I was able to expand it:

Five minutes later, in a staff cloakroom on the other side of the school, a small plastic wallet belonging to Miss Smith, a physics teacher, was taken from the pocket of her jacket, where she had carelessly left it. There were four five-pound notes in it, and some credit cards.

The thief was not greedy. Fifteen pounds were left. So were the credit cards, naturally. Mr Tim Atkinson, who had been in the lavatory in the cloakroom, frightened the thief when he pulled the chain. But he emerged too late to catch sight of anybody.

A little later, Miss Smith talks to Tim Atkinson about the theft.

'The door was still open,' he said, 'but when I looked out into the corridor, the bird had flown. I didn't realise he'd nicked anything, though. You should use a bigger wallet, not a plastic billfold. I'd have seen it lying on the floor.'

He said it as a joke, in a nice friendly fashion, because he fancied Judy Smith. She smiled.

Shortly afterwards, they decide to ask around.

'Ah well,' said Tim. 'We can check and see if any boys were skipping classes, can't we? We might track down the culprit.'

They went to ask around the other teachers. Like everybody else, they assumed the thief would be a boy.

'Aren't they little swine,' repeated Judy Smith.

Here the point being made is different — and bigger — than the one I could manage in the television play. In the television script, people were shown as obviously being wrong to blame Kevin, because the culprit was a girl. In the novel they are wrong because they 'naturally' assume it could only have been a boy. Many people subconsciously seem to feel that girls aren't thieves; Kevin Pelham is a boy, and once was a thief — therefore: the thief was Kevin Pelham.

Another problem with film and television is that some actions, however well acted and however long drawn out, cannot actually convey very much about what characters are feeling, thinking or suffering. Kevin and his friends Buzz and Jenny are deliberately locked into a sealed-off part of the caves by an old bombproof door. Kevin thinks he knows a way out, or pretends he does, but in reality they are trapped. This is how they respond in the book:

When the blastproof door slammed shut behind the children, they had been so frightened that for a long moment they neither said nor did a thing. The noise it made was appalling – a hollow, echoing boom, followed by the metallic 'snap' of the bolt going into its socket. Although the sounds were unfamiliar, all three of them knew, instantly, what had happened.

For a long moment, they did nothing. But then – pandemonium.

Buzz leapt at Kevin and snatched the torch from him. With an inarticulate shriek, he stumbled to the passage they had come along, and began to run. He went straight into a wall.

'Stop!' yelled Kevin. 'Buzz! Be careful! We'll be all right!'

That infuriated Jenny, oddly. She shouted at Kevin, something loud and frightened and angry, that did not make much sense. As Buzz began his stumbling run for the iron door again, she pushed past Kevin and rushed after him.

'It's not all right!' she screamed. 'We're trapped, you fool! They've locked us in the caverns!'

Kevin followed them, but more slowly. When they reached the door and began to kick and batter at it, he felt sick. Sick with worry, sick with fear. He knew it was useless, quite impossible. They would hurt themselves, use up their energy.

In the next page or two, the children go through panic, despair, and hope. Kevin persuades them that he can lead them out, and sets off with reasonable confidence to locate an exit he is sure exists. Buzz and Jenny are far from happy, or convinced.

Kevin had to make a show. Otherwise, he knew, the others might collapse. He closed his eyes momentarily, trying to conjure up a picture of his map, the new bits he had coloured in. There was a ventilator leading from this part, he was sure there was. A ventilator in a shaft. If only he could find it . . .

'I know the caves,' he said. He made his voice sound firm. 'I'm fed up telling you. There is a way. Just follow me.'

At first they tried to move without the light, by holding hands and feeling along the walls. But the walls were wet and horrible, and the ground was broken up by holes, some of them deep and dangerous. After only a few minutes, Jenny said they'd have to risk the batteries.

'Yeah,' said Kevin, quietly. 'Go on, Buzz. We'll be all right.'

Buzz switched on the lamp, then shook it. He spoke, and his voice was panicky.

'The torch keeps flickering,' he said.

In the television version, the whole of this action, fear and emotion is conveyed in two tiny scenes. In the first the men who have been chasing them slam the bomb door with a single line: 'Done. No way out.' Later, we see this scene:

70. INT. CAVES. A DARK CHAMBER. SATURDAY 1.15 PM.

A LITTLE LATER. THE CHILDREN ARE AT THE ENTRANCE TO THE SEWER TYPE BRICK CULVERT. THEY ARE FRIGHTENED AND SUBDUED. PANIC VERY CLOSE.

KEVIN: We've got to go along it, I'm telling you. It's the only way.
JENNY: You said there wasn't a way. You said that bomb door . . .
KEVIN: I'm telling you. I know the caves. I'm telling you.
Pause
BUZZ (*whiny*): The torch keeps flickering . . .

It is, of course, impossible to say which is more tense, or expressive: the detailed description on the page, or the sparse words conveyed by good actors, well directed and filmed. But the methods are clearly and completely different, although we arrive at exactly the same point, and the same words, which is probably what successful adaptation is all about. It is impracticable — and would become boring — to have actors stuck in a tunnel conveying 'panic' for any length of time, but on the page we need more than just bare stage directions and a few flat words. Each medium demands its own methods.

Films, scripts, plays and novels

A Game of Soldiers and *The Thief* have both been adapted as stage plays. On stage it is difficult to show the setting realistically, as it can be shown on film – but instead, it can be suggested or conjured up as a stage 'image' which the audience is invited to believe in. In live performance it is also possible to show the *interaction* between individuals very powerfully indeed. In front of an audience, the dramatic tension has to be raised and lowered entirely through the words, actions and sheer presence of the actors.

3. Here is a short scene from the stage version of *The Thief*. It follows on from where the children first discover they are trapped in the caves. Read through the scene, noting how Jan Needle creates the setting and draws out the dramatic tension between the characters.

A stage production showing the dry ice effect. The dry ice stays close to the ground unlike smoke.

SCENE TWENTY-ONE

A dark tunnel. The **children** *are huddled at one end, with a glimmer of light coming through a ventilator hole that has been blocked up from the outside. They have been there for ages, and they are exhausted. No one speaks for some time.*

Jenny It's getting dark outside. Do you think they'll find us soon? It's getting dark.

Pause

Kevin It's not that cold though, is it? *Brief pause* They must've missed us by now, they must've.
Buzz *he's angry and afraid* Why? Why must they? Why should anybody miss us?
Jenny Ssh. Buzz. Don't act daft, we'll be all right.
Kevin Honest, Buzz. My sister knows about the caves. She'll —
Buzz Your sister's as daft as you are! She's a thickie just like you! Just like all the Pelham family! You got us into this, Kevin. You're stupid, stupid!

Pause

Kevin I knew there was a ventilator hole down here. I didn't know they'd blocked it up, that's all.
Buzz *loses his anger, but only to be depressed* That's all, is it? Isn't that fantastic. You knew there was a ventilator but you didn't know it was blocked up, that's all. Just like knowing it was safe to come in through the bomb doors until someone closed them on us and chucked away the key. Isn't that fantastic.
Kevin *also depressed* If we'd stayed out in the passages —
Buzz *interrupting* Why don't you just shut up, eh? Give your brain a rest. It's like everything else about you, Kevin Pelham. Useless. If *you* say we'll be all right, I bet we die. I *bet*.

Pause. **Buzz** *starts to sniff, quite loudly.* **Jenny** *tries to comfort him.*

Jenny *kindly* Try not to cry, Buzz. It doesn't help. If —
Buzz *strangled* I'm not crying, stupid! I'm *cold*.
Jenny Oh.

Pause. With a click, **Kevin** *turns the torch on.*

Kevin Maybe there's enough to signal with. Maybe if . . .

The torch glows for a moment or two, then fades. The light from the ventilator is dimmer as well.

Jenny   *so that* **Buzz** *won't hear*   Do you really think they'll rescue us, Kev? Soon? I'm cold, too. I'm freezing.

Pause

Kevin   We'd better shout again. Maybe someone's in the woods. A courting couple, maybe.
Jenny   In winter?
Kevin   What else can we do?

Fade to blackout. Then we hear **Miss Smith**, *either in total darkness, amplified, or with her picked out in a spotlight, alone. She is on the telephone.*

Miss Smith   Police? Yes, my name's Judith Smith. Yes, look. I understand there are some caves or something, under Vintners Wood. Yes. Well . . . well, I have reason to believe . . .

Fade to silence and blackout.

■ Now try adapting the scene as you think it might have appeared in the book. Use all the information that you have found out about the situation and the characters earlier in this unit, as well as Jan Needle's comments, to help you do this.

When you have finished, compare your version with other people's. Are there suggestions about the characters, the ways that Jenny and Kevin relate to one another (and to Buzz) that you have all noticed and built upon? How far have you managed to describe the setting, the emotions and the appearance of the children as well as their fear?

Changing media

Jan Needle has looked at some of the many differences between the media of film and stage drama and the novel. He has hinted at the kinds of things which are possible in one medium, but difficult or impossible in another.

4 Pick a story or a play which you have recently read or watched in class or elsewhere and adapt a section of it from one medium to the other. Choose a section which you particularly enjoyed where there is plenty of action or one where the characters are in conflict with one another or are changing in some way.

Read your chosen section through carefully. If it is from video-tape, begin by transcribing (copying down) the words which are spoken. Do not start to write your adaptation until the characters are clear in your mind. Remember to set the characters in a concrete and realistic setting and try not to make them into mouthpieces for the words they say. Remember what Jan Needle said about cutting, or reworking scenes which do not work, and the need to limit the speaking characters in a television script. You may have to add to, or change, the words which are spoken in order to do this.

Tips for Success

◆ When you write script or conversation, read it aloud to someone else or ask them to read it to you and see if it sounds real or false.
◆ In adaptation think about the viewpoint of the audience – the reader or viewer. Think about what they will read or see and from what angle you want them to 'look at' the scene.
◆ In adapting scripts or stories try to keep the atmosphere and feel of the original writing in your own version.

DeSign
AND BUILD

This unit explores some of the ways in which you can apply your English language skills to solve design issues in Technology and Science.

A question of design

The first step in creating a new design for anything is the drawing up of a good **design brief**. A design brief sets out everything that the new design is required to do and, usually, it is prepared by somebody else for the designer to work from.

For instance, the product manager for a company which makes foodstuffs might draw up a design brief for some stylish, attractive and protective packaging for a new kind of biscuit. The product manager has to assume that the designer knows nothing about the company or its products and must make sure that all the relevant details which the designer needs to know are included in the design brief.

The **design criteria** might include constraints like costs, packet size, the kind of protection required, details on the sorts of people who might buy the biscuits and the image which the packets should create.

For a manufacturer, missing out a factor in the design brief may be expensive or dangerous. If a company wanted to market a range of big wooden toys based on animal shapes for use in playgroups, one of the vital factors to include in the design brief would be safety. Model animals with sharp wooden edges could lead to injuries, distress and expensive court cases for the company.

you will be . . . .

 Sharing ideas

 Following instructions

 Presenting non-literary material

 Locating information

 Interviewing another person

 Commenting on language use

 Editing and redrafting

PRODUCT MANAGER
'The pack must be **bigger and brighter** than the competition.'

BUYING MANAGER
'We have to keep **costs down.**'

FOOD TECHNOLOGISTS
'Food regulations require a **more protective** pack.'

COMPANY ECOLOGIST
'The pack materials must be **"green".**'

DISTRIBUTION MANAGER
'It is easier to stack and distribute **square** packs.'

THE CONSUMER
'What about me?'

1. With a partner, discuss and note down the factors you would include in a design brief for:

— sets of replacement cutlery and crockery for the school canteen or cafeteria
— a new system of signs for your school giving directions to, and labelling, individual rooms
— pegs, lockers, seating and floor coverings for a refurbished changing room.

You should be able to identify at least four or five design criteria, which would have to be thought about by a designer who was working to your finished design brief.

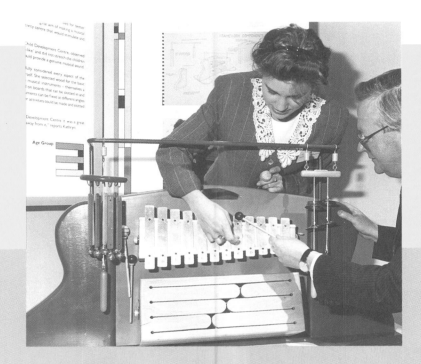

Winners of the Schools Design Award organised by the Design Council

2. Share your ideas with another pair and then with other members of the class. Note the criteria which other pairs have identified which are more unusual or which you should have thought of. Now, write up one of the design briefs for the designer. As you do this, remember that the designer knows nothing about the situation in the school and its requirements except what you tell her. For the brief, you will need to describe exactly:

— what it is you want
— its purpose
— who will use it
— what it has to be able to do
— what it must be resistant to
— what problems it will face up to in use
— how much money you have to spend.

Designing the solution

Now, imagine that you are one of the designers who receives a brief from a manufacturer. For you, the outline of what is required is a kind of puzzle for which your **design proposal** is the best solution.

When you are given a design brief, you will need to organise your ideas and plan what you are going to do in order to solve it. You might need to discuss and explain your ideas to other people, ask experts or carry out some background research or a survey. Doing things in the right order will save time and, for the professional designer, money, so you need to think carefully and to work methodically.

Practical needs and imaginative solutions

1 ASK YOURSELF
What is the task about? What have I got to do? In doing this, sort out the most important things from the things which are less important.

2 RESEARCH
Once you have sorted out the main points, or requirements for your design, you can then find out any information you may need which will help you make decisions about how to tackle it.

3 GENERATE IDEAS
Base your design ideas on your findings. Use them to help you make a decision about what to do.

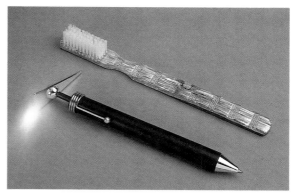

4 PLAN
Most people need a plan to help them structure their work. The plan need not be very long – just reminders of the order in which to work to achieve the best results.

5 MAKE
Only at this stage should you consider carrying out your design. You should already have a clear idea of what it will look like.

6 REVIEW
Once you have carried out your plan then you can look back and evaluate your design. You can ask yourself how well would it work in practice and how close is it to the original design brief?

Meet a designer

Simon Crompton is a product designer. He works for a company which specialises in producing designs for a wide range of products and manufacturers. Below he writes about his work:

❝How would you design a system of providing a bigger choice of paint colours in a smaller space?

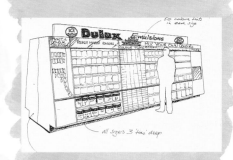

In this instance, we were asked by Dulux to design a system of offering an improved choice of paint colours to customers in large DIY stores. However, although market research had already identified that customers would like a wider range of colours, retailers, on the other hand, wanted to reduce the amount of shelf space taken up by rows of tins.

Next, we put forward a range of concepts to the client. As you can see below, these ideas are not presented as highly finished drawings. They simply provide a means of communicating how the Colour Option system might work. At this stage nothing is hard and fast and the team has to be prepared to modify the design.

This was one of the projects that the company I work for was asked to do. DCA Design Consultants offers its services to anyone who wishes to develop a product. We are a team of skilled people such as engineers, draughtspeople, graphic designers and model-makers. The product designer is the team member who follows a project through from start to finish, communicating ideas and gathering information as it is needed.

The first stage of the project *Colour Options*, as it was called, was to do more research. We needed to understand how people went about choosing colour schemes for their homes *and* any other practical needs from the point of view of the shops.

The concept agreed on was fairly simple. The customer walks into the paint area in the DIY store to be met by some displays. These contain information to help the customer select the colour and correct quantity of paint. A can of 'base white' is picked off the shelf, and a 'tinter pack' is removed from the appropriate rack and clipped on to the can.

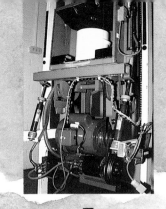

The customer places the base white can with the tinter pack into a specially designed mixing machine which injects the tinter into the base white and mixes the two together. The customer then pays for the mixed paint and takes it home.

3 The point-of-sale display The colour charts and customer information must be presented in the store in a way that is both eye-catching and easy to use.

4 The packaging The graphic design of the paint cans and packs must be informative and attractive.

Before manufacture, we have to produce detailed drawings (often using computer aided design) which specify the size, construction, assembly and material of all the components needed in the product.

Once this concept was selected, the brief could be broken down into much more detail. As this was a large project, with many people working on it, it was subdivided into separate design projects:

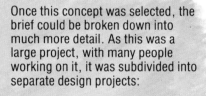

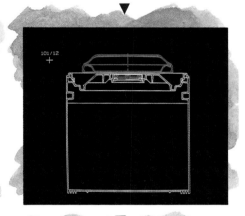

1 The mixing machine The mechanical or electronic design of the machine, its appearance and how it can be safely operated by customers must all be carefully planned.

2 The paint container and tinter pack These need designing in such a way that they will clip together and their contents combine during the mixing process.

Model-making plays an important role in the next stages of the design process. It gives the client a clear idea of the final product and highlights any area which may need modification. In this case, the mixing machine went through several mock-up stages, and then working models to develop the mechanical operation.

In the end, job satisfaction comes from knowing that the product is successful – that it works, that you purchase it and are pleased with it. After all, we are surrounded by products – whatever we do and wherever we go, they affect the way we live. Products should make our lives safer, simpler and more enjoyable. It's my role to provide these tools for living. ,

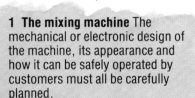

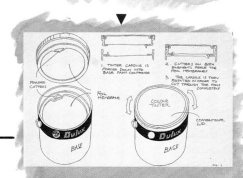

DESIGN PROPOSAL

1

GETTING STARTED

For some people, thinking about the first stage is the hardest part of drawing up a design proposal. Often the easiest way to decide what to do is to brainstorm your ideas with a small group.

Look at the design brief below with your partner:

Many students buy snacks from the school tuck shop at breaktime. These snacks are often high in fat and sugar. Plan, prepare and market a range of healthy snacks which would appeal to the school students who use the tuck shop.

Before you can decide what sort of snacks to plan, make and sell, there are many questions you need to ask such as:

— When can we sell the snacks?
— Which snacks are most popular with teenagers?
— What is meant by healthy?
— How much time have we got to do this in?
— How can snacks be made healthy?
— How can we persuade teenagers to buy our snacks?
— How much will students pay for a snack?
— Will students pay more for a healthy snack?
— Who actually uses the tuck shop?

3 Study the list above and, with your partner, decide on the order in which you think you should set out to find answers for these questions. Think of two or three other questions you would like to ask as well. Report back to the class. As you listen to other reports, decide for yourself on what are the most important *needs* which apply to this particular design task.

DESIGN PROPOSAL

2

FINDING INFORMATION AND USING RESOURCES

Now, look at the design brief below. It is concerned with how young children can learn through constructive play.

Design and make a simple learning toy or game suitable for a child aged between 4 and 6 years.

4 Join with another pair and, in small groups, *brainstorm* the things you would need to do before you could carry out this task. Then decide, individually, on the main points you need to think about and explain your ideas to the rest of your group.

Once you have decided what you need to do, you will have a clearer idea of the kind of information you may wish to find out. The next step is to find out and record that information.

LOOKING FOR INFORMATION AND CHOOSING RESOURCES . . .

5 Suppose that, for the brief above, you have decided that you need to find out about children's likes and dislikes for toys or games. Where and how could you find out this information? With your group, discuss the range of resources you could use to help you find this out. Make a list of them.

It may not be possible for you to use all of the resources you have listed. For example, if you thought of visiting a playgroup to see what children like to play with, then you would need to find a local playgroup and organise time to fit in a visit. That might involve more time and effort than asking an expert for the information or reading about the subject.

Look back at your list of resources and note down the advantages and disadvantages of using each of the resources you have thought of.

RETRIEVING AND RECORDING INFORMATION...

The easiest way to find something out, is to look it up in a reference book of some kind but do not forget that there are many other *paper-based resources* you could use, such as magazines, newspapers, fact sheets and advertisements – all of which may contain helpful information.

[6] Read the extract below with a partner. It is about the kinds of toys and games children enjoy playing with.

Try to identify, and note down, at least five points which the writer makes about toys which could help you in carrying out the design brief.

Toy play

The best toys for your child are the ones she can do lots of different things with. Traditional favourites are still best for encouraging imagination, manual skills, shape-matching and problem-solving (all things your child will be doing in school soon enough); that means dolls, models, building bricks, construction kits, jigsaws, drawing materials, colouring books, cut-outs, sticky shapes and board games.

Pre-school children enjoy simple, co-operative games most of all like Snakes and Ladders, cards and even draughts. These games are good for teaching them about taking turns, counting, being a good loser (or winner) and getting everyone in the family together. If they only cause squabbles and frustration though, they're probably best left until your child is a little more mature.

Don't underestimate your four-year-old. She may be able to join in quite complicated games like Monopoly if the older players are patient and give her some encouragement. And she will, of course, enjoy playing with many of the more modern toys you'll find in your toyshop, and advertised on television.

Maire Messenger Davies

SELECTING SOURCES...

Sometimes you have to be very careful about the information you choose to note down at this stage. First, not all the information presented to you will be that useful and, second, it may contain a bias if it has been produced by a company with a financial interest in a particular product.

[7] Study the three extracts opposite with your partner. Decide what kind of resource each of them comes from and which of them is likely to be most useful to you in developing your design.

Toys

From an early age, a baby needs the right kind of toys to play with. They do not have to cost money: wooden spoons, plastic drinking cups, bowls of water, make perfect learning toys. He does not need too many; this will only confuse him.

Very different toys are not always as much fun as they seem. The child's small world needs small new additions, not sudden great changes. A difficult construction kit instead of his box of old bricks may bring on tears in an 18 month old.

Safety, and other points to consider

1 As babies feel with their mouths, toys must be too big to swallow or choke on.
2 They must be unbreakable, and free from lead paint which is poisonous.
3 They must be easy to clean, as the baby does not have much resistance to germs until he is at the crawling stage.
4 Soft toys must have passed the safety standard. Eyes stuck in on pins and limbs attached by hooks have caused terrible accidents in the past.
5 For older children, toys need to be sturdy and built to last.
6 There must be no sharp edges, no pins or staples, to cause damage.
7 Toys on wheels should be stable, wheels and brakes regularly checked.
8 Water and sand play need to be supervised. A child should never be left alone playing in the bath or the kitchen sink.
9 Plastic bags must be removed from toys and immediately put away. Most bags carry warnings of the danger of suffocation.
10 To avoid bitter disappointment, check there are batteries to fit any battery-operated toys.

Growing up and getting mobile

This clever ball squeaks when squeezed, but has no squeaker to come loose. And that electric socket is protected with a safety socket cover, to keep little fingers out of the holes.

Now baby can support her own weight, and a Toddle Truck encourages good balance while she wheels her treasures from place to place. Note the rounded corners, just in case she takes a tumble.

Strong chip-proof plastic makes this Ball Barrow light and safe for young children. The large ball wheel runs easily over soft ground or sand.

Build it all up, take it all down, start all over again.

Brio-Mec is an exciting range of wooden construction sets for boys and girls from the age of four.

There are six sets full of blocks, beams, wheels and connectors, all smooth and safe for little hands to play with. And there are lots of accessories, too.

The special tools provided make building easy, helping children to develop their co-ordination and creativity.

It all adds up to the most original and imaginative toy. But, what else would you expect from Brio?

GATHERING INFORMATION...

One of the best ways of finding out which toys or games young children like is to ask either the children or their parents!

There are several ways of finding out information from people. You can use surveys, interviews or questionnaires. These are all useful techniques but, for all of them, success depends on the right questions. These need to be clear and easy to understand, short and to the point. You will also need to be able to record the answers in some way and to draw conclusions from the results.

Remember that the sample of people you choose to ask will need to be quite large, otherwise you will not get enough information on which to base your ideas.

8 Design a mini-questionnaire to try out on about 20 of your friends to find out what their favourite toys or games were when they were younger. Try to find out what it was they actually liked about them. Think hard about the questions to ask and about the information you will need about the friends you survey. Will it help to know their approximate ages, for example?

Decide how to record their answers and note them down clearly. Then try out your questionnaire. Finally, study the answers and state what conclusions you can draw from them.

A good way of organising information is to use a computer database. It does not need to be expensive or complicated.

When you record the information on the database make sure that the same words are used each time to describe the same things. For example, if one person gives 'building bricks' as a response and another puts 'building blocks' you need to record both of them with the same name, e.g. 'blocks' or 'bricks'. It will also be important to spell the information correctly or the computer will not be able to find out what you want to know.

Toys and Games

Name: Joanna Farmer
Age: 4
Sex: F
Favourite toys: Bricks, jigsaws, books
Favourite games: Ludo, snakes & ladders
Outdoor toys: Tricycle
Outdoor games: Skipping, hide & seek

Think carefully about the headings you use in your questionnaire as it is helpful if they can also be the headings in your database.

When you have enough records entered in the database, you will be able to search it very quickly for answers to questions such as: How many girls liked jigsaws? How many children who enjoyed books also liked football?

DESIGN PROPOSAL

PLANNING A COURSE
OF ACTION

You should now be ready to use all your information to generate a design proposal. In your group, *brainstorm* ideas for specific toys or games you could make. Discuss each idea. Explain what you think the child will be learning. Be ready to decide on one idea for yourself and explain why you think it is the best one.

Having decided what you want to do, you now need to plan your work. If your work is well planned you will be more organised and waste less time. It is useful to work out a sequence in which to work, then you will know exactly what to do next and what equipment you might need.

9 Below is a jumbled up sequence of work for someone making a storybook for a child. With a partner, sort out the sequence into a sensible order of work.

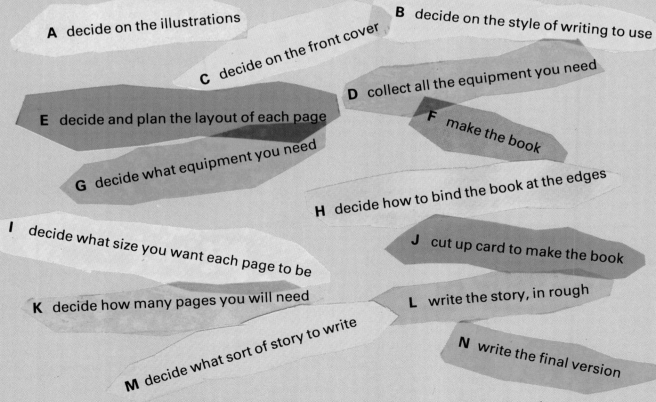

A decide on the illustrations

B decide on the style of writing to use

C decide on the front cover

D collect all the equipment you need

E decide and plan the layout of each page

F make the book

G decide what equipment you need

H decide how to bind the book at the edges

I decide what size you want each page to be

J cut up card to make the book

K decide how many pages you will need

L write the story, in rough

M decide what sort of story to write

N write the final version

Now work out a similar sequence for the toy or game you have decided to make.

DESIGN PROPOSAL

4

HOW WELL DID I DO?

When you talk or write about what you have learned and how well you have done, you are **evaluating** your design. It is not always easy to do this well, yet it can be the most important part of the whole learning process. An evaluation is an opportunity to show what you have learned and, more importantly, it offers you the chance to say how you would do better if you did the task again. An evaluation involves being able to:

JUSTIFY: Explaining what you did, what happened and why you think it happened.

ANALYSE: Working out why things went well or badly.

HYPOTHESISE: Being able to say 'what might happen if . . .' and suggesting what to do differently next time.

Part of your evaluation will involve discussing the product you have made and deciding how well it answered the task. This means looking back to the original design criteria and using them to assess the end-product. For example, if you had made a storybook, one of your criteria might be to see whether the story appealed to the child. If the child got bored half way through the story then you could say that it did not meet this criterion.

10 With your partner, study these evaluations of their work made by a group of technology students. Where can you find these students justifying, analysing and hypothesising about their work? Where are they making the mistake of just describing what they did or making general statements which are not justified?

Well, I didn't take it to 5A in the end as they were always away or ill. So I decided to take my item to a playgroup. I told a boy called James that I had a book and his friend, Simon, asked if I'd read it to him. I said 'yes'. I went to go and get it from my bag in the back room.

I followed the plan that I had written out all the way through and carried it out successfully. My results were very pleasing, both to me and the child. I wrote my plan in rough first and took it from day to day putting down what I was going to do each day. I spent little time on each bit, so that I had time to change any parts if I wanted to. I spent roughly 20–30 minutes each day and I found I could fill in quite a bit of information in that time.

Soon after, I went out and chose the material at the same time. I wish now that when I bought the material I had bought all of the 'activities' at the same time. I found it very inconvenient having to stop what I was doing all because I had not bought a certain activity.

As I progressed through the weeks I kept a diary of everything that I did each lesson. Looking back over it, I realise that my main problem was sewing on all the pockets and activities. With each pocket I had to measure where it had to go; and then sewing on the pocket I found very tricky because I kept going off the edge of the hem!

I gave Megan her apron last October half-term. When she first saw it she smiled and her hand went straight towards the pockets and different activities. She asked me if she could put it on. I gave it to her and she put it on over her head. I noted the hole for the head was about the right size because Megan did not have any trouble getting it over the head. After about the first 20 minutes the novelty of using the pocket wore off. I wish I had sewn more on but I could not because it was an apron and I could not fit anything else on without it looking too much over the top.

If I made the apron again, I would choose the same colours because they were bright and attractive. Also, I would put the pocket that was at the top, slightly lower, so that it was not awkward to reach. There is nothing else I would change about the apron.

Looking back I wish I spent more time on the book, so that I could have put a few more pages in and also a lot more ideas. I felt I could have produced a lot more work and put a bit more effort into it. When I had a look at some other people's pieces of work, I could see that they had put a lot of hard work into them and spent a lot more time on their work than I did.

Now, write a brief evaluation of the work you have done so far for this unit. Try to explain what you set out to do (justify), what went well or badly (analyse) and how you could have (hypothesise) improved your work. Swap your evaluation with your partner's and ask them to comment on the good points about your evaluation and ways in which you might improve it.

As you have worked through this unit, you may have thought of other ideas for learning toys or, perhaps, for one which does not already exist. For example, you might have started to think about making learning play-aids for children who are blind. In other words, you have identified a new need . . . and so you are ready to write your own brand new design brief.

Tips for Success

◆ As you talk and discuss use large sheets of paper to jot down your ideas as they occur to you.

◆ Read a design brief carefully, thinking about the implication of what it asks for as well as what it actually says on the surface.

◆ Write notes and plans as your work progresses and modify them where necessary. Try to be flexible and organised. Designing questionnaires and writing design evaluations need plenty of careful thought and planning before you begin to write.

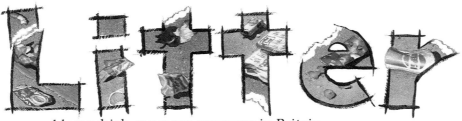
Litter

This unit focuses on a problem which concerns everyone in Britain today – litter. You will be asked to think about the kinds of waste left around in a typical town, who is responsible for it and what can be done.

you will be....

- Sharing ideas
- Recounting events
- Responding to a range of texts
- Arguing a point of view
- Locating and selecting information
- Solving problems

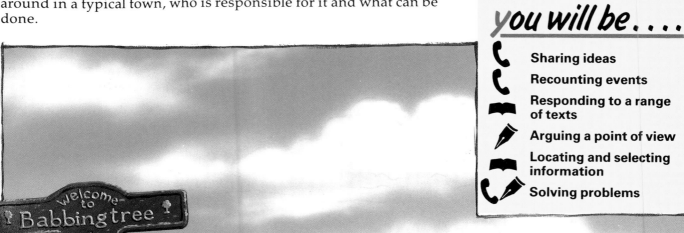

Welcome to Babbingtree

This is Babbingtree, a town in the Midlands with a population of 70,000. Babbingtree is 25 miles north of Northurst which is the third largest city in the country and a major industrial, business and cultural centre.

Babbingtree has several small, flourishing industries including electronics, frozen vegetable packing and light engineering. The headquarters of a large insurance company, Midland Mutual Insurances (MMI), have recently relocated there. It has a further education college, a horticultural college, three secondary schools and several primary schools.

The centre of the town is a mixture of the old and the new. Some buildings date back to the eighteenth century and the remains of the castle to earlier, Norman times. Ten years ago, a new shopping precinct was built in the centre of the town with a multi-storey car park adjoining it.

Saturday and Wednesday are the busiest days in town. Frequently, on Saturday there is a queue to get into the car park. Wednesday is market day; on that day the Market Place is closed to traffic and the streets around the market are very busy.

The Breakaway Guide to Britain

Babbingtree

The town stands at the point where the River Babbing meets the Dorring. Little now remains of the castle which dates back to the Norman period. Sir William Pennington, at one time a favourite of Elizabeth I, was imprisoned in the castle for 15 years until his death in 1574 for his alleged part in the Catholic plot. The castle was destroyed by fire in 1803.

St Matthew's Parish Church has a fine flint tower dating from the fifteenth century. The brasses to Margaret and Hugh Bostock, parents of the poet Charles Bostock, are among the noteworthy monuments of the church. Although Charles Bostock rarely returned to Babbingtree as an adult, he recalls the town in the following lines from his poem *Harmony*:

Peaceful thoughts soothe my troubled mind,
As I remember those waters clear
Of Babbing Brook . . .

Just outside the town is Babbing Hall which was built by Robert Adam in the mid-eighteenth century. It is still the family home of the Childs, but the gardens, with their exquisite orchids, are open to the public throughout the summer months.

The town of Babbingtree offers good shops and services.

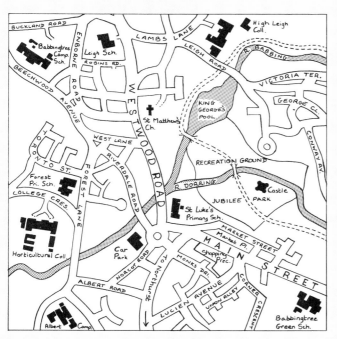

A load of rubbish

Babbingtree is undoubtedly a pleasant town. But the view of the town on the previous page does not give the full picture. People are becoming increasingly aware of a growing problem in Babbingtree – litter.

There are three main trouble spots in the town – as well as some more general problems.

LITTER PROBLEM 1

Maxiburger's – the best burgers in the Midlands

Two years ago, Maxiburger's opened a take-out hamburger shop in the shopping precinct, close to the cinema and a short walk from Babbingtree Green School and High Leigh College.

Open from 10 o'clock in the morning until midnight, Maxiburger's is very popular with young people.

Opposite the take-out in the precinct is a circular flowerbed surrounded by a low concrete wall. Many people sit on this wall to eat their hamburgers. There are also two seats nearby which are in constant use by Maxiburger's customers.

There are litter bins outside Maxiburger's. However, hamburger cartons and paper bags litter the precinct and surrounding streets.

LITTER PROBLEM 2

The Market Place

Wednesday is market day in Babbingtree. It is a popular market which sells almost anything from toys and clothes to meat and vegetables. There are usually more than 30 stalls.

The market traders set out their stalls before nine in the morning and pack up by about 4 o'clock in the afternoon – sometimes earlier on a cold or wet day. They leave whatever they do not want to take away – empty boxes, papers, waste vegetables and fruit – on the street. This is taken away by refuse collectors who start work at 5 o'clock. Market Place is usually then sprayed with water.

LITTER PROBLEM 3

The river

The most popular part of the river flows past St Luke's Primary School and Haw's shirt factory to the Jubilee Park and Recreation Ground, widening into King George's Pool, a popular fishing spot. The towpath is edged by trees and in the spring the flowering chestnuts and hawthorn make a lovely sight.

Just beyond King George's Pool, the river flows close to Victoria Terrace. Here, several houses have been boarded up before modernisation plans are put into action. The fence dividing the park and river from Victoria Terrace is low and broken in places. Rubbish – large household items such as prams, mattresses, bikes and chairs – is frequently dumped here.

There are two small bridges over the river in the park. These are used by pedestrians and cyclists. Both bridges are covered with graffiti – slogans and names sprayed in paint.

GENERAL LITTER PROBLEMS

There are other litter worries:

— dogs fouling the pavements, particularly near the park
— dogs fouling areas in the park where children play
— litter around the bus station, outside certain shops (particularly sweet shops), near the bingo hall and cinema
— graffiti on the telephone kiosks and on the walls of the public lavatories.

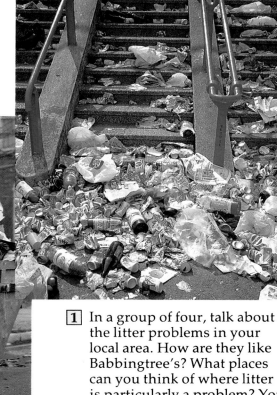

1 In a group of four, talk about the litter problems in your local area. How are they like Babbingtree's? What places can you think of where litter is particularly a problem? You might think about where there are take-away food shops, rail and bus stations, shops close to school or about the places where rubbish is frequently tipped into rivers or on to wasteland.

POINTS OF VIEW

Many people in Babbingtree are aware of such problems. Their opinions vary, however, about who or what is to blame and what can be done about the problems. Below and on the next three pages, some of them give their views:

A Police Community Liaison Officer

'Illegal dumping and littering are real problems in the town. The trouble is finding the culprits. We couldn't possibly draft police officers all over the town and get them to lie in wait all night in the hope of catching people who dump things. However, our best officers are liaising with community groups to discuss the problem and ways of letting people know that it is illegal – and that if we catch them we won't have any hesitation in prosecuting. Most people behave well and don't litter. It's the same old problem of a few people spoiling things for the majority.'

Some adult residents

'You see children coming out of the sweet shop eating a chocolate bar and just dropping the wrapper in the street.'

'It's not just children who drop litter. I've seen all age groups drop litter.'

'Cleaning up litter is the work of the street cleaners. It's not my job.'

'It's not Babbingtree people who drop litter. On market day and Saturday the town is full of people from all over the place. They don't have an interest in the town so they don't care where they throw their litter.'

'What can you expect from the way young people are brought up today!'

'People just don't care anymore about how the town looks. Years ago you never saw the mess you do nowadays.'

'I know I'm only one person, but if we all play a part there won't be a litter problem.'

'Generally, I think people try to be tidy. But the street cleaners leave a lot to be desired.'

'People go on about dogs fouling the pavements, but most dog owners control their animals very well. I think it's a problem which is very much exaggerated in this town.'

Gus Warner, Manager of Public Health and Safety Services

'During the last two years, we've set up two bottle banks – one near the shopping precinct and one on the edge of the town. They've been very successful. We're now looking into other possibilities, such as an aluminium can bank which would work in a similar way. People would deposit their used cans in bins for recycling. The Aluminium Recycling Can-paign is advising us on this. I have also had discussions with other groups about the possibility of collection points for newspapers and magazines. But that won't overcome the sort of problem we've got in parts of the town. We have easily enough litter bins for the town's needs, but still people throw their litter anywhere. We've somehow got to make people more aware of their actions and the role they can play in making this a clean town.'

A park keeper

'You wouldn't believe the stuff that gets dumped here – beds, bikes, prams, anything people don't want. There was even a three-piece suite here the other day. And it's not children doing that. Each week we have to get it taken away. There's a proper place run by the Council at the bottom of Toronto Street where you can dump stuff. Or, if you can't get there, you can ring the Council and they'll come and collect it for you. But I don't know if people know about that service. It would stop a lot of dumping if they mended the fence so that people couldn't just toss rubbish over from Victoria Terrace. It would also help if the park was patrolled regularly at night.'

Leonora Watson, a Councillor with responsibility for refuse services

'I'm prepared to admit that we haven't solved all the problems of littering, but we've made huge strides. This Council must have one of the best records in the area for public services – and refuse collection is just one of those. We are planning a poster campaign in the autumn, though, to make people more aware of their responsibilities in keeping Babbingtree clean.'

William Doyle, an opposition party Councillor

'It's my view that this Council simply isn't moving with the times. The numbers of street cleaners involved in cleaning the market is the same as years ago when there wasn't half the volume of rubbish that there is today. And where are all the litter bins? I walked the full length of Main Street yesterday and the only litter bin was a small one attached to a lamppost. At eleven in the morning it was already overflowing. It's all right going on as Leonora Watson does about changing people's attitudes. If you don't provide the services and facilities you can't blame people if they fail to keep the town clean.'

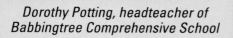

Dorothy Potting, headteacher of Babbingtree Comprehensive School

'We're very keen to encourage the right attitudes in our students. Litter is a constant theme in assemblies and we've had two sponsored clean-ups of the streets around the school. Certainly, students act responsibly in school – the school site is very clean.'

Camilla Logan, manageress of a natural beauty product shop

'We now have a sign up saying "Do you really need a bag?" and describing the need to cut down on the amount of packaging we use and waste. But people are slow to change their ways. They've taken their goods home in a bag for years and they'll go on doing that! The young people seem more aware of the issues.'

Abdus Shahid, owner of a sweet shop

'There's one waste bin inside the shop and one just outside, but some people still drop their wrappers in the street. I think they ought to design new bins, though. Some of the ones we have in the town are completely the wrong shape and size for the job they're supposed to do. They're either too small or the part where you drop the litter in is in the wrong place or at an inconvenient angle.'

Doreen Morris, owner of a shop selling newspapers and magazines

'I see my job as selling newspapers, magazines, sweets and cigarettes. There is a litter bin just outside the shop and I keep the shop really neat and tidy. But what people do with the stuff they buy from me is no concern of mine. I'm not going to go around telling them what to do with their wrappers or their newspapers – that's up to them.'

Jim Murphy, chairperson of Willowtree Street Tenants' Association

'People who live in streets like this feel forgotten. They can never get repairs done in time. No one seems to care. It's no wonder that people don't take a pride in the area. That piece of land there in front of those houses could be made into a proper play area for the kids, but it isn't. It's just left year after year – and then people dump their rubbish on it.'

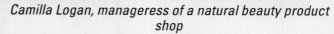
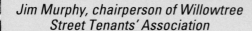

Local school students

'As usual, we get blamed for everything! I don't reckon we drop any more litter than anyone else, but it's convenient to pick on us.'

'Well, we hang about the bridge in the park because it's somewhere to meet. Sometimes, people write their names on it or draw a bit on it. It's just something to do, that's all.'

'It's awful if people dump glass. Animals get cut by it – and it looks so terrible.'

'We read about a Junior Friends of the Earth group in London and we wondered about getting a group together here.'

'Of course there's more litter around Maxiburger's because people eat there, but it's not a big problem. Most people put it in the bins.'

Elizabeth Butcher, Green Party representative

'We've run two successful campaigns in the town; one to get another bottle bank established, and one to get the aluminium can bank set up. We've also been campaigning to get shops to introduce biodegradable plastic bags. Every month we have a stand outside the supermarket on a Saturday to inform people of some of the issues – and there's a lot of interest in "green" issues now. I think people have got to feel that they have a say in what happens around them. Then they take more interest in the environment.'

George Grimstead, local MP

'Several people in the constituency have raised the matter of litter in the precinct in Babbingtree. I've written to the Council about it. It's not a question of having more people employed to clean the area, but of making sure that those who are supposed to do the job really do get on with it.

'There's always a problem where you get these hamburger places. The packaging they use may serve their purposes all right but it's a disaster if it gets on to the streets.'

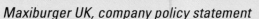

Lina Daley, student at High Leigh College

'As a vegetarian, I don't eat at Maxiburger's. It isn't just the business of eating meat I object to, though. Look at what the burgers are packed in; a polystyrene box which is used for a few minutes but takes hundreds of years to disintegrate. If you burn it, no doubt it adds more poisonous gases to the atmosphere. Generally, though, you just see them cluttering up the streets.'

Maxiburger UK, company policy statement

'Aware of its environmental responsibilities, Maxiburger UK has invested heavily in a comprehensive programme of research to explore alternative packaging forms. The present packaging form for our burgers is the polystyrene clamshell container. This ensures hygiene, protects the food from damage and is cheap to produce. Since 1988, no CFCs have been used in the manufacture of these packages.

'Our current research programme involves trials with alternative fully degradable packaging forms. So far, these have not proved as cheap and efficient as the polystyrene clamshell. The company is, however, confident that future developments will reduce costs and overcome other current problems such as heat loss.'

Kevin O'Shea, manager of Maxiburger's, Babbingtree

'We have two large litter bins on each side of the doors of Maxiburger's. We also have a large poster above the counter reminding customers not to drop their litter. As an environmentally aware company, we take the question of litter very seriously. We are considering printing an anti-litter slogan on our chip bags – which, incidentally, are made from recycled paper.'

Lisa Williams, environmental health inspector

'Some people say that we get the rats we deserve. A bit of burger and a greasy chip paper are a banquet to a rat.'

Bert Parker, market inspector

'The market cleaners do a good job – that's for sure. The difficulty stems from the different times that people choose to pack up their stalls. Some are gone by 2 o'clock – often the ones selling food leave quite a lot of rubbish. Other stall holders are still there two hours later. It's pointless trying to clean up the area until the last one has left. On a windy day, though, some of the litter does start to blow around before the street cleaners have got into action.'

Dr Shoona Patel, local doctor

'Dog mess can be dangerous. The main health threat is through a little bug called *toxocara canis*. If someone catches *toxocara canis* they can go blind or suffer brain damage. And the people most at risk are children who play where dogs roam. It's essential that owners act responsibly, keeping their dogs away from areas such as sandpits where they know children play.'

Maggie Rivvington, representative of the Clean Up Babbingtree group

'The fouling of pavements and grassy areas in the park is a problem in Babbingtree. I think we need to set aside – and mark it clearly – 'dog toilet' areas in the park. But we also need a poster campaign warning people of the fines which they might receive if their dogs foul the pavements.'

Dave Hatcher, youth leader

'Not all the graffiti you see about is vandalism. I've seen fantastic art produced by kids as graffiti. But more commonly, graffiti is done to deface a building. Look at the public lavatory walls in Babbingtree. They're a mess. But that's not just young people who have done that.'

Wilson Prescott, community artist

'We've had projects with one of the secondary schools and with the youth club to encourage more awareness of the environment. In both cases we produced 'organised graffiti' – wall paintings which were planned and executed by a group and which expressed a message or theme. In these projects we covered dull, grey walls and the results were terrific. I think the kids became very aware of the difference between this kind of art form and scrawling your name on the wall.'

Talk rubbish!

2 In a group of four, look back over these different views and facts.

- Make a list of all the reasons put forward to explain why there is a litter problem in Babbingtree. Then put the reasons into a ranked list, with the reasons which you think are most important at the top, and those which you think are least important at the bottom.

- Then, list all the possible solutions to Babbingtree's litter problems which are mentioned and others you can think of. Rank these in the same way, putting them in order of priority – with the thing that should be done first at the top of the list.

JUNK JOURNALISM 1

The Sunday News

Pressure groups like Greenpeace and political parties like the Green Party have made people become interested in issues like waste disposal. Now they are news.

For several weeks, *The Sunday News* – national tabloid newspaper – has run articles featuring various litter and waste issues. This week, the editor has decided that the approach will be to show what a common problem litter is throughout the country. She wants to make the point by showing these trouble spots in a typical English town. Her brief for the story is 'The scandal of our dirty towns'.

The editor asks you to write the article. You look on the map and decide on Babbingtree.

---

3 From the information about Babbingtree on pages 190 to 193 and the opinions of people on pages 194 to 197, select those which you feel could support the line of your article and make some notes from them.

■ Remember that your article intends to put a one-sided view; that towns in Britain like Babbingtree are being spoiled by litter. You want to make this case as strongly as you can so be quite selective about the information you use.

■ Choose a headline for your article. It should catch the reader's eye and give strong clues as to what your article is about.

■ You have been told by your editor that your article will be the main one on the middle page of the newspaper. The headline will spread across the top of the page. Your article should fill almost half of the page and should be between 500 and 600 words.

■ Write the article. Plan and draft it carefully.

AS
YOU
REPORT

JUNK JOURNALISM 2

The Babbingtree and District Gazette

Many people in Babbingtree are outraged to see their town featured in a national newspaper as a litter problem! The local weekly paper, *The Babbingtree and District Gazette*, decides to counter *The Sunday News*. The editor decides that a front-page article is needed – one which argues strongly against the damaging view put forward by *The Sunday News*.

The editor asks you to write the article.

4 As you plan and draft, you will need to emphasise the lack of litter in most parts of the town and stress the responsible attitude taken by most people towards the problem. You will have to describe the measures which the Council and other groups are taking to deal with any litter problems which do exist.

■ Now write the article. Give it a headline which captures the angle of your story. It will take three-quarters of the front-page space of the newspaper – between 750 and 800 words.

■ Remember that this a local newspaper. You can describe places in more detail. Certain people, such as councillors, will be known to readers.

● *Include quotations from some of the people involved as if you have interviewed them.*

● *Select the information and views which support the point you are making. Be ruthless about excluding anything which supports the other side of the argument.*

● *Open the article with a 'strong' first paragraph which will catch the reader's attention. Write it in capital letters in your final draft.*

Different views

The editors of both newspapers know that it is important to illustrate the articles on the Babbingtree litter problem with photographic material. Both editors ask you to select the main photograph.

5 Choose the photograph for each article from the photographs on this page. Write a caption of about 50 words for each chosen photograph which supports the style and argument of the article it will illustrate.

Cleaning up

6 While litter is a national problem there are many common-sense ways it can be tackled. Work with a partner on the following simple, yet practical, local solutions.

▬ The manager of Maxiburger's Babbingtee mentioned that his company was thinking of printing an anti-litter slogan on the chip bags used in the shop.

Write and design that slogan.

▬ Several people in Babbingtree mentioned litter bins. Abdus Shahid pointed out how unsuitable some of the bins were for the job they were supposed to do.

Design a litter bin for use in the precinct in Babbingtree. Before you start, draw up a design brief which says something about the need for the bins to be noticed, to be wind and animal proof, and so on.

▬ One Babbingtree resident talked of the need for a poster campaign directed against the fouling of pavements by dogs.

Design the poster. Think of a message or slogan which conveys the meaning of the campaign and is easily remembered. Illustrate the poster with your own drawings or pictures cut out from magazines and colour supplements.

In your own back yard

7 Use all the ideas you have encountered in thinking about Babbingtree and see which of them could be used to do something about the problem of litter in your own area.

Follow this outline:

— Locate the problem. Describe the area and the kinds of litter involved. A sketch map, drawings or photographs may help.
— Say what can be done. Write a plan and timetable for cleaning up the area. Say who it will involve and describe any special equipment required.

Tips for Success

◆ As you discuss the causes of litter pollution and what can be done about it, do not just blame the people you think are responsible. Talk about the problems *objectively* and look for practical solutions which could work.
◆ As you read about Babbingtree, try to relate what is happening there to your own experience and see how different places compare.
◆ As you write about litter pollution, remember that everyone drops litter sometimes. Do not let your writing preach to people – recognise the problems and suggest ways that individuals can tackle them.

poems and paintings

This unit is about poems and paintings and the similarity in the ways we react to them. The poems and pictures featured here are closely related but in different ways. Sometimes, a poet has written about a particular painting or the painter has interpreted some well-known poetry. At other times, poet and painter are one and the same person.

In this unit, you will be looking at some of the connections in the way we 'read' poems and paintings, and at how our reading of one form can help extend our understanding of the other.

Read and respond

Poems and paintings come in all shapes and sizes and convey many different messages to readers and viewers alike. So, learning to read them means responding to an enormous variety of thoughts, feelings and ideas.

One way to start to look at poems and paintings is by thinking about the ideas and questions they raise in your mind rather than trying to decide at once what they are about or what they show.

1 With a partner, look carefully at the painting opposite by René Magritte and jot down your thoughts about it before reading the accompanying poem by R S Thomas. Talk about your reactions to both of them. Some notes and questions have been jotted down already. They may help you to get started.

you will be . . . .

  Responding to a range of texts

  Responding to literature

  Writing a narrative or poem

A long, thin poem, perhaps like the missing model?

Victim of a firing squad?

Ghoulish humour playing on the idea of down-at-heel and ingrowing toenails.

The Red Model
by R S Thomas

Given the boots
solitary against
the boards, I construct
the body, kneed
and hooded, perforated
with dark, taken
away at dawn on
a barrow to be provender
of a grave.
　　　　Tall
and shapeless, too
(as they deemed)
big for them, he
left them behind,
not for robins
to build nests in,
not for the dust to tell
boneless time; for his out-
at-toe ghost to walk
onward for ever against
an ingrowing thought.

Why this title? — 'THE RED MODEL'
Where's the red? by René Magritte
The picture
makes me uneasy.

Change taking
place.
Is a person
about to appear?
Or is s/he just
disappearing?

Empty space
implies a
missing, ghostly
figure.
Horror film
image.

Why is the
right foot
turned outward?

Human feet and leather boots.
Humans kill animals for their skin.

203

2 Now, study the painting below and read through the two poems. Choose the poem you prefer and make your own list of the ideas and questions the painting and the poem raise in your mind. Compare your ideas with someone who has chosen the other poem.

Then write a short piece about how you and the poet of your choice each responded to the painting. How far do you share the poet's reading of the picture?

'The Badminton Game'
by David Inshaw

The Badminton Game
by Connie Bensley

That morning, I awoke and went down
just as I was, in my green slippers
to look at the hydrangea mariesii –
the only flower Clifton allows in the garden,
for he must have his trees and shrubs.

Out I crept, my slippers darkening in the dew,
and hearing a movement behind me
I turned and found Ruth. She was carrying
the racquets: and so – smiling, not speaking –
we ran between the great bushes to the net,

and there we played (quietly, of course,
so that Uncle Edward might not hear)
until the breakfast gong recalled us.
We ran up the back stairs en deshabille,
and down the front ones, decorous but tardy,

and kissed Uncle Edward: but I took care
to embrace him as he likes best, to forestall
reproof. Colour rose up behind his moustache
and his face worked silently, but then he vanished,
as usual, behind *The Times*.

The Badminton Game
by Heather Harvey

This is a green planet.
  We can see Earth from here,
  Ringed with light in the clear air,
  Where wind-shattered clouds give way
  To the blue curve of open sky.

The evening slowly revolves,
  The shuttlecock drifts.
  Arms lift, and shadows stretch
  Down over the wide lawns.

The trees are here today.
  Inquisitive but wary,
  It took them three days to move
  Up from their long meadows,
  And round the corner of the house,
  As if on huge, invisible wheels.
  Now they watch us, leaning together,
  Looking over each other's shoulders.

The day is ending.
  Beyond us high walls wrap themselves
    with leaves,
  The pale hydrangeas droop in sleep,
  And dusk flows over the cool hills.

This is a green planet,
We can see Earth from here.

Different readings

Each reading we make of a painting is unique. This section invites you to think first about *how* you look at a painting, and then to consider two 'readings' of it by the same poet.

3 Look at the painting. How does your eye move about the picture? Which details do you notice and in what order? Make a quick sketch of the picture as on page 206 and number and note down your thoughts as you go.

■ Compare notes in small groups and notice the variety of ways in which people look at the painting and the different interpretations they have.

'The Poet Reclining'
by Marc Chagall

Time of day?
Think about the
trees silhouetted
against the
pink sky.

Think about
the colours.
What atmosphere
do they create?

Animals - figments
of the reclining
poet's imagination?

What's his
head against?

Elongated figure, awake or dreaming?
Why does he lie along the bottom
of the picture?

■ Now, read through Gerda Mayer's two versions (below) of her response to the picture. Talk about her interpretation and decide which version you prefer.

■ Using your own notes on your sketch and any ideas you have from Gerda Mayer's poems, write your own poem to express your reading of Chagall's painting; or, if you prefer, write an essay comparing the two versions.

THE POET RECLINING
by Gerda Mayer

The poet dreams himself willowy and at rest
In a rural retreat: it is what all poets dream of.
The sky is a dusky rose, night enters the trees;
He lies in a heartache of grass, it is so green.
Who's minding the beanrows, though? Who mucks the
    pig out?
Will the horse amble up to inspect him and slobber his
    face?
What if the neighbours (there's a fence) turn the radio
    up?
No – this is Arcadia, Vitebsk, the Garden of Eden;
The horse stands for peace, the pig is a piggy-bank
    merely;
What every good pastoral needs is a background of
    shelter and grub;
As for the poem – it searches for solitude
Before it can saddle the horse and make for the Seine.

THE POET RECLINING
by Gerda Mayer

All poets dream of this: the rural retreat,
The meadow stained-glass, a piggy-bank in the background.
A horse standing for freedom. The simple life.

Who's minding the beanrows, though? Who mucks the pig out?
Will the horse amble up to inspect him and slobber his face?
What if the neighbours (there's a fence) turn the radio up?

The sky is a dusky rose; night enters the trees.
He lies in a heartache of grass, it is so green.
Later, he'll saddle up and make for the Seine.

Poet and painter

William Blake was both a poet and an artist, who worked almost 200 years ago. He was not content to see his poems only as written texts. For Blake, each of his poem-pictures was a single work of art and he composed the pages of his books so that the poem and the picture both complemented and explained one another.

The example below, 'A Poison Tree', shows how Blake used natural things, like trees and plants to frame his poems and to symbolise his ideas. Study it with a partner.

4 Then, with your partner, discuss the poem and the picture. The design of the page is an illustration of the last verse. Talk about your answers to these questions:

— What is the argument of the poem? What is it saying about anger?
— How could you describe the mood of the poem?
— Do you read it as a moral poem – a warning, or one where Blake is gloating?
— How do the picture and the poem work together?
— How could you re-interpret the poem with an illustration of your own?

5 Now, write your own poem. Use a feeling or emotion as the subject for your poem and illustrate your page as Blake does.

A page from Blake's book of poems
Songs of Innocence and Experience

Paintings from poems

The death of Ophelia in Shakespeare's tragedy *Hamlet* was a favourite subject of Victorian painters.

Ophelia feels rejected by Prince Hamlet whom she was expected to marry. Upset to the point of madness, she collects wild flowers and, while arranging them over some branches, she falls into a shallow stream where she drowns – too disturbed to appreciate that she is in any danger.

The Queen's moving description of what happened has inspired many artists:

Arthur Hughes 'Ophelia' (1910) (below); John Everett Millais 'Ophelia' (1852) (top right); John William Waterhouse 'Ophelia' (1894) (bottom right).

There is a willow grows aslant a brook,
That shows his hoar leaves in the glassy stream;
There with fantastic garlands did she come
Of crow-flowers, nettles, daisies, and long purples
That liberal shepherds give a grosser name,
But our cold maids do dead men's fingers call them.
There, on the pendent boughs her coronet weeds
Clambering to hang, an envious sliver broke;
When down her weedy trophies and herself
Fell in the weeping brook. Her clothes spread wide,
And, mermaid-like, awhile they bore her up;
Which time she chanted snatches of old tunes,
As one incapable of her own distress.
Or like a creature native and indued
Unto that element. But long it could not be
Till that her garments, heavy with their drink,
Pulled the poor wretch from her melodious lay
To muddy death.

(Act IV Scene VII)

6 The three painters have each taken a different moment in Ophelia's death scene. With your partner, study the paintings carefully and jot down a few notes about the atmosphere and details of each one. As you talk, compare the paintings and decide which one you prefer and why.

Re-read Shakespeare's description. How do you visualise this scene? Jot down your thoughts and ideas, including any words and phrases from the text that particularly strike you. Make a collage of one of Ophelia's last moments, using words and pictures. Or, if you prefer, describe how you imagine the scene in a piece of writing.

ART GALLERY

7 Choose one of the following paintings or sculptures which appeals to you, or find another one in a book or in postcard form, and write about it in your own way. Think carefully about how to make your writing communicate the ideas, moods and feelings that the painting suggests to you.

For example, you could be a person in the painting or sculpture and could write down his or her thoughts; you could be the artist creating the work; you could try to capture the overall mood, or concentrate on some small detail.

Present your writing, and a copy of your chosen picture if possible, as a wall display or for your folder.

WEEPING WOMAN
PABLO PICASSO

A BAR AT THE FOLIES BERGÈRES
EDOUARD MANET

ROCKING CHAIR NO. 2
HENRY MOORE

ST GEORGE AND THE DRAGON
PAOLO UCCELLO

THE DOG
ALBERTO GIACOMETTI

Tips for Success

◆ As you and your group ask questions about pictures, sculptures and poems, do not feel you *have* to answer them. Rather, use the questions as the starting point for moving your talk into new areas.

◆ The way you read a poem or a work of art can be very important in helping you make sense of it. Think about what could be happening in the poem, or what impression the artist might want you to take away from a painting, rather than trying to state exactly what it is about.

◆ As you start to write in response to poems or works of art, let your ideas flow thick and fast. Only try to organise and structure them when you redraft.

FAIR IS FOUL

In this unit you are going to look closely at part of Shakespeare's play, *Macbeth* and see how a witch's prophecy corrupts an honest man. You will also see how, as a reader or a member of the audience, you can identify and follow particular *themes* in the course of a play.

Reading the future

People always think that they would like to know what is going to happen to them in the future. You might not read tea leaves in a cup or go to the fortune-teller at a fair but you have probably played simple prophecy games when you were younger. One famous game – 'Tinker, tailor, soldier, sailor . . .' – is played with cherry or plum stones. Or, you may have played other games, like the ones based on the letters and numbers on bus tickets which are supposed to reveal the initials of the name of the person you will marry.

Games like these have been played for centuries. Kings and other rulers often kept their own personal fortune-tellers or soothsayers, who were supposed to be able to see into the future. Fortune-tellers were once to be found in most large towns, while the accusation that they looked into the future was commonly used to justify the burning of women as witches.

Now, people are more realistic about such matters but personal horoscopes, based on the star constellations and the movements of the planets, are still a very popular way in which many people sneak a look at their futures in magazines or newspapers.

1. As a group, talk about your own experiences of prophecy, or retell stories you have heard your families tell. Also, look at the different examples of horoscopes on this page. Where and how often do you look at your horoscope? Does it ever seem to contain an element of truth? Has there been a day, or a time, when your horoscope seemed to be particularly accurate?

you will be . . . .

- Relating personal experience
- Responding to literature
- Locating and selecting information
- Commenting on language use
- Writing a narrative

Setting the scene

One thing you may notice about horoscopes and about similar kinds of prophecy is that they often hint at the likelihood of both good and bad things going on in any one person's life at the same time – that is why the advice contained in them can often seem to fit with what eventually does happen.

Many myths and stories revolve around the theme of prophecy. Several of Shakespeare's plays use this idea, and none more so than *Macbeth* in which an honourable Scottish noble is destroyed by the prophecy that he will be king.

Macbeth, the leading character in the play, has his future told to him by a group of witches but, like someone reading their horoscope in a newspaper, he notices only the points of the prophecy he wants to hear. Part of what the witches say comes true very quickly so Macbeth is then eager to make the rest of it happen.

As the play begins, the audience sees the witches as they plot their meeting with Macbeth:

First Witch When shall we three meet again?
   In thunder, lightning or in rain?
Second Witch When the hurlyburly's done,
   When the battle's lost and won.
Third Witch That will be ere the set of sun.
First Witch Where the place?
Second Witch Upon the heath.
Third Witch There to meet with Macbeth.
First Witch I come, Graymalkin.
Second Witch Paddock calls.
Third Witch Anon!
All Fair is foul, and foul is fair
   Hover through the fog and filthy air.

The prophecy

Shortly afterwards, Macbeth enters with his friend and fellow soldier, Banquo. They are on their way home after fighting loyally for Duncan, King of Scotland. Macbeth's opening line 'So foul and fair a day I have not seen' echoes the last words of the witches. On one level, these words could mean the weather is terrible and the battle was won but Shakespeare is hinting at more than that. Just as in the average horoscope there are good and bad elements, so there are two forces in Macbeth's life at this stage. The audience is meant to notice that the words he uses are the same as the words used by the evil witches. So, the theme of prophecy begins to unfold.

Now, read the scene below aloud, working in groups of five. Use a large space like a hall so that you can project your voices and have room to move around. Angus and Ross are other Scottish nobles and the castle at Forres is where the travellers are heading for.

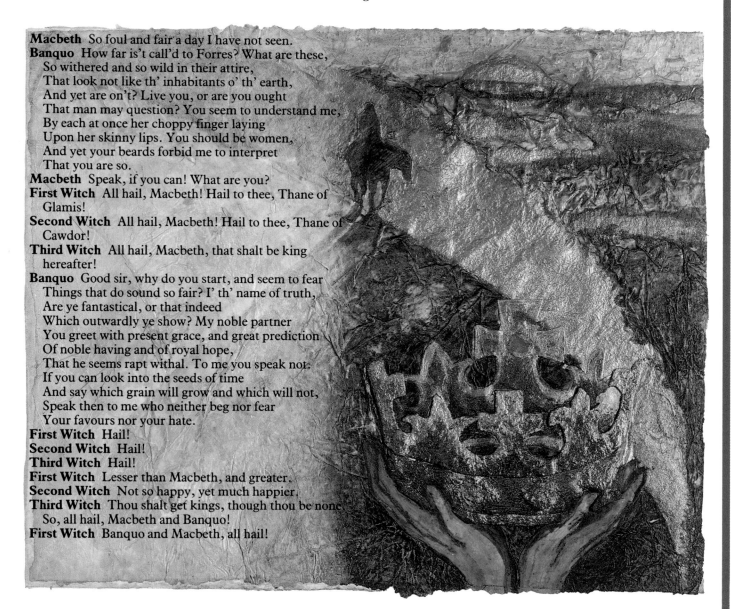

Macbeth So foul and fair a day I have not seen.
Banquo How far is't call'd to Forres? What are these,
So withered and so wild in their attire,
That look not like th' inhabitants o' th' earth,
And yet are on't? Live you, or are you ought
That man may question? You seem to understand me,
By each at once her choppy finger laying
Upon her skinny lips. You should be women,
And yet your beards forbid me to interpret
That you are so.
Macbeth Speak, if you can! What are you?
First Witch All hail, Macbeth! Hail to thee, Thane of Glamis!
Second Witch All hail, Macbeth! Hail to thee, Thane of Cawdor!
Third Witch All hail, Macbeth, that shalt be king hereafter!
Banquo Good sir, why do you start, and seem to fear
Things that do sound so fair? I' th' name of truth,
Are ye fantastical, or that indeed
Which outwardly ye show? My noble partner
You greet with present grace, and great prediction
Of noble having and of royal hope,
That he seems rapt withal. To me you speak not.
If you can look into the seeds of time
And say which grain will grow and which will not,
Speak then to me who neither beg nor fear
Your favours nor your hate.
First Witch Hail!
Second Witch Hail!
Third Witch Hail!
First Witch Lesser than Macbeth, and greater.
Second Witch Not so happy, yet much happier.
Third Witch Thou shalt get kings, though thou be none
So, all hail, Macbeth and Banquo!
First Witch Banquo and Macbeth, all hail!

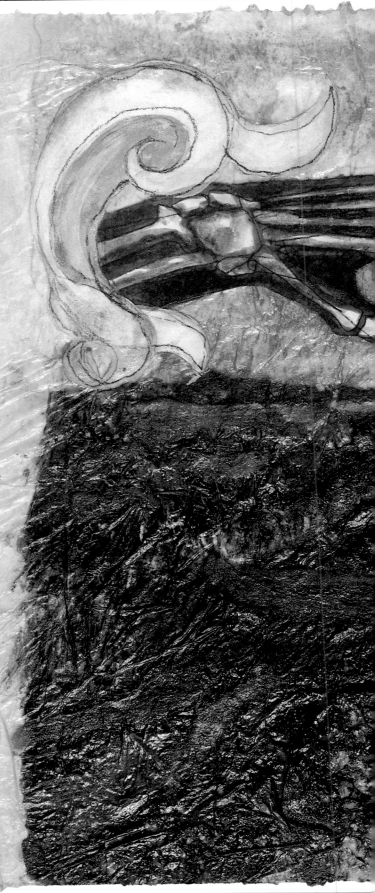

Macbeth Stay, you imperfect speakers, tell me more.
By Sinel's death I know I am Thane of Glamis;
But how of Cawdor? The Thane of Cawdor lives,
A prosperous gentleman; and to be King
Stands not within the prospect of belief,
No more than to be Cawdor. Say from whence
You owe this strange intelligence, or why
Upon this blasted heath you stop our way
With such prophetic greeting? Speak I charge you.

Witches vanish

Banquo The earth hath bubbles, as the water has,
And these are of them. Wither are they vanish'd?
Macbeth Into the air; and what seem'd corporal melted
As breath into the wind. Would they had stay'd!
Banquo Were such things here as we do speak about?
Or have we eaten of the insane root
That takes the reason prisoner?
Macbeth Your children shall be kings.
Banquo You shall be King.
Macbeth And Thane of Cawdor too; went it not so?
Banquo To th' self-same tune and words. Who's here?

Enter Ross and Angus

Ross The King hath happily receiv'd, Macbeth,
The news of thy success . . .
     . . . And, for an earnest of a greater honour,
He bade me, from him, call thee Thane of Cawdor;
In which addition, hail, most worthy Thane!
For it is thine.
Banquo What can the devil speak true?
Macbeth The Thane of Cawdor lives; why do you dress me
In borrow'd robes?
Angus Who was the Thane lives yet;
But under heavy judgment bears that life
Which he deserves to lose. Whether he was combin'd
With those of Norway, or did line the rebel
With hidden help and vantage, or that with both
He labour'd in his country's wreck, I know not;
But treasons capital, confess'd, and prov'd
Have overthrown him.
Macbeth *aside* Glamis, and Thane of Cawdor!
The greatest is behind. – Thanks for your pains.
     Aside to Banquo Do you not hope your children
          shall be kings,
When those that gave the Thane of Cawdor to me
Promis'd no less to them?
Banquo *aside to Macbeth* That, trusted home,
Might yet enkindle you unto the crown,
Besides the Thane of Cawdor. But 'tis strange;
And oftentimes to win us to our harm,
The instruments of darkness tell us truths,
Win us with honest trifles, to betray's
In deepest consequence. –
Cousins, a word, I pray you.

Macbeth *aside* Two truths are told,
  As happy prologues to the swelling act
  Of the imperial theme. – I thank you, gentlemen.
  aside This supernatural soliciting
  Cannot be ill; cannot be good. If ill,
  Why hath it given me an earnest of success,
  Commencing in a truth? I am Thane of Cawdor.
  If good, why do I yield to that suggestion
  Whose horrid image doth unfix my hair,
  And make my seated heart knock at my ribs
  Against the use of nature? Present fears
  Are less than horrible imaginings.
  My thought, whose murder yet is but fantastical,
  Shakes so my single state of man
  That function is smother'd in surmise,
  And nothing is but what is not.
Banquo Look how our partner's rapt.
Macbeth *aside*
  If chance will have me king, why, chance
  may crown me,
  Without my stir.

2 In your group, talk about your reading. First, look back through the text and identify exactly where:

— Macbeth realises that there may be some truth in what the witches have foretold and his attitude to them changes
— Banquo is startled and realises the same
— Macbeth realises that what he and Banquo have been told is dangerous and treasonable information which they must keep to themselves
— Macbeth argues with, and finally persuades himself, that the prophecy may come true for him.

Secondly, talk about how you can bring these reactions across in a reading of the scene. Think about how you might give the witches' words an almost unreal or evil sense so that they become sounds as well as words.

Rehearse, and then re-read the scene for the group.

Making it happen . . .

You may have noticed from the anecdotes and stories you shared earlier, that sometimes it is possible for people to do things, almost unconsciously, which make a prophecy come true. For example, if your horoscope says that this is a good week for foreign travel, you may think about planning a holiday. As Macbeth speaks about the prophecy to his wife and thinks about its implications, he begins to turn the fantasy that he could be king into the possibility that he will be.

3 With a partner, write the letter which Macbeth sends his wife on his arrival at Forres Castle. Try to communicate what you think his version of events might be and his mixed feelings about what has happened. Include as much relevant detail as you can from the part of the play you have read.

Later . . .

In the scene below, Lady Macbeth is reading a letter which Macbeth has sent to her. It describes his meeting with the witches.

Read it carefully with a partner.

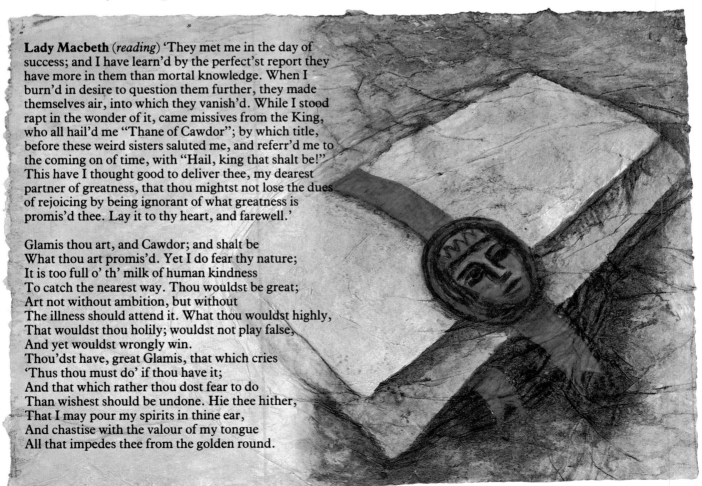

Lady Macbeth (*reading*) 'They met me in the day of success; and I have learn'd by the perfect'st report they have more in them than mortal knowledge. When I burn'd in desire to question them further, they made themselves air, into which they vanish'd. While I stood rapt in the wonder of it, came missives from the King, who all hail'd me "Thane of Cawdor"; by which title, before these weird sisters saluted me, and referr'd me to the coming on of time, with "Hail, king that shalt be!" This have I thought good to deliver thee, my dearest partner of greatness, that thou mightst not lose the dues of rejoicing by being ignorant of what greatness is promis'd thee. Lay it to thy heart, and farewell.'

Glamis thou art, and Cawdor; and shalt be
What thou art promis'd. Yet I do fear thy nature;
It is too full o' th' milk of human kindness
To catch the nearest way. Thou wouldst be great;
Art not without ambition, but without
The illness should attend it. What thou wouldst highly,
That wouldst thou holily; wouldst not play false,
And yet wouldst wrongly win.
Thou'dst have, great Glamis, that which cries
'Thus thou must do' if thou have it;
And that which rather thou dost fear to do
Than wishest should be undone. Hie thee hither,
That I may pour my spirits in thine ear,
And chastise with the valour of my tongue
All that impedes thee from the golden round.

4 Now, study the speech more closely. Try reading it using various tones of voice – soft and gentle, harsh and irritable, scornful and persuasive – as the speech changes in mood and tone. Decide between you:

— what Lady Macbeth thinks of her husband and his personality
— what impression the speech gives of the character and personality of Lady Macbeth.

What comes next?

5 Now, join with another pair and predict what may happen in the rest of the play. Use the events you know have already happened as your starting point.

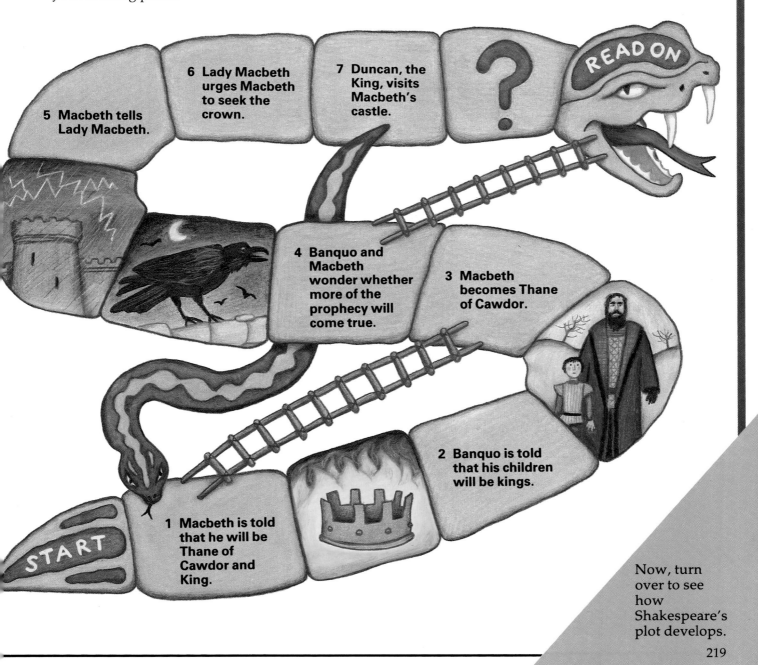

Now, turn over to see how Shakespeare's plot develops.

Back to the future

Coincidence brings King Duncan to Macbeth's castle. Encouraged by Lady Macbeth, Macbeth kills him and takes the crown for himself. Although he is now king, the witches' second prophecy that Banquo's children will be kings continues to haunt him. He has Banquo murdered but his son escapes. Macduff, another noble, starts to organise the opposition to Macbeth with the aim of putting Duncan's young sons back on the throne.

All around him opposition to Macbeth's rule is growing. The people around him are suspicious and he is now uncertain of what to do next. In a near panic he decides to go back to the witches, but this time he seeks them out. They have prepared their spells and are ready for him.

Read this scene in your group of four. Four ghostly apparitions are conjured up in front of Macbeth by the witches.

Second Witch By the pricking of my thumbs,
Something wicked this way comes. *Knocking*
Open, locks, whoever knocks.

Enter Macbeth

Macbeth How now, you secret, black, and midnight hags!
What is't you do?
All A deed without a name.
Macbeth I conjure you by that which you profess –
Howe'er you come to know it – answer me.
Though you untie the winds and let them fight
Against the churches; though the yesty waves
Confound and swallow navigation up;
Though bladed corn be lodg'd and trees blown down;
Though castles topple on their warders' heads;
Though palaces and pyramids do slope
Their heads to their foundations; though the treasure
Of nature's germens tumble all together,
Even till destruction sicken – answer me
To what I ask you.
First Witch Speak.
Second Witch Demand.
Third Witch We'll answer.
First Witch Say, if thou'dst rather hear it from our mouths,
Or from our masters?
Macbeth Call 'em; let me see 'em.
First Witch Pour in sow's blood that hath eaten
Her nine farrow, grease that's sweaten
From the murderer's gibbet throw
Into the flame.
All Come, high or low;
Myself and office deftly show.

Thunder. First Apparition, an Armed Head

Macbeth Tell me, thou unknown power –
First Witch He knows thy thought.
Hear his speech but say thou nought.
Apparition Macbeth! Macbeth! Macbeth! Beware Macduff;
Beware the Thane of Fife. Dismiss me. Enough. *Descends*
Macbeth Whate'er thou art, for thy good caution, thanks;
Thou hast harped my fear aright. But one word more –
First Witch He will not be commanded. Here's another,
More potent than the first.

Thunder. Second Apparition, a Bloody Child

Apparition Macbeth! Macbeth! Macbeth!
Macbeth Had I three ears, I'd hear thee.
Apparition Be bloody, bold, and resolute; laugh to scorn
  The pow'r of man, for none of woman born
  Shall harm Macbeth. *Descends*
Macbeth Then live, Macduff; what need I fear of thee?
  But yet I'll make assurance double sure,
  And take a bond of fate. Thou shalt not live;
  That I may tell pale-hearted fear it lies,
  And sleep in spite of thunder.

Thunder. Third Apparition, a Child Crowned, with a tree in his hand

What is this
That rises like the issue of a king,
And wears upon his baby brow the round
And top of sovereignty?
All Listen, but speak not to't.
Apparition Be lion-mettled, proud, and take no care
  Who chafes, who frets, or where conspirers are:
  Macbeth shall never vanquish'd be, until
  Great Birnam Wood to high Dunsinane Hill
  Shall come against him. *Descends*
Macbeth That will never be.
  Who can impress the forest, bid the tree
  Unfix his earth-bound root? Sweet bodements, good!
  Rebellion's head rise never till the wood
  Of Birnam rise, and our high-plac'd Macbeth
  Shall live the lease of nature, pay his breath
  To time and mortal custom. Yet my heart
  Throbs to know one thing; tell me, if your art
  Can tell so much – shall Banquo's issue ever
  Reign in this kingdom?
All Seek to know no more.
Macbeth I will be satisfied. Deny me this,
  And an eternal curse fall on you! Let me know.
  Why sinks that cauldron? And what noise is this?
First Witch Show!
Second Witch Show!
Third Witch Show!
All Show his eyes, and grieve his heart;
  Come like shadows, so depart!

A show of eight Kings, and Banquo last; the last king with a glass in his hand

Macbeth Thou art too like the spirit of Banquo; down!
  Thy crown does sear mine eye-balls. And thy hair,
  Thou other gold-bound brow, is like the first.
  A third is like the former. Filthy hags!
  Why do you show me this? A fourth? Start, eyes.
  What will the line stretch out to th' crack of doom?
  Another yet? A seventh? I'll see no more.
  And yet the eighth appears, who bears a glass
  Which shows me many more; and some I see
  That two-fold balls and treble sceptres carry.
  Horrible sight! Now I see 'tis true;
  For the blood bolter'd Banquo smiles upon me,
  And points at them for his. *The show vanishes*
  What! Is this so?

6 Study the scene together. Decide between you:

— the message which each apparition brings Macbeth and whether
  he is pleased or worried by it
— how this scene differs from Macbeth's first meeting with the
  witches
— how the events of this scene should cause you to change your plot
  plan. Revise it as necessary.

The final solution?

As the play goes on, Macbeth orders Macduff's wife and children to be killed and his castle destroyed. However, Macduff himself has already escaped. Lady Macbeth turns mad and dies.

With the ending of the play, most of the prophecies are fulfilled. The army led by Macduff besieges Macbeth's castle. To conceal their numbers they camouflage themselves with branches from the wood of Birnam and as they move 'a wood comes toward Dunsinane'. Finally, Macduff kills Macbeth after telling him he 'was from his mother's womb/untimely ripped'. He was born by what we know as a Caesarean section where the womb is opened and the baby released without the mother going into labour and having her baby naturally.

But, even as Duncan's son Malcolm invites the nobles to see him crowned, one prophecy remains to come true. Banquo's son can now return from exile and for long-term peace in Scotland the outlook remains bleak.

Following up the theme . . .

The power of prophecy played a major part in the downfall of Macbeth and his progress from being an honourable noble to becoming a despised and hated tyrant.

7 Now, write your own story, set in modern times, to parallel Macbeth's. Introduce the idea of prophecy at the beginning of the story and give your central character a partner like Lady Macbeth. Make your story develop in the same kind of way as Shakespeare's so that the hero returns for more guidance when things go wrong.

These ideas may help you get started:

■ A rock singer at the height of her career is persuaded to visit a fortune-teller who says that with a change of manager she could get to Number One . . .

■ An ambitious politician is persuaded by a strange visitor that chance may make him Prime Minister . . .

■ Playing games with a pack of cards and a glass, makes a teenager believe that she can make a fortune in stocks and shares with her father's credit cards . . .

Macbeth killed by Macduff at Dunsinane, in the BBC television production of Shakespeare's play.

Tips for Success

◆ As you speak Shakespeare's lines you will find your understanding of them gradually increases. Saying the words out loud can often help you to make sense of difficult sections.

◆ As you read the text, try first to understand the gist of it and do not worry if odd words are not clear. When you perform your reading, remember to project your voice and to speak slowly and clearly.

◆ As you follow the development of a theme like this, expect to find it reflected in the events and language of the play – not obviously, but in a subtle and suggestive way.

Acknowledgements

We would like to thank the following English teachers, advisers and others, who have prepared units, trialled material and otherwise contributed to the COLLINS ENGLISH PROGRAMME.

Karen Alexander, Sandra Anstey, P. Baldwin, J.M. Barker, Phyllis Bell, Sue Bowles, Cathy Boyle, Graeme Burton, Robin Brabban, Glyn Bradbury, Mary de Caires, Peter Catmull, Mary Clark, Lorna Cocking, Alan Combes, J. Coward, S. Crocker, Susan Daniels, J. Dawson, Reetha Desai, K. Downs, Kevin Eames, Philip Ellis, Alan Ellison, Dave Farrar, Liz Fincham, Angela Fitzgibbon, Jerry Fitzgibbon, Peter Foster, Gill Fox, Garrick Fraser, Pandora Gabidon, Janet Gaskell, Liz Gerschel, Dave Gilbert, Joan Goody, Arthur Graley, Sue Hart, I. Hathaway, Ken Haworth, Geoff Hill, A. and J. Hinchcliffe, J. Hitchcock, David Howe, Shelagh Hubbard, Chris Hunt, Mike Jones, Bridget Joslin, A. Khan-Cheema, E. Kircher, P.B. Knott, Stephen Kruger, D. Langford, Roger Lane, Margaret Leal, Patricia Lennon, M.J. Lunn, Sheila McCann, Norman Madden, John Mannion, D. Margett, Chris Miles, Diti Mukherjee, Peter Murray, Vaya Naidoo, Mike Newman, Mark Ormiston, M. Parker, Paul Patrick, Christine Peters, John Proctor, Jacqueline Purdie, Jacqueline Pyper, P. Quirke, Jeremy Radburn, Stephen Richardson, Graham Robertson, Jessica Rood, Andy Roughton, Pauline Rudman, Sean Russell, Angela Sinfailam, Patsy Spiller, P. Stock, John Sweetman, Enid Vaughan Edwards, Ian Wall, Andrew Ward, A. Webb, Judi Webb, Keith West, S. Woodmansey.

Units for the Collins English Programme were trialled in the following schools: Top Valley School, Nottingham; The Holy Cross School Broadstairs; Bedwas Comprehensive School, Newport; St Michael's RC School, Watford; Myton School, Warwick; Northlands High School, Preston; Williamwood High School, Glasgow; Wilcombe Middle School, Tiverton; Monkwearmouth School, Sunderland; Kings High School, Warwick; The Hurst School, Baughurst; Salesian College, Farnborough; Thirsk School, Thirsk; The Aylesford School, Warwick; The Friary School, Lichfield; The Mountbatten School, Hemel Hempstead; Broomfield School, Havant; Claverham Community College, Battle; Chapter School, Rochester; Brookhill and St Leonards, Hythe; Stratford School, Newham; Camphill High School, Paisley; Ullapool High School, Ross and Cromarty; Pensby School for Girls, Wirral; Olchfa Comprehensive School, Swansea; Walton Comprehensive School, Peterborough; St Bede's High School, Blackburn; Oakfield School, Frome; Test Valley School, Stockbridge; Brookway High School, Wythenshawe; St Michael's School, Watford; Stratford High School, Stratford upon Avon; The National Comprehensive School, Hucknall; Wheeler's Lane School, Birmingham; Westhoughton High School, Westhoughton; Southam School, Southam, Warwickshire; Crofton School, London; Fort Hill School, Basingstoke; Bramhall High School, Stockport; Garforth Comprehensive, Leeds.

Special thanks to the following for their contributions to these units:

Lori Reid for *The future in your hands*; Edwin Morgan for *Photo poems*; Julie Wales for *Household soap*; Alan Combes and the students at Pinder School, Scarborough for *Home ground*; Mary Vass and Lorna Cocking for *The Struggle*; Andy Tricker and John Mannion for *Life story*; David Griffiths for *Voice plays*; Shelagh Hubbard for *Sugar and snails*; Mary Vass for *Time management*; Andy Roughton and Lorna Cocking for *War stories*; Sue Butterworth and Marion Rose for *Hold the front page*; Nigel Turner and Marion Rose for *All in a day's work*; Lorna Cocking and Anne Brogan for *Burning issues*; Lorna Cocking for *Write from the heart*; Jan Needle for *The book of the film*; Jan Coles and Simon Crompton for *Design and build*; Lorna Cocking for *Litter*; Michael Benton for *Poems and paintings*; Liz Fincham for *Fair is foul*.

Also thanks to the following for their various help and advice: Stephen Attmore, John Boult, Stephen Cockett, Lorna Cocking, Information Technology Consultant Trevor Millum, Phoenix Antiques at Menai Bridge, Gareth Price, Carla Turchini, Claire Hartas, Christian Jarvis, Gillian Saville, Natalie Davey, Janine Ledger, Kamaldip Randhawa, Gill Newham, Jennie O'Connor, the parents of Stephanie Holmes, Curtis Reeve, Akira Newlands, Verdha Walikhan.

The following are thanked for permission to reproduce their material:

Penguin Books Ltd for the extracts from *Children Dreaming: Pictures in My Pillow* by Brenda Mallon, the covers of *Is That It?*, *Clinging to the Wreckage* and *My Childhood* and the extract from *Hiroshima* by John Hersey; Pat Arrowsmith for *The Day I Once Dreamed* from *Ain't I a Woman?* published by Virago Press; Jacqui Deevoy for Dreams extract; *Living* magazine for our adapted version of the *How to read your palm* feature from the December 1989 issue; Express Newspapers plc for the article from *Daily Express* and the front page and article from *Daily Star*; *Glasgow Herald* for two articles; *Hornsey & Muswell Hill Journal* for the article; Mirror Group Newspapers for the article from *Daily Mirror*; Raleigh Industries Ltd for the advertisement (applies to UK in 1991 only); *Just Seventeen* magazine for Best Mates material, the *Just Seventeen* cover and the horoscope; *Cambridge Evening News* for the article *Comical capers boost charity*; FISA (UK) Ltd for the postcard; *TV Times* for the soap update material; Horwitz Grahame Pty Ltd, New South Wales for the soap logo from *TV Soap* magazine; A.P. Watt Ltd on behalf of Graham Swift for the extract from *Waterland*; Pan Books Ltd for the *Waterland* cover; Oxford University Press for the extract from *Eagle of the Ninth* by Rosemary Sutcliff, the Toys extract from *All About Children* by D. Baldwin and *The Poison Tree* from *Songs of Innocence and Experience*; Brian Catchpole for the extract from *The Clash of Cultures*; Johnathan Cape Ltd for the poem by Hyllus Maris from *A Secret Country* by John Pilger; IDAF for *Hector P.* by Tembeka Mbobo, the extract by Dumisani Kumalo, *For A Dead African* by Dennis Brutus, *Dedication* by Mzandile Mguba, all from *The Child Is Not Dead*; B. Feinberg for *A Dry White Season* from *Poets to the People*; Heinemann Publishers Ltd for the extract from *No Easy Walk to Freedom* by Nelson Mandela; André Deutsch for the extracts and cover from *Accidents Will Happen* by Andy Tricker and the extract from *Crick Crack, Monkey* by Merle Hodge; *East Anglian Daily Times* for the extract *Crash victim's fight to succeed*; Virago Press for the extract and cover from *Gather Together In My Name* by Maya Angelou; Sidgwick and Jackson for the extract from *Is That It?* by Bob Geldof; Valentine Mitchell & Co for *The Diary of Anne Frank* cover; Octopus Publishing Group plc for *My Left Foot* cover and the extracts and illustration from *Bill's New Frock* by Anne Fine; by kind permission of Abacus Books for *If This Is A Man – The Truce* cover; Phillip Taylor for the autobiographical work; Sony Music for the *War of the Worlds* record cover; Madeleine Sotheby for *I Cried At Your Wedding*; John Murray Publishers Ltd for the 1857 and 1869 *Jane Eyre* covers; Thames Publishing Co. for the 1952 *Jane Eyre* cover; Fontana Lions, a division of HarperCollins for extracts from *No End To Yesterday* by Shelagh McDonald, *Going Out* and *A Game of Soldiers*; Equal Opportunities Commission for the employment by occupation information from the *Labour Force Survey 1988*; The Controller of Her Majesty's Stationery Office for statistics from *Statistics of Education School Leavers GCSE and CSE 1988*; Sheil Land Associates Ltd for *The Robot Who Looked Like Me* by Robert Sheckley, published by Sphere Books; Jane Waller and Michael Vaughan-Rees for the advertisement, article and recipe from *Women in Wartime* published by Macdonald and Co.; Grafton Books, a division of HarperCollins for two extracts from *War Wives* by Colin and Eileen Townsend; *South Wales Evening Post* for the front page material; Lois Clark for the poem from *In Time of War* published by Blackie and Son Ltd; William Collins Pty Ltd for the extract and illustrations from *My Hiroshima* by Junko Morimoto; James Kirkup for *No More Hiroshimas* from *These Horned Islands: A Journal of Japan* published by Collins and the Macmillan Company of America; *The Guardian* for the front page, masthead and cartoon; *The Independent* for the front page and article; *Today* for the front page and article; News Group Newspapers Ltd for the *Sun* masthead; Associated Newspapers Ltd for the *Daily Mail* masthead; United Kingdom Atomic Energy

Authority for the extracts; British Nuclear Fuels for the extracts; Friends of the Earth for the extracts; Evening Standard Company Ltd for the extract and the horoscope material; Spellbound Cards for the postcard; Grace Nichols for *Waiting for Thelma's Laughter*; A.L. Hendriks for *The Fringe of the Sea* from *The Blue Foot Traveller*; © Edward Kamau Brathwaite 1973 for *South*. Reprinted from *The Arrivants* (1973) by permission of Oxford University Press; Hamish Hamilton Ltd for the extracts from *The Thief* by Jan Needle; Thames Television for the extract from the television script of *The Thief*; Collins Educational for the play extract from *The Thief*; Maire Messenger Davies for the extract *Toy Play* from the article *It's fun to play*; Mothercare for the Growing up and getting mobile leaflet; Brio-Scanditoy Ltd for the advertisement; The Tidy Britain Group for the Tidy Britain Year 90 poster; Poetry Wales Press for *The Red Model* by R.S. Thomas from *Ingrowing Thoughts*; Connie Bensley for *The Badminton Game* from *Central Reservations* published by Bloodaxe Books; Heather Harvey 1990 for *The Badminton Game*; Gerda Mayer for *The Poet Reclining*; Peterloo Poets 1988 for *The Poet Reclining* by Gerda Mayer from *A Heartache of Grass*; Grizelda Holderness for the horoscope illustration from *Cosmopolitan*; *Best* for the horoscope; Reprinted courtesy of Dell Magazines © 1991, a division of Bantam Doubleday Dell Publishing Group, Inc., the front cover from Dell Horoscope Purse Book (1991).

Every effort has been made to contact the holders of copyright material but if any have been inadvertently overlooked the publishers will be pleased to make the necessary arrangements at the first opportunity.

ILLUSTRATORS

Catherine Denvir: 4, 5, 6-7, 8-9
Jack McCarthy: 10-12
Diane Fisher: 13, 14-19
Stuart Hughes: 20, 26, 48, 51, 53-5, 67, 79, 83, 85, 88, 99-100, 101, 102-9, 113, 167
Delyth Jones: 34-5, 191
Fiona Macvicar: 48-52
Evelyn Bartlett: 70, 72, 75, 76
Viv Quillin: 79
Emma Whiting: 96-7
Colin Robson: 101
Paul Reynolds: 110
Product First: 134, 136-41
ML Design: 143, 145, 169, 172-3, 175, 185, 191
Peter Clark: 154-5
Jane Human: 158-63, 166
Lorraine Harrison: 165
Christie Archer: 177, 180-1, 182, 183, 187, 188
David Chambers: 189
Patrick Garland: 190
Barry Rowe: 210-12
Alice Woods: 213, 214, 215, 216-17, 218, 220-1
Nick Sharatt: 219

PHOTOGRAPHS

Science Photo Library: 4; David Hambly Photography: 13; Associated Press: 20 (Thomas Kienzle), 21TL (Morten Hvaal), 21B (Gill Allen), 112L, 112R, 114; All Sport: 21TR (Mark Becker); *Glasgow Herald*: 24; *Hornsey & Muswell Hill Journal*/Mark Moody: 25; Grundy Television: 26; Kobal Collection: 27T, 29C, 57T, 116; Granada Television: 27C; © Thames Television: 27B, 174; *Cambridge Evening News*/Chris Morton: 28; Portman Entertainment Ltd: 29T; Copyright © BBC: 30T, 30B, 56L, 222; J. Allan Cash: 33T, 33BL, 33BR; Frank Bird Photography: 38, 58, 64B, 65B, 66T, 66B, 69, 99, 118, 121, 127, 128, 129T, 129B, 132B, 133, 153, 169, 171, 186; Simon Warner: 40-1; National Maritime Museum: 42; Ancient Art and Architecture Collection/Ronald Sheridan: 43R; C.M. Dixon Photo Resources: 43L, 44B; Mary Evans Picture Library: 44T; ZEFA Picture Library (UK): 45T, 45B; IDAF: 47, 54-55; Rex Features/Sipa Press: 53 (Junan Kuus), 54T, 55T, 65T, 192, 193R, 194, 200BR; Network/Franklin: 56R; Sally and Richard Greenhill: 57B, 84, 137, 138, 139, 140, 193L, 195, 196, 197, 200TL, TR, BL; *East Anglian Daily Times* and Associated Papers: 62; Nick Dutton-Taylor: 80, 132, 133; Nigel Luckhurst: 83; Brontë Parsonage Museum: 86L, 87B, 88, 89, 90; Hulton Picture Library: 86-70, 94; Marion Rose: 87T; GLR Office: 91; The Vintage Magazine Company: 92B; Topham Picture Library: 117, 119, 120; Ros Drinkwater/Times Newspapers Limited, London: 125T, 130C, 130B; Independent Television News Ltd: 125B; Stephen Attmore: 130T, 175; John Walmsley Photo Library: 136, 184; picture courtesy of Bradford Enterprise Service: 142; British Coal: 144T, 144B; British Gas: 145T; Greenpeace: 145B (Staans), 147 (Zindler), 148 (Midgley), 149R (Gleizes); British Nuclear Fuels: 146, 149L, 156TL; National Trust Photographic Library/Olive Kitson: 150; Centre for Alternative Technology/Canolfan y Dechnoleg Amgen: 152B; National Power plc: 151, 152T, 156TC, 156B, 157C; National Electric plc: 156LC; Ann Bolt: 164; Design Council: 178; Chris Ridgers Photography: 179; DCA Design Consultants: 180-1; by courtesy of the Swedish National Art Museums © ADAGP, Paris and DACS, London 1991: 203; Tate Gallery, London: 204; Tate Gallery, London © ADAGP, Paris and DACS, London 1991: 205, 209T; by courtesy of the Library of Congress, Washington D.C/Bridgeman Art Library, London: 207; Manchester City Art Galleries: 208; Pre-Raphaelite Inc/ by courtesy of Julian Hartnoll: 209B; Courtauld Institute Galleries: 211T; Henry Moore Foundation: 211B; National Gallery: 212T; Kunsthaus Zürich, Alberto Giacometti Foundation © ADAGP, Paris and DACS, London 1991: 212B.